★ ★ ★ ★ ★ ★ ★

THE SINGIN' SALMON MAN

from *Cornet Bay*

by Arnie Deckwa

with Rob Simbeck

©2011 by Arnie Deckwa. All rights reserved.

Published by Cornet Bay Publishing
    251 Cornet Bay Road
    Oak Harbor, WA 98277

Book and cover design by Terri Morris,
McClearen Design, Nashville, TN.

Publisher's Cataloging in Publication data
Deckwa, Arnie, with Rob Simbeck.
The Singin' Salmon Man From Cornet Bay
p. cm.
ISBN-10: 0-9642991-4-3
ISBN-13: 978-0-9642991-4-6
LCCN 2010937949

1. Deckwa, Arnie, 1941- ; 2. Cornet Bay Foods
3. American entrepreneurs ; 4. Grand Ole Opry
5. Nashville, TN ; I. Title

11 12 13 14 15 16   10 9 8 7 6 5 4 3 2 1

For more information about the Cornet Bay Company
contact Joanne Deckwa at 360-675-6331
and be sure to visit us at www.cornetbay.com.

···· *Dedication* ····

[Mom and Dad on their honeymoon on Ben Ure Island in Cornet Bay]

To my best friends, Dad and Mom, Oliver and Rena Deckwa

[Over 40 years later, still in love]

❖❖❖ Foreword ❖❖❖

Once in a lifetime someone comes along who doesn't fit any kind of mold. They are true self-starters who go against the grain and are relentless when the impossible needs to be done. One such person is a salt-water cowboy I've known for twenty-plus years named Arnie Deckwa.

You may have heard the song that says "I did it my way"—well, that song could have easily been written especially for this wrangler who has been my best friend for the better part of my musical career. Deckwa—that's what his friends call him—rode into Music City U.S.A. with a dream of making it big as a singer/songwriter, and after ten years left town with a much bigger dream that has become a national reality. He's a larger-than-life character who lives every minute of every day like it was his last.

I have worked with and around many recording artists and stars in my thirty years in the music industry, including Garth Brooks, Anne Murray, Trisha Yearwood, Isaac Hayes, Blake Shelton, Brad Paisley and many more. But I have never, I repeat *never*, met anyone who has the personality, drive and desire that this Whidbey Island entrepreneur cowboy possesses.

The Singin' Salmon Man from Cornet Bay is a wonderful read that keeps you captivated every second with true stories that seem to parallel the lives of Mark Twain's Huck Finn and Tom Sawyer. It's an amazing and inspirational account of what someone can do when they won't let anything stand in the way of making their dream come true. For anyone who doesn't know what songs and salmon have in common, this book will truly be an eye-opener.

It's great, it's entertaining, it's funny and most of all it's PURE DECKWA.

—Tom Long, former membership director of ASCAP, VP of Anne Murray's publishing company, and president/owner, That-A-Fly Music, Nashville, TN.

Tom Long; Rick Butler; me, in the truck; ?; Christi Wright; Belinda Long; Jeff Crossan; Joanne Deckwa; Kim Tribble; ?; Hobo Jim; Jimmy Gray; Allen Shamblin; Renee Coale Willis, holding daughter, Catherine; Gerald Coale

In the late '80s, I was a head seafood clerk at the Kroger Bellevue Store near Nashville. One day a cowboy walked up to my counter and asked to speak to the seafood manager. I told him I was the manager and asked how I could help him. He replied with a big wide smile that he hoped he could help me. That was not a usual response, but I would soon learn there was nothing "usual" about this cowboy.

Of course the cowboy was Arnie Deckwa. He talked a few minutes about "hot smoked salmon" from the great Northwest. (Please understand that in the late '80s we had never heard of hot smoked salmon in Nashville, Tennessee.) I was late for a meeting with the store manager, so I thanked him, but explained I needed to end the conversation. He understood and was very polite. When I returned to the shop about an hour later, there was the cowboy still waiting patiently to continue our conversation.

I admired that kind of determination, so I decided to listen to him more. Eventually, we tried to sell hot smoked salmon in my shop. After this failed, Arnie told me about a smoked salmon dip he was making. We got all the ingredients and made it right there in my shop. We started sampling it. The response was phenomenal! We realized we finally had the right vehicle to sell Arnie's hot smoked salmon.

Those first few years were hard on Arnie, but his determination and inspiration carried him through. He never gave up, no matter what happened. Arnie found a silver lining in every defeat. Years later, I became the fresh seafood buyer for the Kroger company. One of the first things we did was develop Arnie's recipes into our private label Kroger brand seafood dips. Now, we sell several of Arnie's recipes every day at Kroger. Every time I see Kroger Smoked Salmon Dips in the seafood case, I think back to the time I first met him and how we mixed everything by hand. He is an inspiration to us all.

—**David Long, Seafood Coordinator, The Kroger Company**

Arnie is a true American original and I count it one of my great blessings to have met him when I first moved to Nashville as a "hungry songwriter." Not only were there times when "Arn" literally showed up at my apartment door with a bag of groceries, but there were many other times when he nourished my soul with one inspiring, funny and heartwarming story after another. As I read the stories in this book, I caught myself bursting with laughter one second and trying to swallow a big lump in my throat the next.

This book captures the spirit of a man who lives with as much passion, gusto and love for life as anyone I've ever met. I'm proud to call "Arn" my friend and I hope this book is the beginning of many more.

—Allen Shamblin, writer of "He Walked On Water," "Don't Laugh At Me," "I Can't Make You Love Me," and "The House That Built Me"

One day while I was working in the seafood shop at Kroger, I saw a strange man talking to my boss. Later, I was called over and introduced.

"Glenda, this is Arnie. He is from Washington and he is promoting smoked salmon for our stores." Now, this was a strange mix, I thought—a cowboy with a hat and boots, a country music singer, selling smoked salmon.

We got the product in, but there was not a big market for it in the South, and so Arnie decided to make a dip out of it. This consisted of hand-chopping everything. Arnie would arrive at all hours, carrying his big green bowl. Feeling sorry for him, I would help him chop. After days of chopping, singing and getting acquainted, one night we had a brainstorm. Why not use our food chopper to chop the onions? Instant success! This cut down on time and manpower, and what a friendship we developed!

I am extremely proud to say that Arnie's seafood dips and spreads have been private labeled by Kroger and are being sold in Kroger stores nationwide; this country music-singing cowboy rode into Nashville on a salmon and became a lifelong friend. Thanks, Arnie, for including me in your success.

—Glenda McClurkan, former head seafood clerk, Green Hills Kroger, Nashville

Back in 1988, I was working at Kroger in Belle Meade, near Nashville, as seafood manager. One day Arnie showed up with a cowboy hat on, saying, "Hey, I'm here in Nashville riding in on my smoked salmon, trying to sell it at Kroger." Back then we never had any kind of smoked salmon line to sell, so I decided to help him sell his. When Arnie came back to the store to see how it was going, I told him it wasn't selling that great, so he decided to start making smoked salmon dip out of it. He would come back there in the shop with me, and we would take the salmon and skin it, debone it, cut it up, and mix in the other ingredients, putting it all into eight-ounce cups with lids. All the while, we'd be cutting up, singing, and having a good time.

Along with his smoked salmon dip, Arnie came up with a Southern Style Crab Dip and a Cajun Style Smoked Salmon Dip, and we'd put out samples with crackers on top of the seafood case. He talked to customers, telling them about the dip, and it really started to sell great. Arnie eventually had to put together his own manufacturing facility to make it, and he'd ship it out to our stores. It doesn't seem like it's been twenty-three years since we were having all that fun. I really enjoyed those times with Arnie and I'm really glad that Kroger has their name on those dips. Ya did good, Cowboy.

—**Tim Woodard, assistant meat manager, Belle Meade Kroger, Nashville**

It seems like just yesterday that I first laid eyes on a character by the name of Arnie Deckwa—and he is a character, defined as "someone who has a certain quality or trait that distinguishes him as an individual." I say that with respect and love for the man I grew to know.

In the spring of 1987, I was employed in a large grocery store chain as head seafood clerk. I had completed my display set-up and was policing the area, putting the finishing touches on the shine of the stainless steel display case when something told me to look up. Here came this cowboy, five-foot-six or so, slightly bow-legged, dressed in blue jeans and boots, a suitably western shirt and his ever-present grey-colored felt cowboy hat. He waltzed right up to the counter, looked me in the eyes, and with a big swift slap brought the palm of his hand to rest on the stainless steel counter top I had just polished.

"Pardner," he said, "I've got the best-tasting smoked salmon you ever did put in your mouth."

Boy howdy, was I surprised! Never in all my born days did I expect that. I brought the palm of my hand down on the very same stainless steel display case with as much vigor and noise as he had and said, "Well, Pardner, then why don't you bring me some so I can taste it, and then I'll tell you if it's the very best smoked salmon I ever did put in my mouth." He did, it was, and a professional and personal relationship began at that moment. It is a friendship that is as strong as ever to this day. For ten years we worked together in and out of the field prior to his move back to his home in Washington State, establishing a business that is still thriving today. We have experienced many good times together, and I take pride in the fact that I played a very small role in his food business but shared a big role in his life. And even though today he lives over 2600 miles away, we remain Pals & Pardners Forever.

—**Buddy Hayes, former head seafood clerk, Brentwood, Tennessee, Kroger**

Introduction

"THE FIRST AND ONLY COWBOY EVER TO RIDE INTO THE HISTORY OF NASHVILLE'S COUNTRY MUSIC ON SMOKED SALMON"

Hello, Pardner. I'm Arnie Deckwa. Chances are, since you've picked this book up, you're familiar with one or more of my seafood dips, spreads, sauces and seasonings. My family and I produce them under our own Cornet Bay label and under the Kroger label, among others. They're part of a line of products that was launched backstage at the Grand Ole Opry, believe it or not—and there are times when I can hardly believe it!

It's an amazing story, if I do say so myself. Actually, it's a bunch of amazing stories from a life with more twists and turns than an eight-second bull ride. Along the way, I've been a commercial fisherman, a deputy sheriff, a rodeo contestant, a building contractor, a land developer and a singer who took a five-piece band halfway around the world. Eventually I went to Nashville to seek fame and fortune in country and country/gospel music. One thing led to another and, as you'll see later on, pretty soon I was a backstage regular at the Opry. I was able to hang out with some of the greatest pickers, singers, and entertainers ever to grace a stage, from Roy Acuff to Garth Brooks, and I spent some of the best times of my life there.

It was also there that God put together two great loves of mine—music and food—and turned them into something big and wonderful. I started bringing smoked salmon from back home to the entertainers backstage, and before long they were telling me, "Arnie, you need to get this in stores and sell it!" That's just what I did, and before long I came to be known as "the first and only cowboy ever to ride into the history of Nashville's country music on smoked salmon." Ten years later, I went back home as the head of a growing nationwide business based on the best smoked salmon dips that ever tempted a palate. Sometimes I wonder how on earth a kid born in a log house on an island in Washington State and raised like Tom Sawyer in the woods and on the water near our tiny home on Cornet Bay managed to pull it all off.

You'll find the answers in this book. You'll also meet some really wonderful people, including my great-aunt Goldie, who crossed half a continent in a covered wagon and built her own log house; my boyhood friend Buddy Rodgers, who was Huck Finn to my Tom Sawyer; Brent Burkett of the Four Guys, who planted the seeds of a dream; a dressing room full of country music legends; the Magnificent Seven, made up of seven head seafood clerks in seven Kroger grocery stores who provided encouragement and business savvy enough to help me turn the dream into a profitable business; and many, many more.

This book is my way of sharing the adventure with you. I'd love to be able to tell you these tales in person, and I hope one day soon we'll meet up and I'll be able to do just that. In the meantime, friends have been urging me for a long, long time to collect them in a book, and with a little help from my good friend Rob Simbeck—a writer who's worked with plenty of country legends himself—I've finally done it. So, pull up a chair and get comfortable. I sure hope you enjoy it.

•••• Thank you ••••

To my beautiful and wonderful wife Joanne:

There are not enough words, Hon, to express my feelings to you for your understanding of my being away so much in this last year and a half while writing this book. Whether it was simply up in the office until early morn, in the back room, or actually gone from our home, I was still away. Thank you for all your help and input and for being the rock that is so much needed in my life.

You are a wonderful lady and I'm a very lucky guy.

All my love to you,

Arnie

Contents

Photo & Illustration Credits

Cover shot of Arnie with Lady—Tony Locke; i, 161, 165—Wayne Lewis;
iv, 168, 176—William A. Kimmins; 50—Herb Bittman; 54—Wallie Funk;
56, 57, 60, 78—Diana York; 82, 88, 92, 130, 160, 171, 185, 190—Arnie
Deckwa; 97—Tom Burrier; 122, 126—Judy Mock; 134—Eddie Malone;
147—Ashli Shamblin; 156—Barbara Miller-Hughes; 163—Joe Loesch;
183—Joanne Deckwa; 184—Laurie Deckwa; 191—Scott Worden; 196—
Karen Griffith; 207—Scott Deckwa.

[Great-aunt Goldie and her sister, my grandma Effie Deckwa]

★ ★ ★ ★

Chapter One

AUNT GOLDIE AND MY BEGINNINGS

I came into this world on April 10, 1941, in a log house my great-aunt helped build. Goldie Wayman, a midwife by trade, chopped down and barked some of the trees herself at the age of fifty-one, living in a lean-to while working on the place with her husband and son-in-law after they'd moved to Whidbey Island, Washington, from California in 1934.

That log house was the launching point for quite a few of the children of north Whidbey Island. Goldie and I visited it when she was in her nineties, and she pointed out the very spot where she had helped my mother, who was twenty at the time, through my difficult birth.

Aunt Goldie was a multi-talented free spirit and I could tell stories about her all day and half the night. In most families, she'd be a rarity. In mine, she was just one of a wagonload of real characters. They never had much money to speak of, but they left me a legacy of high adventure, rugged individualism, and hard work that I hope to live up to every day of my life. And, Pardner, they sure made my childhood an interesting place.

Goldie and my grandmother, Effie Gipe Deckwa, left Culp Creek, Kansas, in a covered wagon in the spring of 1894 when they were just kids. They traveled with their parents, David and Harriet Gipe, across the prairie to the town of Cedaredge in the mountains of western Colorado, where David got work in the silver mines.

It was quite the caravan. The family, like many setting out on such journeys, was already taking its horses, cows, and goats, but Goldie, a ten-year-old with a mind of her own, wanted one more item—the family's pump organ. Her parents told her that because of its size and weight, they'd be leaving it behind.

"If the organ isn't going," Goldie told them, "neither am I!" She finally said she'd give up her place inside the wagon if they'd load the organ and take it, and eventually they agreed. That organ, by the way, is still in the family.

David heard there was a way to help ensure the family's safety as they crossed land held by Native Americans, and so every evening he took food to a ridge outside the camp and left it to demonstrate his peaceful intentions. Although several times they saw tribesmen watching them from a distance, they were never harassed.

Goldie, true to her word, walked most of the time, riding one of the horses when she could. Sometimes she would climb onto the back of one and ride it bareback into the hills just to burn off extra energy. It was a passion she never lost. Once when I was ten or twelve and she was in her late sixties, she asked if she could ride my horse. I gave a little laugh, the way a cocky kid does in a situation like that. I didn't know what she knew about horses, and I pictured her taking a slow little stroll around the yard. I was riding bareback, and I jumped down and said, "Sure, Aunt Goldie. Go ahead." She grabbed the reins and a handful of mane and swung up on that thing in one smooth motion. She kicked that sucker with a blue-jeaned leg and went up the hill wide open, then turned around and came back.

"I like your horse," she said, jumping off and handing me the reins. "It's very nice."

My jaw was on the ground. I was just plain dumbfounded, and from that moment until she died at the age of ninety-five, I never thought about her the same way again.

[Our Cornet Bay headquarters]

★ ★ ★ ★

Chapter Two

THE LITTLE YELLOW HOUSE ON CORNET BAY

When I was born, my dad was logging in the high country of the northern Cascades, and shortly after that he began managing an apple orchard in Yakima. I was baptized in a Methodist church in nearby Selah and was still a baby when we moved back to Whidbey Island. I grew up three miles from Aunt Goldie's place, in a 494-square-foot yellow house on a dead-end road that skirted a beautiful body of water named Cornet Bay, which empties into Puget Sound. My father, Oliver Deckwa, built that house from the ground up, installing the wiring and the plumbing himself, and over the years he built five of his own commercial fishing boats. Dad was a tall, thin man who took a no-nonsense approach to work—he was always busy—and to child rearing.

"Are you gonna stand there and talk about it all day, or are you gonna do it?" he'd say when my mouth was moving faster than my muscles. "Talk is cheap," he'd add, looking over the top of his glasses. "If you want it, go after it."

I couldn't argue with him, because he practiced what he preached. He knew more ways to bring a little income into our household than you could keep track of, and there wasn't much in a home or on a boat he couldn't do.

Dad was a gentle and very well-liked man. I saw him lose his temper only three times in my life—twice at me and once during a night out fishing. The first was when I decided to run away. I was around ten, and I made it a couple of miles to the house of Dad's cousin, Cliff Deckwa. Of course, Cliff called Dad and told him I was there. That's when I found out what a willow switch across the back of my thighs was all about. I never ran away again.

My mother, Rena, was the daughter of Russian immigrants and an amazing combination of culture and earthiness. She stood 5'2" and looked a little like Rita Hayworth, and she could grab a shovel and dig a ditch from here to Timbuktu, then put on a gorgeous dress and go out with Dad to dance the night away to the Big Band music she loved so much.

————★★★★————

Mom and Dad were as close to my sister, Charlotte, and me as any parents could be. They were my best friends.

Both were survivors, tough yet tender people who loved the Lord and taught me to love Him. Mom took me to Sunday school when we still lived in Selah, and all of us went to a local Lutheran church back on Whidbey when I was a young boy and then a teenager. At some point we all drifted away from churchgoing but I never lost contact with the Father. I remember praying as I hitchhiked home after football practice, and out on that fishing boat, asking Him to keep an eye on us. It wasn't until much later, though, that I grew into the adult faith that means so much to me now.

Mom and Dad were as close to my sister, Charlotte, and me as any parents could be. They were my best friends. They had the know-how to do whatever it took to make a living, the discipline to stay at it, and love enough to make sure those traits were passed on to their children.

I was about five when Dad built the house. I remember it like it was yesterday because of how much I always wanted to help him. He'd mix cement in a big mixer powered by an electric motor, then carry it in a five-gallon metal bucket as he poured the floor. The first few times, I hung onto the sides of the bucket and walked beside him, but that didn't last long. The bucket was heavy enough without my "help" adding to the weight. In later years, he and I shared a lot of laughs about those days.

The front door led into the kitchen. You'd take a right and walk six or seven feet past the sink and wood stove, then turn left through the living area. Once you passed the end of Mom and Dad's bed—they got their privacy by pulling a curtain across the living room—you'd take another left into the bedroom I shared with Charlotte, with me in the top bunk and her in the bottom one. There was no door to our bedroom, which you had to walk through to get to the bathroom. As a little kid at bedtime, I would listen as much as I could to what was going on in the living room, especially when the folks had company.

The pathway through my parents' bedroom to mine gave my mother a way to slow me down when I was a teenager in the '50s. I still have the high-backed rocking chair Mom put at the end of their bed with its seat facing me as I walked toward it. Trying desperately to be quiet while sneaking in late one night, I walked smack dab into that chair, falling into its seat and riding it down to the floor as it tipped over with a crash at the foot of their bed. I believe to this day she put the chair there for just that reason. Of course, the alcohol on my breath didn't help matters any, and after Mom had a good talk with my dad, I got my final look at his temper.

There were just three families on our end of the Bay—the Deckwa, Lang, and Rodgers families, all of whom made their living in one form or another from the sea. They had commercial fishing boats and tugboats, and they supplemented their incomes with everything from beachcombing logs they sold to the mills to guiding bigger vessels through nearby Deception Pass.

The Lang and Rodgers families made regular visits to our little yellow house. My parents loved company and loved having folks come over for dinner. "Uncle Bill" Lang, as we kids called him, was one of my favorite guests. He and my dad were partners in Cornet Bay Boat Works, and he and Aunt Connie lived close by the county dock. We saw each other almost every day. After he'd get off work, he'd drive up our driveway and honk the "oooo-gah" horn on his old green and black Model A pickup. That meant, "Hurry up and get out here if you want to go with us—and, yes, you get to drive." Well, sort of. I was only six or seven, but he always let me sit on his lap and steer as we drove the mile and a half to the end of Cornet Bay Road and back. He was a good man who treated me like a son.

Uncle Bill also let me shoot his twelve-gauge shotgun before I was big enough to reach the trigger. After I got up off the ground, he decided I'd better grow a little more before we did that again.

There are so many memories that little house brings back. I can remember the wonderful meals Mom cooked on our old wooden stove. I recall practicing my accordion lessons and my sister practicing organ and tap dancing. Mom was our Cub Scout den mother, and we held all our troop meetings and did a lot of our projects there. Of course, many of our friends stayed the night. It was and is a wonderful, magical place, and the adventures I had and the lessons I learned there are priceless.

[Hammering as my friends Barbara "Sis" Miller and Buddy Rodgers look on]

Chapter Three

❖❖❖❖❖❖❖❖❖❖❖❖❖❖❖❖❖❖❖❖❖❖

BUDDY AND ARNIE'S RAFTING ADVENTURE

❖❖❖❖❖❖❖❖❖❖❖❖❖❖❖❖❖❖❖❖❖❖

Buddy Rodgers, who lived up the hill, was Huck Finn to my Tom Sawyer. We were as close as brothers, and we shared all sorts of adventures. Not a day went by that we didn't meet each other at the dock, on the beach, or at one of the hideaway forts we had built in a tree or in the hollow under a log. The fishermen were used to seeing us looking for red crabs under rocks or sitting on a log laughing as we planned a campout. They were also used to answering question after question about boats, fishing, and the sea from two kids with lots of energy and plenty of big dreams.

Buddy and I had little boats before we had bicycles. That, of course, made us experts in our own minds when it came to watercraft, and it convinced us one time that we could make the Northwest's equivalent of the raft that took Huck down the Mississippi.

The two of us didn't have to read novels to find adventure when we were growing up. There was plenty of it all around us. Commercial fishing takes muscle and know-how, and the people who do it have to face nature at its most elemental—tides and wind and rain are just part of the bargain. That's one of the reasons we spent so much time at the dock, talking to adventurers we could meet without ever setting foot in a library.

Buddy's grandfather, George Rodgers—"Pa," as we called him—and his brother Johnny had thirty-foot tugs. Their business was assisting the large tug companies in getting tows of logs, which could stretch hundreds of feet, through the tricky tides of Deception Pass, one of the most treacherous narrows anywhere in the region. A big tug would pull the tow, which was held together with boom sticks—logs tied end-to-end and encircling the tow—and Pa and Johnny would stay to the side or at the rear of the tow, guiding it to keep it from drifting into and breaking up on the rocks. There are few things worse than logs adrift when you're running a fishing boat at night through rough waters. It was tough, exacting work that relied on an intimate knowledge of the changing tides. Slack tide, when the direction of the tide started to reverse and there was very little water motion for thirty minutes or so, was the time to tow logs through the pass.

When we were nine or ten, Buddy and I decided two of those boom sticks would make a great starter for a raft, which was just what we needed for some new adventures. We went to Buddy's family's dock, up the road from my house about a quarter of a mile, took two of the thirty-foot boom sticks, which were chained together at one end, and set the other ends about twelve feet apart. We nailed boards from one to the other until we had a solid framework, then built a little platform that would hold a chair. One of us would sit in the chair, the other would push us around the bay, and we really felt like somebody. Then we decided it would be really cool to build a little house on that raft. As luck would have it, Buddy's grandfather had dismantled an old outhouse, and he told us we could have it. The walls were still intact. If we nailed them back together, BINGO! We'd have our house. We thought it was a great idea, and we placed the outhouse smack in the middle of that raft.

The roof was in one piece too, but the two of us were too small to lift it onto the walls. Shingles and all, it was pretty heavy, so we came up with another idea. Buddy's mother and father were having a home built right on the beach next to their dock. One day when they were gone, we talked the carpenters, Cliff Nienhuis and John VanKal, into carrying the roof down to the dock and lifting it up onto the walls. They really got a charge out of that.

So here we were, the Huck Finn and Tom Sawyer of Cornet Bay, using long poles to push ourselves around the shallows of the bay in what had to be the only raft anywhere with its own outhouse—an empty outhouse, thank goodness.

We'd push ourselves out a ways in front of Buddy's house, drop anchor, and sometimes stay there all night, talking, cutting up, and getting really spooked when the blue herons would land on the roof and make their loud, shrill cries. We'd laugh and talk until finally we dropped off to sleep.

For a while, we were just two kids fooling around, going on adventures without a care in the world. We never thought to bring life jackets, and we still had a lesson or two to learn about the difference between a river and a bay. Rivers get deep gradually, whereas Cornet Bay can get awfully deep rather quickly. There came a moment when, as we pushed ourselves along with our poles, we ran out of bottom. We plunged them down as far as we could reach and—nothing. All of a sudden we were aware of the possibility of disaster. We knew we could drift into deep enough water that we'd be completely unable to control the raft. We could be drawn around Goose Rock and then—who knows?—maybe all the way out through Deception Pass, where the whirlpools could spin us around and smash us into the rocks.

★ ★ ★ ★

We were just two kids fooling around, going on adventures without a care in the world.

Fortunately, there was a difference between Huck and Tom and Buddy and me, and it was in the level of parental supervision. Around Cornet Bay, any family could let Buddy's or my parents know what we were up to if that seemed like a good idea, and our own parents knew to keep half an eye and half an ear tuned in our general direction when they were around. This time, they were nearby, and they came to tow us back in. That episode, of course, really made us appreciate the advantages of boats with motors.

[Buddy Rodgers and me, cleaning fish]

★ ★ ★ ★

Chapter Four

THE WORLD'S SLOWEST JUMPING BOAT

The episode with the raft was one of those that came along every now and then to teach me something new about boats or water or my own abilities. I'd had one a couple of years earlier when I was seven or eight.

My grandfather had a fourteen-foot boat with a 2.5 horsepower Lawson outboard motor. In fact, I still have the motor, although the boat is long gone. It was a very heavy boat, slow enough that I could take it out pretty much any time I wanted. My folks never seemed to mind, because it kept me occupied.

Around that time, I'd seen newsreel footage about Florida that showed speedboats zipping through the water and shooting up and over ramps, then thumping back down and roaring on. One day I was out running Grandpa's boat around when I decided it would be fun to jump over something. This was a boat, mind you, that might have topped out at three or four knots on smooth water with a brisk tailwind.

Not far from our home was the county dock, and one side of it was waterlogged, so it tilted down at a good angle and sat partly in the water. It seemed like a perfect makeshift ramp to me! I figured I'd launch myself onto that sucker and into the wild blue yonder I'd fly, just the way they did it in Florida.

I made a big, slow turn between the dock and Goose Rock, and with the wind and the roar of that motor I convinced myself I was really kickin' up a rooster tail. Running wide open, I aimed at my pretend Florida jump ramp, gritted my teeth, and narrowed my eyes. I hit the edge of that dock, but instead of roaring into the wild blue yonder, the boat slid halfway across it and stopped. The motor, which was barely out of the water, didn't—it was screaming and echoing all over the bay. I scrambled as fast as I could to shut it off.

"Uh-oh" was about the extent of my musings. There I was, with part of the bow of Grandpa's boat hanging off one side of the dock and part of her stern hanging off the other. I was high and dry, and in trouble in more ways than just being stuck in the middle of the dock, standing out like a duck on a picnic table. I knew Grandpa's eyes had to be on me because he always sat by the living room window and watched the goings-on in the bay, and I certainly couldn't hide. I climbed out and began pushing as hard as I could, but there wasn't enough of me to push that boat anywhere.

Sure enough, while I was grunting and groaning, trying to get the boat to move, here came Dad and my grandfather. "What are you doing?" was the first thing I heard. I decided to try to explain. Believe me, it didn't go well. Both of them helped me push the boat back into the water, and after that little incident, I had plenty of time ashore to think about the lessons I'd learned, since my dad restricted me from running the boat for a good while.

As I look back, I get a kick out of those wonderful memories, but most of all I cherish the fact that until the day they passed on, Dad and Grandpa were always in my life watching out for me.

[Learning to rope and singing to the seagulls]

★ ★ ★ ★

Chapter Five

THE SINGING COWBOY

I've done a lot of things, but the two I do now are the ones I've loved since I was old enough to hear the radio and pick up a fork at suppertime—music and food. Music was the dream that led me to Nashville, and food was the passion that turned into a great and exciting way of life.

Music was always in the air around the Deckwa household. When I was lucky enough to go fishing with my dad, I'd hear country music on the old radio in his boat. The first song I ever learned well enough to sing was Roy Acuff's "Wabash Cannonball," so you know country music runs deep in my veins. Back home, Mom would play Big Band music—Glenn Miller, Tommy Dorsey, Benny Goodman, and vocalists like Frank Sinatra and Bing Crosby. I learned to like that kind of music as well. When it came time to pick, though, the choice was clear. I wanted to be a singing cowboy. I'd seen Gene Autry and Roy Rogers at the movies, and I knew that's what I wanted to be a part of.

I had a little black and white dog named Trigger, and I had Dad's old child-sized saddle up on top of the doghouse. I'd sit there holding reins that were tied to the bottom of the eaves, singing cowboy songs at the top of my lungs to the seals and seagulls. Mom encouraged my dream, making me some embroidered cowboy shirts flashy enough for the movie screen and plenty flashy for first and second grade, where I wore them as often as I could.

Given how much I idolized cowboys, I couldn't help but be drawn to a piece of authentic cowboy history that showed up one day in our little house. I remember like it was yesterday Dad and his cousin Cliff sitting in the living room talking about guns and hunting. I was five or six, perched on Dad's knee and taking in every word.

Cliff was Dad's hunting partner and a terrific gunsmith, and this particular day he was absorbed in a gun Dad was showing him. It was a .41 Colt Single Action six-shooter that my great-grandfather Whitlow—my grandmother Effie Deckwa's stepfather—had owned. It was a cowboy's gun for sure, and it looked just like the pictures in my cowboy comic books.

It also had its own story. My great-grandfather carried that gun in his belt, and my dad said he could take the head off a weasel from the porch to the chicken house with it. Grandma told me they were sitting in the house in Kansas one cold and snowy night when she was a little girl, and Mr. Whitlow said, "Effie, go see what the dogs are barking at."

She went out on the porch and looked toward the barn.

"What did you see?" he asked her.

"Nothing but the fence posts," she said.

Quick as lightning, he was on his way out the door. The snow was so deep the fence posts had nearly been buried. He didn't know for certain what the dogs had been barking at, but he knew something was up—and he was right. The Dalton Gang was at that moment in the process of stealing their horses.

There are so many questions I should have asked. Did she hear gunfire? Did she hear yelling? I didn't, and it just breaks my heart how many old family stories and how much real history I lost along the way.

Anyway, Dad was explaining the gun's hair trigger to Cliff, telling him how Grandpa had filed its release pressure down so far you could fan six rounds and never touch the trigger. Dad showed Cliff by firing it empty. He cocked the hammer and pulled it back beyond its holding position. When he let go, it slammed down to the firing position, and the trigger hadn't been touched.

Being the rambunctious, exuberant kid I was, enamored of cowboys and always wanting to be part of whatever was going on, I said, "Dad, let me do that! Please! Please!"

"No," Dad said. "Your hands are too small."

"I can do it, Dad," I assured him. "I can do it. Please, let me try! Please!"

My pleading and whining worked, because he gave in, although I soon wished he hadn't. Dad held the gun steady, giving me room to clasp both hands around the pistol grip. Then, with both thumbs, I slowly pulled the hammer back. Meanwhile, my left thumb slid down into the hammer's path, and when I released it, it came slamming down on it, taking a big piece of flesh with it.

The blood flew, and the pain was excruciating. I'm sure my screaming could be heard all over the bay. My mother was on the scene immediately, and this became one of those extremely rare occasions when my dad was in trouble for letting me get too involved.

As much as I loved cowboys, I was a lot more cautious about their hardware after that, and it would be years before I held that gun again. Today, the gun is in my collection, and it reminds me of that day on Dad's knee every time I see it. It also reminds me of the importance of asking the older members of our families to tell the younger ones their stories so they can be passed on.

[Dad's project, the ROCA]

[Dad, launching his project next to my slowest jumping boat]

★ ★ ★ ★

Chapter Six

FROM STEM TO STERN BETWEEN THE TIDES

The romance and adventure of the sea—and there are plenty of both for a curious kid growing up in a fishing village—are quickly tempered by the fact that it's a life with plenty of hard work attached. I helped Dad work on his boats from the time I was a little guy, and I couldn't begin to count the hours I spent on one chore or another while my buddies were headed toward the swimming hole in the nearby rock quarry.

One of the biggest, toughest chores was scraping and painting the boats, something we did in May or June as we prepared for the fishing season. It required both elbow grease and precise timing, since you needed the boat out of the water, which meant you had to play the tides and the sun to your advantage.

Dad would bring the boat in at high tide and run it up over the "ways," a set of concrete strips the boat settled onto as the tide went out. They allowed the boat to sit high enough that we could work under it and scrape all the barnacles and seaweed off the bottom before we painted. It was a delicate process. Done wrong, it could make matters interesting in a heartbeat. The boat was tied to the dock at high tide, and you adjusted the lines as the tide went out. Keep the lines too tight and the boat would be left completely out of the water, attached as an unwelcome weight to the dock. A big enough boat could do serious structural damage. Keep them too loose and the boat could settle incorrectly onto the ways, perhaps damaging the baskets designed to keep the nets out of the rudder and propeller.

Often the first I'd know of the impending task was when Dad began putting on his rain gear on a sunny morning. Mom would give me my rain gear and start pulling out the scrapers and paint brushes. We'd carry them down to the boat, which was usually sitting perfectly on the ways, just out of the water and ready for action. Dad's boats were cleaned regularly, so the job was nowhere near as tough as it could be for a boat that hadn't been cleaned in a while.

Dad would be on one side and Mom and I would be on the other, dipping our long-handled scrub brushes into the water we were standing in and scraping and scrubbing for all we were worth. High tide follows low by six hours, so you've got to be fast as well as thorough when you're working on a hull. For me, keeping up with Mom was a real chore, and she was never slow about pointing out the spots I missed.

We'd start at the bow and work our way toward the stern. At first, the job wasn't bad, since we'd be standing, but the farther we went toward the stern, the more we were crouching, complicating our task considerably. We had to keep moving, though, because the object was to get that bottom cleaned and still have water to work with.

We'd also have to keep an eye on the weather. Once the hull was clean and before the tide came in, we had to do the painting, so we wanted the sun to help the hull dry after we'd scraped it.

Sometimes after the scraping, I'd try to think of an excuse to get out of painting. After all, those buds of mine were still at the swimming hole! Asking was normally useless, but I figured it was always worth a try. Yet, no matter how tired I was, or how young, for that matter, I wasn't going to escape doing that job.

We'd take our positions, starting at the stern this time, for the painting. Brushes in hand, Dad still on one side and Mom and me on the other, we'd get after it. By then, the tide would be reminding us of the need for speed. We'd often start on our backs, lying on beach rocks in the mud, working over the bottom of the stern. Then we'd go back to crouching as we moved forward, painting as fast as we could, trying to outrace rising water that was already nudging at our boots or lapping at our pant legs.

By the time we'd get back to the bow, we'd be tired, but extremely proud and happy. We'd stand back and watch as the tide came up and covered that freshly painted hull, sometimes in the company of other fishermen who'd come by to offer their approval or their stories.

As my little sister, Charlotte, got old enough to help, all four of us would be involved, and as hard as that job could be, it was great to be part of a family project that made us a living and was so bound up with our identity.

[Log tow going under Deception Pass Bridge]

[Dad's catch, a sixty-eight pound king salmon]

Chapter Seven

FISHING WITH DAD

Dad and Uncle Bill Lang were the first two fishermen to lay a net out on the west side of Whidbey Island. They fished in an area we call West Beach, just outside Deception Pass, and people called them crazy for taking their small boats to the outside waters and risking some of the roughest seas anywhere. What's more, in those early days, which were before my time, they didn't have hydraulic reels to pull the net in; they had to pull it in by hand.

As a youngster fishing with my dad, I was able to experience a piece of history I will forever cherish. His patience was extraordinary—I would be practically under his arm as I helped him pull the net in, both of us in the stern of the boat, him standing on one side of the cork line and me on the other, getting wet and tired and sore. There were times when this was not at the top of my list of fun things to do, but I certainly knew with every fiber of my being that I was in good hands with Dad. Those waters were as familiar as our yard to him. He knew he would have to pick the net up at a certain time and allow for a run of an hour or so to get to the pass in time for a slack water drift. He knew that if he was late, he would be able to lay out only part of his net, fish for a spell, then get the net back in the boat before the tide began running through the rocky cliffs of Deception Pass. The tide waits for no man.

I fished with Dad from the time I was old enough to walk. I went out with him on four of the boats he built, and I remember the habits of each. Yes, boats have habits, and sometimes if you don't treat them and their engines exactly right, you can end up in a mess. And at two o'clock in the morning, with eighteen hundred feet of net hanging off the stern or bow, a mess is something you don't need. Bucking the tide, running in rough water—the sea is big and beautiful, but she can eat you in a heartbeat. Looking back, I realize just what kind of dangers my dad faced and how impressive his ability to react and make a living from the depths really was. It was wonderful to be a part of that.

By the time I was ten or so, I was always thrilled to go out fishing with Dad. I felt like I was contributing my fair share when it came to the scraping and painting—not to mention all the other chores around the house and gardens—and it seemed only right that I should go out and take part in the family business.

He and I would walk from our house to the dock, and I'd want to do everything—untie the boat, start the engine, and take her out to the fishing grounds. I was a very persistent kid, and my dad was a wonderful man. Like I said, he was filled with patience, and he usually let me do most of it. The only time that changed was when the going got a little rough. Bucking a seven- or nine-knot tide under Deception Pass Bridge in a boat that tops out at nine knots is a tricky proposition, and at moments like that he took over.

Once we were set out somewhere, with that net strung out from the end of the boat, I would be fine until around 2:00 a.m., when my eyelids would have a terrible time staying open. I'd be sitting in Dad's chair in the pilothouse, watching for other boats coming toward our net or anything else that was out of the ordinary. Dad would relax on the bunk down below. He'd never sleep while fishing, but he would break for a while and rest his eyes. During those moments, I felt in control. I knew I'd been given a very serious job, and I was in heaven.

After the net had been in the water a while and the engine was shut off, we would drift, and when he'd come back on deck I might go lie down in that bunk. The heat from the engine would make me drowsier and drowsier, the boat would rock gently back and forth like a cradle, and before I knew it I would be in dreamland. All of a sudden the quietness would come to an end with a bang as Dad cranked up that engine. Then, though, it would begin purring like a big kitten, and it would once again lull me fast asleep.

I'm sure those moments had to be the most peaceful time of night for Dad. He must have sat in the pilothouse and thought, *Ah, finally. The kid is out for the night and won't be walking around the cabin checking out this and that.* I was always looking to see if everything was okay, opening the cabin door to look around, then shining the spotlight down the cork line along the net.

———— ★★★★ ————

I felt like an admiral with the wind blowing in my face and the boat plowing through the waves.

Once we'd pick up the net, Dad would sometimes let me steer the boat while he looked around for our next fishing spot. For a kid, that was big-time stuff. I was naturally under his direction at all times and the boat was not a fast one, like the one he built later, which did around forty knots. When I was at the wheel, we were not going to get into trouble, because as much as I would have liked to believe I was in total control, Dad was right there. More than once—without asking, I might add—he would take the wheel from me and turn us in another direction. He was always close enough to take over if needed, and down deep inside I knew that. It made me feel safe.

Quite often he let me turn on the radio while we were under way. It was the one piece of technology on the boat in those days. We didn't have radar or a fathom meter or a short wave radio. It was a beauty, though, a 1947 Pontiac tube AM model that Dad had installed under the dash of the pilothouse. He loved country music, and we'd listen as long as the boat battery would let us. He knew just how long he could let the radio run with the motor off and still conserve the battery. When the engine was running, he could keep the radio cranked, so we usually had music aboard. Sometimes we couldn't hear much over the static of the running engine, but that was okay because I could hear enough to be satisfied. Dad was a big Eddy Arnold fan, and he loved it when "Bouquet of Roses" or "Cattle Call" came on the air.

I always steered the boat the way Dad did, hanging halfway out of the pilothouse window. The only difference was that I had to stand on the chair to get enough height to reach it. I felt like an admiral with the wind blowing in my face and the boat plowing through the waves, moving up and down, the radio blaring away. Dad got a kick out of watching me grow to like that feeling more and more with every night we fished.

When Dad decided where he wanted to lay out the net—it was called "making a set"—he usually told me to steer the boat toward a certain light coming from a house on the beach, or toward an island or a star. One night we were fishing around Padas Island, nearly at the Canadian border. We had no sooner laid out the net, around 8:00 p.m., than we hit a mess of dogfish. The minute Dad realized it, he began pulling the net back in. We were into them in a big way, though, and he knew it was going to be a long night.

Dogfish, which are related to sharks and have no commercial value to a fisherman, average two or three feet in length. They have razor-sharp teeth, and hidden behind the dorsal fin is a spear-like horn you don't want to tangle with. They'll swim into the net, take a mouthful of webbing, and begin twisting. Soon the horn and their tail are caught in the webbing, and they continue to twist around and around until they are hopelessly tangled. Dad estimated we had caught well over a thousand dogfish that night, and that many can wreak havoc on a net.

Dad told me we were going to get out of the area as fast as we could and I was to steer toward a light he pointed to. He waited until I acknowledged I understood exactly what he wanted, then he went aft, working hard to pick those fish out of the net. It's a painfully slow process untangling and taking them out without losing several meshes of net because of their sharp teeth.

Hours and hours went by as he struggled. He picked out as many as he could and then rolled a few more yards of net, fish and all, onto the roller. Then he'd pick more out, and we'd keep moving, towing hundreds of feet of net, still loaded with those smelly, tangled, good-for-nothin' fish.

The exhaust pipe from the engine went up through the rear of the inside of the cabin, just behind the chair I was sitting on, out the roof to a muffler. That three-and-a-half-inch galvanized exhaust pipe generated a good deal of heat inside the cabin, and the next thing I knew I was being shaken back and forth and a loud voice was asking me, "Where is the light I told you to head for?"

"There it is! That's it, right there!"

"That's not the light I told you to head for!" Dad said. "It's over there. The one you've been steering toward is taking us to Canada!" I have no idea how long I'd been steering in the wrong direction, but you can bet I didn't drift off to sleep again that night.

We finally made it to calm water in Birch Bay, where Uncle Bill came and helped us. We laid the net back out and picked dogfish until around 11:00 a.m. It had been fifteen hours of nothing but hard work, and it didn't stop there. After the net was back on the reel, we headed for the docks in Blaine, Washington, to wash the net in the bluestone tanks and then put it on the rack for mending. We sewed and patched for all we were worth. Even though we had no sleep, we were ready to go back out that night. It was all part of a fisherman's life.

[Dad and the ROCA, which made many trips north]

Chapter Eight

THE BELL AND THE STORM

One night when I was ten or so, Dad and I were fishing the *Charlotte D,* a twenty-eight-foot gill net boat he had converted from a tug and named after my sister. It was a fairly clear night, and the water was as smooth as glass. We were sitting off the end of the Whidbey Island Naval Air Station runway on the west side of the island, near the lighted pylons that help guide the Navy jets in. The engine was shut off, and an eighteen-hundred-foot net was lying straight as a moonbeam through the water. Everything about the night was perfect. I was sitting in the pilothouse, feeling on top of the world. Dad was down below resting, and I was in charge, watching the net and keeping my eyes open for anything out of the ordinary.

All of a sudden, that black sky lit up like God had turned on all the lights in the world, and then it went black again. I looked around for a moment, and then it happened again, bright as noon, then dark again. After the longest time, the boat started swaying ever so slightly and slowly. The swaying kept up and gradually turned into rocking.

Now, just before the Charlotte D had been launched, Dad attached a brass bell to the mast at cabin height. Its purpose was to signal that the water was getting too rough to fish, that it was time to pull in the net and go home. That's the way it was supposed to work, anyway.

In rough water the boat would rock up and down and from side to side. At first you'd just hear the water splashing on the sides of the boat, a few creaks and groans from her hull, and maybe a cup that hadn't been put away sliding around in the sink. The higher the waves, the more the boat would rock, and sooner or later I'd hear, ever so slightly, the soft ding of the bell now and then.

Yes, I would think. *Dad's surely going to pick up the net and head for home. It's getting nasty out there and that's the rule.* That was more wishful thinking than anything. Dad wasn't about to move yet. Same thing when the bell began to get good and loud. I started telling myself it had become rough enough to think about picking up the net and going to calmer waters where we could drop anchor and wait for a tide change, or maybe even going home and calling it a night. Those bright moments had been lightning, far enough away that I couldn't hear the thunder but brilliant enough to signal a powerful storm. The rain and rough waters were nearly on us.

Through trial and error, though, I had learned that if the bell wasn't banging loud enough to be heard all the way to England, we weren't going anywhere, least of all home. On this night, I thought if it wasn't reaching England, it was at least waking up people on the East Coast. I yelled, "Dad, it's gettin' kinda rough and the bell's been ringing for a long time. Can't you hear it?" By this time I was hanging on to whatever I could to keep from falling off the chair in the pilothouse. Finally, the answer came from down below: "Yeah." And that was it.

We bounced up and down for what seemed an eternity, and then I yelled, "Dad! That bell is really getting loud!" I was thinking, *Is he going to lie there forever? I know he's not asleep. How can he stay on that bunk in this stuff? I guess it'll just have to get rough enough for him to fall off. Maybe then we'll get out of here.*

Deep down inside, no matter how many times I became scared, which was often, I knew somehow he was in control and would know exactly when it was time to pick up the net. Now and then, though, I felt he should be reminded, and that's what I was doing.

All at once, the storm was on us like gangbusters. We had drifted toward the beach to the point where I could shine the spotlight and see the waves beating on the shore, and that was bad news. It meant we were in shallower water, which would kick the waves higher. Dad bolted up the stairs and onto the deck, and amid the whitecaps he started winding the net into the boat.

My job was to keep the boat pumped out, and I was on the deck beside the cabin, working like crazy with the old-fashioned manual pump while Dad was winding that net onto the big, wide roller. All of a sudden a monstrous wave crashed over the stern of the boat and knocked him down. "We're in trouble," I said to myself. It just scared me to death.

In those days, Dad wore black rain gear, and for the longest moment I couldn't see him. I knew how hazardous winding in that net could be at times like this. Your hands could get caught, and you could get pulled onto the roller or knocked clean off the boat.

Finally, he came up from the bottom of the boat, yelling at the top of his lungs, "Get a life preserver on!" That's when I realized he was scared, and I got even more scared. I pulled on a life vest and kept pumping.

Perilously close to the shore, with the waves crashing and the rain pelting us, he got the net in and was able to turn the *Charlotte D* toward home. That little twenty-eight-foot boat, which had a tendency to go straight into waves rather than over them, was not the best place to be in a big storm. We battled our way into Bowman's Bay, where we dropped the hook—my dad's term for the anchor—and rode out the storm.

The next morning, in calmer weather, we chugged through Deception Pass and back into Cornet Bay. As the sun rose, we jumped onto the dock and tied her up. Dad and I started walking to the house. As we walked by their place, I said, "Dad, those waves last night were almost as tall as Grandpa and Grandma's house."

He looked down at me and said, "Yep."

He was like that. He didn't need to say anything else. The sea was that way sometimes, and his was a life that pitted him against it now and then. It was just another day at the office. When you came through an event like that, you'd earned a story you might tell one day, but in the meantime there was nothing else to do but rest up and get ready to go back after it tomorrow.

★ ★ ★ ★

Chapter Nine

THE ACCORDION AS A CAREER STARTER

When people ask me how far back my experience as a musician on the road or in the studio goes, I can honestly tell them I've been doing both since I was six. It's all because of a versatile instrument that doesn't get nearly the respect it deserves—the accordion. My friend Buddy and I were six when our mothers decided we needed to learn how to play one.

I'm not sure what inspired Mrs. Rodgers, but my mom's father, a Russian immigrant, was a terrific accordion player, among many other things, and my dad loved the accordion. Buddy and I were taken to Hugo Helmer's music store in Mount Vernon, Washington, and had our first twelve-bass accordions placed in our hands. We began taking lessons, and I quickly learned the extent of my mother's desire to instill in me a work ethic and a sense of discipline. She made me practice one hour a day, every day. If my attention lapsed, I had only to look at the willow switch that lay on the warming oven on our old stove. Buddy and the other kids would come by sometimes and sit on the lawn in front of the house, yelling, "Come on, let's go!" Asking for permission to break early was futile. My mother would say, "You have twenty-five more minutes."

I'd practice and practice, and as much as I sometimes thought I wanted to be anywhere else, I learned as much about discipline as I did about the accordion. If you want to do something well, and you want it badly enough, you'd better stay at it and just do it. Nobody's going to play that accordion or get that business off the ground for you, or do any of the other things you want to get done. I'm not saying you're not going to need help, because you will, but if you want to make something happen, you're going to have to do it yourself.

Mr. Helmer was also the founder and leader of a fifty-piece aggregation called Hugo Helmer's Marching Accordion Band. Buddy and I were enrolled right away, and because of our age and size, we were put together in the front row. We'd jump into Mom and Dad's 1939 Chevy and head to Mount Vernon for our once-a-week rehearsals at the Moose Hall, which had dance floors big enough to allow the band to go through all the drills. There was also a stage where the band members sat in pretty much the same positions we had when we were marching, and we'd practice polkas, schottisches, marches, and popular songs. Every summer we did a whole circuit of recitals, fairs, carnivals, parades, and community events in Washington and Canada. I did that until I was sixteen, and although we didn't make any money, it was a chance for a green kid to learn something about showmanship, hard work, and travel as a musician.

One of the first songs I learned was "My Wild Irish Rose," which both my parents loved. My dad encouraged me to take the accordion onto his boat, and I'd practice when things were quiet.

I especially remember our trips into Bowman's Bay, where Dad sold his salmon to buyers in boats anywhere from 60 to 80 feet long. The fishing boats tied up alongside the buyers, and one at a time the fishermen pitched their fish onto the buyer's boat. They'd weigh your fish and give you a ticket for the night's catch. In the galley, Dad and the fishermen he always liked to visit with could get coffee, donuts, and rolls.

I remember one morning tying up to the buyer's boat and the skipper looking down at us and saying, with his thick Norwegian accent, "Ollie, did the boy bring the accordion?"

"Yes, he did," Dad said proudly. They lifted the accordion up and onto the big boat and then hoisted me aboard. They sat me up on the counter in the galley, and I played "My Wild Irish Rose" for all those fishermen while they drank coffee and ate donuts. I remember something clicking inside me when they applauded—I really liked that.

When my first grade teacher, Dell Bryson, a precious lady and a wonderful influence on me, learned I could play, she talked my mother into having me bring my accordion to school. I was proud to be in the same old three-story school my dad had attended, and I loved the feel of that crowded old building, which housed everyone from us newcomers to the high school kids. Let me tell you, I was scared to death, though. I got off the bus and my mom met me there with my accordion, and she and Mrs. Bryson walked alongside me down the hall. I was wearing the embroidered western shirt my mother had made, and into the eighth graders' class we went. They got me up on top of the piano, both of them assuring me that I could pull this off. I looked out and saw all those older kids staring at me as the room turned quiet. I don't know how I did it, but somehow I did, playing "My Wild Irish Rose" on that twelve-bass accordion as well as I knew how.

That song became a staple for me, and it was the first thing I ever played in a recording studio. It was at KBRC in Mount Vernon, and I played my heart out into a microphone hooked up to an acetate that became my first record—a commemorative single I wish I could lay my hands on now.

The only thing I didn't really like about the accordion experience was my music teacher. Gus was one of several people working for Hugo, and, like all of them, he was an amazing player. The guy could play anything—standards, jazz, boogie, Cajun. He had once finished fifth in the world in a competition. If I could have played like him, I'd have thought I'd died and gone to heaven. But he was an old school, single-minded disciplinarian who stuck to a rote teaching style that drove me nuts. Don't get me wrong; I learned a lot. You don't learn "Lady of Spain" and "Dizzy Fingers" without a good teacher and lots and lots of that hour-a-day practice, but I wanted more than just to be able to play those songs well. I wanted to be able to back somebody up, to fill in behind a singer or join in with a band and just pick it up. I think Gus could sense my frustration, because from the beginning he treated me like somebody who didn't have his heart into it and who was going to need to drill, drill, drill.

More than once I left a session so frustrated I was crying. As just one example, if you made a mistake, you couldn't start over or pick it up someplace simple. You had to get a running count and start on that note, on the beat. I could spend my whole lesson just trying to get in on the count. I hated it.

Overall, Gus was a mixed blessing. He taught me plenty of things, including how to play a lot of complicated songs, but to this day, I can't fill the holes behind a singer the way other people can. I would have loved a teacher who could have taught me a little bit of both.

I will give him this—Gus was part of an amazing musical journey I took as a boy. I look back and know how blessed I was along those lines. Plenty of times in Nashville recording studios I thought of my dad and that old radio, of my mother, who taught me to dance to the Big Band sound, and of my boyhood desire to sing country music and be a singing cowboy. Then there was everything I learned on that accordion. All of a sudden I realized how fortunate I was to be exposed to such a round-robin of music. I watched bands that were trying to make it, struggling to get an authentic country feel. They knew the pop and rock they'd grown up with, but they hadn't heard all the real country, going back to Roy Acuff and Eddy Arnold, that had come through those speakers at home and on my dad's boat. Some of them didn't have the Big Band exposure that let them round out their feel for Western swing. Some bands with great ability out there aren't very musically rounded, but because of the variety and the discipline of my childhood, I had a big advantage when I finally moved to Nashville.

[Ron Christensen, me and Denny Hoff]

★ ★ ★ ★

Chapter Ten

ROCKIN' IN THE BROOM CLOSET

As hard as it may be to believe, two of the places that put indelible stamps on my musical development were a boiler room and a broom closet. I should probably explain that. After several years of playing the accordion, I became interested in the guitar. My grandpa bought one and gave it to me, and I fooled with it every chance I got. The closest I got to lessons came from Hank Zeilstra, a school janitor I called Uncle Hank. He played guitar in a band for years and was another tremendous influence on me. Years later, we had a yearly party, and it seemed half the town showed up. I invited musicians from all over, and Uncle Hank always rounded up some of the old-timers he used to play with. I remember the steel guitar player well, because he had to use a walker to get across the floor, but his playing and the overall sound were amazing. During trips back and forth from Nashville, I'd always visit Uncle Hank and tell him stories about the Opry and the people I met there.

Anyway, I'd bring the guitar on the bus to Clover Valley Grade School, and when recess came, I'd take it to the boiler room. I could feel the heat coming from behind that door as I opened it. Hank would be waiting for me, and he'd light up a cigarette and take a break so he could help me learn how to play.

I'd bring a piece of lined notebook paper, and he'd draw six strings and then draw the finger positions for a chord on them. We started with a G chord. He showed me how to play it, and then I took the guitar and the paper home and just beat that thing to death. At first, I'd sing everything I knew and never change finger positions. Then I'd go back and play the chord for him, and when he was satisfied I knew it, he'd show me another. It went on that way until I got to be pretty good at it.

Once you learn a few chords you can sing a lot of songs, which of course was just what I wanted to do. That meant I didn't always see eye to eye with Mr. Young, the school's choir director, who more or less stuck to the book. It was a process that didn't have as many immediate rewards, and the stuff we did wasn't always to my liking. They offered both choir and band to us, and I started out in choir, where it didn't take long for Mr. Young and me to bump heads.

Once two other guys in the choir and I were put together to do a song for a school program. Mr. Young told me how the song was going to be done, and I just didn't like it that way. I really thought it needed extra pep. So, one day the other two guys—Ron Christensen, a great tenor, and Denny Hoff, a baritone who could charm anyone—and I were holed up in the broom closet rehearsing. I had spiced up the arrangement, and between that and the natural reverb in that tiny room, I thought we sounded great. We were really rockin' along when all of a sudden that closet door flew open and there was Mr. Young. He'd been walking by and heard us. We got quite an earful about the relative merits of the arrangement he preferred, and it was becoming clearer that he and I were never going to see eye-to-eye and that he was the one calling the shots.

Another time we were rehearsing a song with a really good piano player who had been working with the choir. Once again, I thought Mr. Young might not mind a new arrangement—I was only changing things a little. One day before he got to the rehearsal, I talked some folks into, shall we say, adjusting the tempo. The piano player got a little more Little Richard into his playing, and he and a bunch of us were really rockin'. I'd never have believed we could make it sound that good. Of course, when Mr. Young got there, he took exception to my conducting ideas, and I was asked to leave the choir. My days as a bandleader were over, at least during my early years in high school.

Looking back on it, though, I doubt if our parting of the ways hurt either Mr. Young or me in the long run, and it's funny how things turn out. At my twenty-year class reunion I was asked to put a band together and play the dance portion of the evening. The band and I spent quite a bit of time getting set up and going over the show, so I missed a good portion of the evening's program. Up to that time I really didn't know who all was there. After the evening got rolling and everybody began to dance, an older gentleman walked up to the stage. He just stood there watching me and listening. It was Mr. Young. After the song was over, I jumped off the stage and shook his hand. He was all smiles as he said, "Arnie, if I hadn't seen it with my own eyes, I never would have believed it." We had a great visit before the night was over and had a lot of laughs. After all those years, it turned out he was a great guy.

[Dad, Grandma and Grandpa Deckwa]

★ ★ ★ ★

Chapter Eleven

◆◆◆◆◆◆◆◆◆◆◆◆◆◆◆◆◆◆◆◆◆◆◆◆

NATURE'S BOUNTY AS A WAY OF LIFE

◆◆◆◆◆◆◆◆◆◆◆◆◆◆◆◆◆◆◆◆◆◆◆◆

If I'm going to talk about music, I need to talk about my other passion too—food. You know, for a family that didn't have any money to speak of, the Deckwas of Whidbey Island, Washington, had an awful lot of the bounty of nature on their table. Our freezer was usually filled with venison and elk from hunting trips I took with my dad starting when I was seven or eight; there was salmon, cod, crabs, clams, oysters, shrimp, and more from the sea; and we had vegetable gardens, apple and cherry trees, and a berry farm next door on my grandparents' place that brought us raspberries, blackberries, boysenberries, and loganberries. It makes my mouth water just thinking about it.

Grandpa Deckwa's house was exactly 660 feet from ours, and as a kid, I always seemed to be headed there. Grandma usually had raspberry or blackberry cobbler on the wood stove. What a delicious smell that was, and what a treat it was walking in their door!

There weren't a lot of kids in our small fishing village, but you could generally find all of them at Grandma's house at one time or another during the course of a day. When friends came to visit from the city, that was the first place I'd take them. Grandma's kitchen was special for far more than just the cobbler, although that was always a prime attraction. The stove required a good deal of wood splitting, and from the time I was a little guy I got to help Grandpa split wood and carry it in to the wood box beside the stove. That box also held the broom Grandma used to chase me out of the house if I tried to steal samples while she cooked!

Everything that came from that stove just seemed to taste great, from the wonderfully thin hotcakes Grandma made for breakfast to giant Thanksgiving turkeys that knocked your socks off. We ate at a big round table with lion claws at the bottom of each leg. Sometimes it was just the three of us, with Grandpa and me seeing who could eat the most pancakes. Sometimes it was that big holiday feast with the entire family and maybe a neighbor or two. Either way, it was a wonderful place to sit down together over whatever Grandma cooked.

✦✦✦✦

The aroma of that alder-smoked salmon floating on the breeze to my nostrils was absolutely heavenly.

Plenty of dishes ended up on that table. Grandpa and Grandma raised chickens and big white rabbits. They had hutches from one end of the place to the other, and I have never seen as many rabbits in all my life. Most of them went to market, and we ate the rest.

Much of the time, there was one kind of fish or another for the main course, and a lot of that came out of the twelve-by-fourteen-foot smokehouse Dad built behind their house. Ah, that smokehouse. The aroma of that alder-smoked salmon floating on the breeze to my nostrils was absolutely heavenly.

All of that work, by the way, was what Grandpa called "retirement," because he started farming berries after he "retired." Actually, the concept was foreign to him because it implied quitting, a word that wasn't in his vocabulary. That farm, like everything he did, combined hard work and nature's bounty into an absolute work of art. Coming in off the Sound by boat under Deception Pass Bridge and turning into Cornet Bay, you'd look up and see the most picturesque berry farm you ever laid eyes on sitting on a hill that rose up out of the water. Those rows ran straight as arrows all the way from the road at the edge of the water to the top of the hill, a distance of a little more than four hundred feet. During harvest time, everybody in the family picked berries, and many times I made the trip with Grandpa to take them to market.

Grandpa also had a giant vegetable garden that was just as beautiful, although I can vouch for the fact that beauty is relative after you spend a few hours working in the middle of it. As a kid, I worked with him a lot from spring to fall, whether I wanted to or not. Much of it was hard, and I'll be honest and tell you I wasn't always thrilled about doing my share. Those rows of berries seemed to stretch out forever.

On the other hand, I always enjoyed having my own cucumber garden. Actually, I helped Mom and Dad plant it but called it mine. I loved Mom's dill pickles. She made the best in the world, and if I could sell a few cucumbers to the neighbors, I did. I was around twelve then and also had a garbage route. I'd use Dad and Grandpa's Farmall Cub tractor, hook the old net trailer on behind, go to the neighbors' homes, pick up their garbage cans, and head to the local dump, which was toward the end of the road about a mile. At fifty cents a can I was also on my way to being prosperous. The only problem came after I returned all the cans, unhooked the trailer, and parked the tractor, when it was time to count the money. There weren't many neighbors, and Dad and Grandpa were always there holding out their hands for what they called "expenses," like gas and equipment. It took me a long time to understand why I was doing all that work, and they were getting most of the money. I think their laughter when they took it was what got me the most.

Still, that was my entry into the world of commerce, my way to be a money-making part of a family that turned food and ideas into a wonderful way of life. As I look back on it, I wouldn't trade an ounce of that lifestyle for love or money.

★ ★ ★ ★

Chapter Twelve

HOW TO GET SICK OF DONUTS

When I was fifteen or so, my friend Willard Gaddis drove a bakery truck. He was a neat guy and I'd ride with him once in a while, enjoying the smells as much as our conversations. We got to talking about what I was going to do once fishing season ended in the fall, and he suggested I apply for a job at the bakery, which was in Oak Harbor. I could work nights and earn a little spending money until fishing season started again in the spring.

George Dixon, who owned the place, was a terrific businessman and a very smart manager. I'll never forget my first day. I was younger by far than everyone else there, and George had his arm around my shoulder, saying, "Come here, son. I'm going to show you our bakery."

My teenage eyes saw the place as a big commercial operation. All the bread ovens stood on one side of the building near the tables where people were rolling out dough for bread, biscuits, cinnamon rolls, and other sweets. Nearby were the deep-frying vats for donuts. There were big tubs of dough rising, and people sliding trays in and out of ovens and taking baskets of donuts out of the grease. Then there was the area where they did the packaging, putting all of this great food into cellophane and boxes, getting it ready for delivery or for sale out front. The place smelled like heaven.

"See all these pastries?" Mr. Dixon said, pointing toward the big table where the donuts—plain, frosted, glazed, filled, chocolate-covered and sprinkled—and cinnamon and maple rolls, éclairs, and all the rest were waiting to be boxed up.

"Yes, sir."

"You help yourself," he said with a kindly smile. "Eat as many as you like, on the house."

"Oh, wow, thanks!" I said, scarcely believing my good fortune. The tour went on and he showed me the rest of the place, but my mind never left that table full of pastries.

"Just help yourself," he told me again when the tour was finished.

What a job! Let me tell you, I was a natural when it came to eating pastries. I gorged myself on them.

Well, he was a brilliant man. Within two weeks I couldn't stand the smell of the stuff. It got to where I'd walk in and they'd kid me: "Hey, Arn, want a donut?" "No," I'd say. Who'd have thought you could get sick of donuts? For the cost of a few dollars' worth of flour and grease he had bought himself an employee who had no interest in eating up the profits.

My job was to cook the donuts. I was stationed at a huge vat—probably three feet by two feet by eighteen inches deep—filled with hot grease. I'd lower the donuts in a huge basket, and they'd float on top as they cooked. I'd use two cedar sticks to flip them over, then take the basket out and dump them on a table for whatever they needed next. It wasn't rocket science, but it was a pleasant-enough job.

For a time I also worked with the biscuit dough, which sat in what looked like a bathtub on wheels. Once it had risen, you'd punch it and knead it, roll it back and forth, then put it back in there. After it rose again, you had to get it from there to the hopper that emptied into the machine that actually made the biscuits. I'd watch George and all the others do it, and they'd just pick up this great big ball of dough and move it in one easy motion into that vat. The trick was, you had to have your timing just right to do it without having the whole thing start this slow, goopy drip toward the floor.

Now, besides being the youngest, I was also the shortest guy in the building, and this vat was way up above my head. *How do they get it up there?* I'd ask myself. I'd gotten the kneading part down, but every time I picked up that dough, it started drooping. If I held it for more than an instant, the dough started to stretch, and I'd have to set it back down again. I tried it a couple of times, and soon everybody turned to watch. Of course, nobody was coming to help anymore. They figured it was time I did it on my own, and they were more interested in a good show than the chance to perform a good deed.

I looked down into the tub of dough and up at the vat, and finally I thought, *Well, I'd better get this thing up there somehow.* I picked it up and walked over, reaching and stretching, and this great big blob of dough just started drooping down my arms and onto my face. I was draped with dough, trying to hold it together and push it up there. Obviously my method wasn't going to work. Slowly, it drooped down the side of my body; part of it went all the way to the floor. The gang got a great show.

Eventually, I got the hang of it—the trick is speed—but from then on when it was time to lift that dough out of the tub and up into the vat, I usually got a little help.

Then there was the night I was in front of the hot grease with the donuts cooking away when all of a sudden the lights went out. After a long moment or two, people started lighting candles and lanterns, and I decided I needed to help salvage what we could. I walked over to the ovens, and we started pulling bread and biscuits out of them like crazy, setting them anywhere we could. Then at some point I heard somebody yell, "Arnie, your donuts!"

"Yeah, what about them?" I said. I took a whiff, and, sure enough, I could smell smoke, which was just pouring out of the vat. I got myself over there, grabbed the basket, and pulled them out of the grease. My co-workers thought it was a hoot that I'd forgotten that grease doesn't get cold just because the power goes off and that the donuts would keep cooking. It wasn't the first or last time they had a laugh at my expense.

All in all, working for Mr. Dixon was quite an experience. The people there may have laughed at some of my mishaps, but they were a good bunch and they taught me a lot. Although my time there made me realize I didn't ever want to work in a bakery again, I learned some things that helped me later on when I started cooking and taking part in food shows—something I never dreamed I'd be doing one day.

★ ★ ★ ★

Chapter Thirteen

◆◆◆◆◆◆◆◆◆◆◆◆◆◆◆◆◆◆◆◆◆◆◆◆◆

HITCHHIKING NEVADA:
THE PINK STUCCO ADVENTURE

◆◆◆◆◆◆◆◆◆◆◆◆◆◆◆◆◆◆◆◆◆◆◆◆◆

One of my bigger adventures—involving several cars, a bus, a shuttle, and a tractor-trailer rig that pulled mobile homes—led me all the way to Nevada in the summer of 1956.

I was fifteen, and the dream of being a cowboy and working on a cattle ranch was so real I could taste it. A pal of mine, Art Edwards, had moved to Fallon, Nevada, to live with his dad, who was stationed there as a chief in the Navy. Art's brother Bill, another pal, told me Art had been working on a cattle ranch and said he was sure he could get me a job there. I wrote a letter to Art but never got a response, which seemed a little puzzling because he was such a good friend.

But I threw caution to the wind and, with what money I had saved plus a $10 stake from a neighbor, I jumped into a 1951 Ford with a lad named Jim

Dallman. Jim was driving home to Florida, and I rode just far enough to catch a bus that would take me all the way to Reno.

I arrived in Reno before daylight, then caught a sixty-mile shuttle that dropped me off at a little café in Fallon, where I began making calls, trying to find Art. No one was at his house, so I called his dad on the Navy base. That one didn't go very well either—he hung up on me. I came to find out Art's dad had received the letter I'd written, but as near as I could tell, Art never read it. I didn't know that then, and it was time to make a decision. I only had $4.25 to my name by then, and being frugal had become of utmost importance. I looked around that café and realized I had no idea where to look for Art. Since he hadn't been in Fallon that long, no one seemed to have heard of him, and my odds of finding him appeared to be very, very slim. Having been taught that making any decision was better than not making a decision at all, I pondered for a bit, then decided to go back home.

I walked down the road, back toward Reno, and stood in front of a pink stucco building, hitchhiking for what seemed like hours, trying without success to get a ride. Across the road was a ranch with white fences along both sides of a very long lane. I decided that if the next car that came by didn't pick me up, I was going to walk down that lane and find a job. I told myself I'd wash dishes, fix fences, feed cattle and horses—whatever it took to earn some money.

★★★★

I told myself I'd wash dishes, fix fences, feed cattle and horses— whatever it took to earn some money.

The next car that came by was an early 1950s, light blue and white Chevy. I stuck out my thumb, it stopped, and I got in. The driver told me he wasn't going far, but he would get me started back to Reno. He also told me I'd be having a tough time finding a ride because not long ago an older couple's car had broken down not far from there and both had been killed by a couple of guys—which explained why I hadn't been getting rides. The man took me about a mile and dropped me off at an intersection. I thanked him and watched as he took the road to the left and drove out of sight. I had made a decision to go home, and that's what I was going to do, so I began hitchhiking with everything I had as I walked down that long, lonely, and very hot road.

I walked for hours carrying my cream-colored, black-buttoned topcoat and my small metal suitcase. I looked about as much like a cowboy as—well,

I didn't look like one at all. I stuck my thumb out at every car that came by. No one even slowed down. By then it was late afternoon, and I had walked holes the size of 50-cent pieces into the soles of my loafers. Things were beginning to get a little serious.

Finally, a truck heading in my direction slowed down and stopped. I jumped in, and the driver said he hauled mobile homes and was on his way to pick one up on the other side of Reno; he could take me that far. As he dropped me off, I thanked him for the ride and pointed myself toward Woodland, California, where I had figured out I would need to take a right to go home, rather than a left, which would take me to Southern California, a mistake I didn't want to make.

I walked and walked. Finally a guy in another Chevy picked me up. He was a strange guy in a big hurry. He kept talking about his wife being in a bus not too far behind him and how he had to beat her home. He kept asking me if I'd like to go home to Los Angeles with him, and the more he talked, the more he worried me. It was a long 150 miles, and when we stopped at an intersection in Woodland, I literally jumped out of the car and ran through the traffic to a Texaco service station. The light changed, and away he went.

By that time it was getting dark and starting to rain, and I was very tired. I stood in front of the service station hitchhiking for hours with no luck. The rain had begun to come down harder; I was drenched. I went into the service station bathroom to get out of the rain and felt like collapsing. I don't know what caused me to do it, but I opened the door of the stall, went in, closed the door, and lay down on the floor. Using my topcoat for a pillow, I promptly fell asleep.

I don't know if I slept for five minutes or an hour, but I do know when I woke up, I charged back out into the dark night and heavy rain and hitchhiked with all I had. I wasn't out there too long before a black 1949 or 1950 Ford pulled up. The driver asked me where I was headed. I told him, "Oak Harbor."

"Where's that?" he said.

I thought that was a little strange—everyone knows where Oak Harbor is. I told him it was up by Seattle. As it turned out, he was in the Navy and being shipped from back East to Bremerton, Washington, not far from where I lived on Whidbey Island.

There was a little restaurant alongside the service station, and he suggested we go there, get a Coke, and get to know each other a little before we began our drive together. I've never forgotten that restaurant, because my Coke cost me 50 cents and that took my finances down to a measly $3.75—and I wasn't anywhere near home yet. We visited for a while and then got under way.

His name was Dick Powell, the same as the movie star, and the back seat of his car had been turned into a bed. He told me I was welcome to crawl back there and get some shut-eye, and I did. I went out like a light.

The jerking of the car woke me up. We were stopped, and I very carefully slid out from under the warm quilts and peered out the side window, only to see Dick changing a flat tire in the snow. Seeing he had it under control, I very quietly slid back under those wonderful quilts and drifted into la-la land again.

Dick drove me to my doorstep in Cornet Bay and stayed with us for several days before checking into his new duty station at Bremerton. He came back and visited us several times after that, but soon we lost contact, and I haven't seen him since. He was definitely a blessing, maybe even an angel. Our God definitely answers our prayers—that's something I know for sure.

Now, there is just one kicker to this story. In the early 1990s, when my wife, Joanne, and I were living in our condo in Franklin, Tennessee, I received a call from the Edwards brothers. Bill and Art were coming in from Georgia to spend a couple of nights with us. We took them backstage at the Opry and took quite a few pictures of them with several of the stars, and we just had a ball catching up. During one of our morning visits around our kitchen table, my 1956 Nevada story came up. It seems Art and his dad didn't get along real well, and Art hadn't read my letter. Still, we had been very close to each other in Fallon and just didn't know it.

Art and his dad had gotten into an argument that turned into a real knock-down, drag-out, so Art's dad had him thrown in jail for a couple of days to cool him off. That jail was the pink stucco building I stood in front of while hitchhiking my way out of town. We had a good laugh about that one.

★ ★ ★ ★

Chapter Fourteen

LIFE LESSONS FROM SOMEBODY WHO USED TO BE COOL

For a while in the mid-1950s, as James Dean and Elvis were just making their marks on the culture, I began turning myself into the epitome of the Whidbey Island hipster. I had my hair greased and combed back into a perfect ducktail, engineer boots polished and shining like a brand-new car, Levi's pulled down just a skosh for that perfect fit. Then, to set it all into motion, there was my leather jacket. Ah, yes, the jacket. That was the key to the whole deal. I'd stand at the mirror, grab the collar with my thumb and forefinger, and, slowly, with the look of someone who would never be afraid of anything, turn it up. The zipper was there only for its silver gleam; I rarely used it—I wanted the front of my jacket to be wide open. Through rain, wind, sleet, snow, or anything else the Pacific Northwest could throw at me, that jacket front was open, exposing the only thing someone as cool as I was would ever wear under it during those exciting years—a plain, white, James Dean-style

T-shirt. When I was in that get-up, you could tell from across the school parking lot, before I ever opened my mouth, that I was as cool as they got.

Cool? The truth of the matter was, when the weather was bad, I was downright cold. Warm, sunny days are the exception, not the rule, around Puget Sound, but would I show it? Not on your life! I'd join the guys in the parking lot, light up a cigarette, and immediately become somebody. I was going places. Where, I hadn't yet figured out, but you could rest assured that I'd get there. In the meantime, I'd light another cigarette and assume the attitude. Then I'd get to thinking, *Just how much good are those classes doing me? This might be just the time to start skipping one every now and then. Then, everybody will notice just how cool I am.*

The first person who noticed, of course, was my teacher, who alerted the principal that young Arnie Deckwa wasn't in class. The next thing I knew, I was being invited to *stay* out of class.

That, I can tell you, was some pressure. "Dad," I could picture myself saying, "it's like this. . . ," and I'd think of all those times I tried to explain the report cards that said, "Arnie could be a good student if he applied himself." There really wasn't any good way to explain something like that to my dad, so there I was, trying desperately to get back into a class I was barely passing. Once I got back in, there was even more pressure. I couldn't just sit there and not be cool, so I'd start acting up, being the class clown. I was spending a lot more time trying to get a laugh than I ever did trying to get smart.

It wasn't that I didn't like some parts of school. When the teacher was good, I applied myself and enjoyed learning. Still, being cool, dressing cool, being somebody, lighting another cigarette, cutting up in class—well, peer pressure and I were teaming up to short-circuit my school career. Plus, I was a little cocky because I had started running fishing boats at 14. It happened to a lot of boys there. Some parents wouldn't let their younger sons operate boats at all when they saw the older kids deciding they didn't need school anymore. All of that was conspiring to complicate my young life, and in my junior year, after a knee injury playing football, I decided to drop out. My parents didn't particularly like it, but they weren't able to talk me out of it either.

[Grandpa and Grandma Deckwa]

★ ★ ★ ★

Chapter Fifteen

MY FIRST LESSON IN ATTITUDE

I should tell you that as much as I love my family and the heritage they passed on to me, there were a few years when I thought it was time for me to rise above them.

It started as I began to develop "the attitude." I knew my cool quotient went down when I was at home, since my mom, dad, and grandparents were nowhere near as cool as the friends I was making in high school. That made the work I was doing for Grandpa Deckwa—a man who knew how to work you—that much harder.

Plenty of times I'd be out fishing by myself or with Dad all night long, and then I'd be expected to help out with the hoeing or harvesting, facing those long, long rows of berries on little sleep. I had started experimenting with the Mr. Cool look, my lip curled into just the trace of a sneer to let everyone know I had that superior attitude. I spent one particularly long day on the tractor cultivating rows, turning up that beautifully rich black dirt, and when I finished, I brought the tractor back to where Grandpa always parked it, alongside the garage.

We didn't have a lot of barns and outbuildings, and Grandpa Deckwa was a perfectionist. He had made a cover that was always to go over the top of the tractor, and once you'd put that on and gotten it secure, you put a little can over the muffler. Well, this time, I just parked it, got off, straightened my hair, and lifted the collar up on my brown leather jacket, then started walking the 660 feet across the field to the house. I figured I'd done all I needed to do.

I hadn't gotten very far when I heard, "Arnold, come back and cover up the tractor." There was a slight edge to his voice. Grandpa was a man of few words, and when he told you to do something, he meant it. He had steel blue eyes that could cut right through you, and I could almost feel them at my back.

For the life of me, I don't know what got into me at that moment. I guess I felt my attitude was something I'd been earning. After all, I had begun running a commercial fishing boat on my own, at the age of fourteen, and sometimes now it was me talking to the fish buyer, like the forty-, sixty-, and seventy-year-old guys who'd been doing it all their lives. I was bucking the same tides they were bucking in the pass, and I guess I figured by then I knew about as much as I needed to know.

I turned around and said, "You want the tractor covered up, cover it up yourself." Then, in a very arrogant way, I turned around and took about three steps before I heard what sounded like a herd of elephants coming up behind me. In an instant I was on the ground, with my beautiful ducktail haircut messed and dirty. Now and then, when I was a younger boy, Grandpa told me in a joking manner that he was going to box my ears in. At that moment I learned exactly what he meant. He took my dignity and just drained it.

He was unbelievably fast. Every time I thought I was beginning to get back to my feet, he'd get his booted foot on my butt and push me right back down into the soft fluffy black dirt, usually face first. It was rougher than football. I literally ended up crawling back to that tractor; he made sure of it.

He never yelled. In fact, he never said a word. But I ended up with my face against one of those tractor tires, ready and willing to put the cover on and, for that matter, to do some wiping and polishing. When I finished with that tractor, it would have passed Marine inspection.

Sometimes I had to learn lessons the hard way, and that was one.

[My Grandpa Henry Sterkel is on the left]

★ ★ ★ ★

Chapter Sixteen

ANOTHER ATTITUDE ADJUSTMENT

I seemed to be a slow learner in those days, because my experience with Grandpa Deckwa boxing my ears didn't stop my bad attitude from surfacing again—this time with the other side of the family halfway across the state.

I was sixteen, and I had it together. I would be spending the summer at Grandfather and Grandmother Sterkel's place, driving to Kittitas, where they lived, in my white 1947 Pontiac, the first car I ever owned. I'd show this branch of the family, living on the outskirts of a town with just a few hundred people in it and working on a nearby farm, how a successful commercial fisherman from the coast could throw bales of hay with the best of them.

There were a couple of problems with the plan as I'd envisioned it. First, those bales weighed 110 pounds each. Second, 180 miles from the breezes off our cool waters, that part of the state of Washington gets awfully hot. Throwing a bale that weighs two-thirds of what you weigh in ninety-degree weather was a good deal harder than anything I'd tried lately.

Then, just as I had when Great-aunt Goldie asked if she could ride my horse, I underestimated the head of the central Washington part of our family. My mother's father Henry Sterkel was in his seventies, and I guess I wasn't taking him seriously. I figured I could handle this old Russian man.

Several of my aunts and uncles still lived at home, and I was working a lot with Uncle Mel and sometimes Uncle Bud and Grandpa. They were competitive workers, always trying to outdo each other to the point that it would have been comical if it hadn't have been such hard work. Uncle Mel took to calling me the "Coastal Puke" because he worked me so hard in that summer heat I would actually get sick and throw up.

Grandpa, believe it or not, worked as hard as they did, even at his age, and he expected me to do the same. If I was going to sleep in his house and eat his food, I was going to work.

We had loaded and unloaded a truck full of hay from one field and were about to start on a second when I realized just how exhausted I was. I was feeling kind of sick, and I wasn't moving very fast. My grandfather walked over to the truck and grabbed a pitchfork. He jabbed it into a bale of hay on the ground and threw it onto the truck at me. It hit me square in the chest. I caught it with the hay hooks and fell backwards into the headboard.

"By God, I tell you to work, you work," he said. I never slowed down again. I grabbed the next bale, starting on the next stack and keeping my misery to myself, realizing as I worked that this old man definitely had something left.

Grandpa Sterkel, born in 1881 in Russia, was raised during the time of the czars. Over the years I've heard many stories, and the one about the Russian women who went out into the fields to work until they were nine months pregnant, had their babies, and then went right back to work still amazes me.

He left Russia before the Revolution and World War I with his pregnant wife, crossing the Black Sea to Turkey in the bottom of a boat hauling cattle. She delivered her baby aboard the ship, and it died. As the story goes, Grandpa wanted to put it overboard, but Grandma wouldn't let him, so he put their baby in a trunk and covered it with blankets. When they reached land, he gave it the burial Grandma wished for. From there, they were able to emigrate to Pennsylvania, and then to Odessa in eastern Washington, where my mother was born in 1917. After the birth of Aunt Peggy, Aunt Mary was next, and then, when my mother was six, her mother died in childbirth. Grandfather had six children by then. Later, he married the woman I remembered as my grandmother. She was twenty-two years younger than Grandpa and the story is that years earlier she had been a little girl he'd chased away from the water trough. Between her three children, his six, and the five they had together—he was sixty-eight, by the way, when his last child was born—there were fourteen kids altogether.

Grandfather was a farmer, a carpenter, and a cobbler. He was also an entertainer who played the accordion and could dance up a storm. On his sixty-fifth birthday, the family gave him a big party at his house. Aunt Mary, who had a country band, got them playing something with a Russian feel, and they talked Grandpa into doing his Cossack dance. As he did, he performed back flips in the middle of the living room floor. When he was seventy-five, at a relative's wedding, Grandpa was again asked to perform. He did his Cossack dance and again turned those astonishing back flips. He was one tough guy, and he certainly taught Cool Arnie Deckwa a few things I've never forgotten and never will.

Uncle Bud, Aunt Shirleen's husband, is a saddle maker and cattleman who once performed a Caesarian on a cow—and saved both the cow and her calf. Of all my uncles, though, I was drawn most to Uncle Mel at that time in my life. He was just five years older than me. I was with him the first night I ever watched an Elvis Presley movie, *Love Me Tender*, in Ellensburg, Washington. I had the D.A. haircut and the leather jacket, and I was as cool as they came. Uncle Mel, like his dad, was also one tough cookie, but underneath that hard exterior he had a heart of gold. He, like Grandpa, also liked to have a drink now and then, and that seemed exciting to my sixteen-year-old brain. I idolized the guy.

I was quite a follower at the time, and this seemed like the cool thing to be doing. We proceeded to go out one night and have some drinks. We had a ball, and got home around four in the morning. It was about the time Grandpa was getting up, and as we sauntered in, he was standing in the doorway of the bedroom. He had on striped bib overalls, and he was leaning against the door jamb, rubbing his back, scratching it to give himself a little relief from the skin cancer he'd gotten from years in the sun.

———— ★★★★ ————

On his sixty-fifth birthday, Grandpa performed back flips in the middle of the living room floor. When he was seventy-five, he did it again.

Uncle Mel walked by, and Grandpa mumbled in his Russian accent, which was sometimes hard for me to understand, something about "damned kids." Mel looked at him and told him something I would never have dreamed of telling my dad, but he got away with it, so I decided to say the same thing.

I did, and just as quickly as Grandpa Deckwa had adjusted my attitude, Grandpa Sterkel adjusted it again. He had hands the size of a giant's, and he was a very strong man. My words hadn't finished leaving my mouth when he grabbed hold of the collar of my shirt and my belt buckle and lifted and threw me across the bed in one clean motion. The back of my head, my butt and the heels of my boots hit the wall at the same time, and I slid down onto the bed. I grabbed covers as fast as I could and just lay there, never looking up, wondering what had just happened.

That instant definitely helped keep my attention, although I always did wonder, *How did Uncle Mel get away with that?* I guess Grandpa and he had worked together for so long that he must have looked at him like just another adult, but he noticed right off that this young grandson of his needed a few alterations, and he flat gave me some in a hurry. I never did talk to him—or anybody else, for that matter—that way again.

Grandpa worked until he was eighty years old. I remember him saying that the foreman on the farm had asked him to quit working—he was afraid one day he would find Grandpa lying out in some row of corn. Grandpa declined, saying, "I can't think of a nicer guy to find me."

Grandpa did retire at eighty, then passed away in 1962, a couple of months before his eighty-first birthday. There are some things in this world I wish I would have done, and one of them is to have visited with all my grandparents more often so I could have heard more of their stories— stories that are now lost forever. I really loved that man, and I know he loved me.

[Uncle Marvin "Bud" Sterkel, my John Wayne]

★ ★ ★ ★

Chapter Seventeen

◆◆◆◆◆◆◆◆◆◆◆◆◆◆◆◆◆◆◆◆◆◆◆◆

THE ACCIDENT: A HUGE LIFE LESSON

◆◆◆◆◆◆◆◆◆◆◆◆◆◆◆◆◆◆◆◆◆◆◆◆

I've already told you how being cool led to some big life lessons, but the biggest and most powerful of those lessons involved automobiles.

Back in 1958, when I was seventeen, I had this 1957 Chevy Bel Air sport coupe. It was a turquoise-colored, two-door hardtop, and it was just beautiful. It could also flat-out fly. I bought it while I was working for Papa Joe Lang after I dropped out of school my junior year. We were scraping the USO building in Oak Harbor, getting it ready to paint, when Don Boyer, who later owned Boyer Chevrolet and Pontiac, brought it over and showed it to me. The car had 23,000 miles on it, but it was like brand new. Papa Joe let me go for a ride with Don, and I drove it a little. By the time we got back, I was mesmerized. This beautiful Bel Air sport coupe was going to be mine! It was all I could think about. I went back to work, and with every stroke of the scraper I pictured that car. It's a wonder I didn't dig right through the wall of the building.

You'd think when I finally owned it, I'd be a thoughtful, careful driver, but that just wasn't me at the time. I was driving home one night from Oak Harbor, and I whizzed by this 1957 Ford. I knew as I passed that it was a Washington state trooper's vehicle. This one was driven by Del Honsberger, who to this day is a very good friend of mine. At the time, though, he was simply a hard-nosed trooper, the first one I really remember coming to Whidbey Island. Of course, once he got there, it seemed he spent most of his time tailing or stopping me.

Now, Honsberger could drive. He should have been a race car driver. To show you how bright I was, I took that as a challenge. I saw him, and I stomped it, thinking, *I'm gonna outrun this guy.* I did, for a while, not thinking about the fact that he knew my car and who I was. I lost him and turned onto Cornet Bay Road, but in just a moment he was right behind me. He stopped me, and I got arrested for speeding—right in front of my house. That wasn't the only time he stopped me, and there was at least one time I wish he would have.

★★★★

They say the car went end over end three times or so and rolled over as well.

My pals Buddy Rodgers and Chuck Jaeger and I were out at a party one night. We'd been drinking, and we decided to go for a ride in my car. We were flying down the road, and we got to a turn the car just didn't make. They say it went end over end three times or so and rolled over a few times as well. Bud and Chuck were thrown out of the car—this was before the days of seatbelts—and both were severely injured. It's a wonder any of us lived. I later found out our friends Dave Milanoski and Kirk Dimmit picked us up in Dave's little '40 Ford and took us to the Navy hospital.

When I woke up, my dad was there. Being the great guy he always was, he didn't lecture me. He just smiled enough to let me know how much he loved me and how concerned he was.

I went home a few hours later, little more than shook up. Buddy had a head the size of a watermelon, and Chuck had a broken neck. They would both recover, but my stupidity had nearly cost them their lives.

The next day my father took me to the Ford garage where my car had been towed. Word had gotten out, and as I went around back, several other people were looking at it, shaking their heads. This once-beautiful sports coupe was so smashed up we couldn't believe any of us made it out without being killed. It was nothing more than scrap.

At one point, Honsberger walked up to me.

"How fast were you going?" he asked.

"I have no idea."

"Come with me," he said. I looked at my dad, who nodded as if to say, "Go."

"Get in," Honsberger said when we got to his patrol car.

He drove out to where this whole incident began, stopping at the driveway of the house where the party had been. We retraced the route the three of us had taken from the party, and as we got to the straightaway leading to that sharp curve, he said, "Those skid marks there in the road yours?"

"I don't know," I said.

He looked at me kind of funny, like he was thinking, I'm gonna have trouble with this kid.

"Were you going about this fast?" he asked me.

"I don't know."

He sped up. "Do you think you were going about this fast?"

"I don't know." This was the day after the accident, and I guess I was still a little shook.

He sped up again, just as we were getting to the corner, and as we made the turn, this older couple was rounding it from the other direction, right in the middle of the road. We were doing a pretty good clip, and Honsie took that patrol car and laid it right onto the shoulder on my side because it was the only place to go. I looked over and said, "I think that was fast enough."

That old couple just scared the fire out of both of us, and it gave me all the respect in the world for Honsie. I'd always heard he could really drive a car, and his quick thinking that day proved it to me. I wish I could say it taught me to drive more carefully and with a little more sense, but that wouldn't happen for a while.

★ ★ ★ ★

Chapter Eighteen

◆◆◆◆◆◆◆◆◆◆◆◆◆◆◆◆◆◆◆◆◆◆◆◆

"YOU CAN'T BEAT US, DECKWA, SO YOU MIGHT AS WELL JOIN US"

◆◆◆◆◆◆◆◆◆◆◆◆◆◆◆◆◆◆◆◆◆◆◆◆

When it came to the law—usually personified by Honsie—I was always touching base because of my driving habits. I was arrested more than once for speeding and once for reckless driving, losing my license and getting an occupational license that allowed me to drive just to work and back.

My friends and I weren't bad kids by today's standards. There was nothing too malicious about what we did, and we were worlds away from things like drive-by shootings. Still, I always seemed to be in more of a hurry to go places than what the law thought prudent, at least judging by the speed limit signs posted in the area. That meant Honsie was fated to remain part of my life, something that's still true today. The real turning point in our friendship came one New Year's Day when I was in my early twenties. I was working for a contractor at the time, building houses, and I was sitting in a house I had just bought, drinking beer and watching the Rose Bowl with my buds Mike Ostrom and Mike Loughlin.

Honsberger pulled into my driveway in a patrol car, turned around, and parked where he could look out his window into my living room. The two Mikes and I were standing there with our beers, looking out the window, and one of them said to me, "What did you do wrong?"

"I don't know," I said truthfully.

Honsberger motioned to me to come out of the house and down to the patrol car. When I did, he said, "Get in." I'd heard that one before. I got in, and without a word he drove out of the driveway and headed toward West Beach. Finally, he said, "You know, Deckwa, you can't beat us, so you might as well join us. There's an opening at the Island County Sheriff's Department for a deputy, and you're gonna go down there and look into this job."

I was just dumbfounded. I looked at him. "Me, a cop?"

"Like I said, you can't beat us. You're going down there."

I looked at him kind of funny. He was dead serious.

At the time, I was working construction and raising some horses, and a few days after our conversation, I was cleaning box stalls when all of a sudden I decided I should go see the sheriff. Honsberger hadn't made a request. He'd pretty much given me an order. I put the pitchfork away, drove down, and walked into the sheriff's office wearing what I'd been wearing in the barn. Sheriff Arnie Freund was around twenty years older than I was, but he was a local, raised on the island just like me.

"Why do you want to be a deputy sheriff?" he asked.

"I'm not sure I do." That was as honest as I could be. Still, the more we talked, the more interested I got, and one thing led to another. I became a deputy, and that's when I got part of my comeuppance. I had to ride shotgun with Del Honsberger for almost a month. Again and again, I heard those words I'd heard so many times since I was a teenager: "Get in the car."

Our lives were intertwined from then on. We built houses together and literally saved each other's butt more than once, becoming the best of friends along the way. Honsie is still like a big brother to me.

I remember a visit with Honsie and his wife, Connie, in Yuma, Arizona, where they moved after retiring. Joanne and I were out checking accounts with Sam's Clubs at the time, and it was nice to stop and relax for a bit, catching up and reminiscing about our rich history together. We had a wonderful time, and one evening we were sitting by the swimming pool having a toddy when they got to telling a story. It seems that when Del was a young guy, Connie saved every ticket he got, putting them in an album. It turned out he'd gotten a ton of them. He was a boxer and a roughneck at the time, and finally one day a state trooper got hold of him and said, "You ain't gonna beat us, Honsberger, so you might as well join us."

I realized at that moment how awesome it was that he had passed the torch to me. I guess he saw in me what that other trooper had seen in him. If it weren't for Honsberger, it's hard to say which direction I might have taken. I will say my years with the sheriff's department were some of the best of my life.

[Me and Wick Peth]

[Wick keeping me safe]

★ ★ ★ ★

Chapter Nineteen

THE GROWN-UP COWBOY DREAM

Ever since I was a little boy, one of my biggest dreams was to be a cowboy. Mom and Dad helped it along, buying me two Roy Rogers cap pistols with a holster, leather wrist cuffs, and a cowboy hat, along with the classic Daisy Red Ryder BB gun. Then, of course, there was the saddle I rode on top of my dog Trigger's house as I sang to the seagulls.

My initial step toward the cowboy life came when I bought my first horse from Joe Short's family when I was about twelve. I paid $25 for it and to this day I tell Joe, who is a very close friend, that I got cheated—I should have had to pay only $20. He says I should have paid $30. It's a problem we'll never solve. It helps to know, as many of our friends do, that the Short family owns twenty or thirty head of good horses that sell for thousands of dollars each. To those who know us, our bickering, which we call the Arnie and Joe Show, has always been a real crowd pleaser.

Joe and I and our friend Les Kammenga rode horses together and dreamed of being cowboys from the time we were little tykes. All of us live on the places we were raised on, and we're still as close as ever. When we get together, often over a weekly game of cribbage, we'll hoist a glass and toast each other. It's always the same and it's always heartfelt: "Friends Forever."

Now, all horse owners have their stories, and the longer you have horses, the more stories you can tell. You soon learn you can't avoid a wreck now and then, and my friends and I all have our tales of being bucked off or maybe pulled off by one of the other kids while we played cowboys and Indians on the sand dunes by Cranberry Lake in nearby Deception Pass State Park. All in all, though, other than one time when I got tangled up with a tree limb, our wounds weren't that bad.

As I got a little older, I knew it was time for me to get more serious about being a real cowboy, so in May of 1960 I took the plunge and entered a rodeo. I'd met a couple of guys from San Angelo, Texas, who were stationed at Whidbey Island Naval Air Station. Besides being characters, both were rodeo cowboys. They helped me a lot with my roping skills, and in no time at all I was throwin' a loop onto buckets, rocks, fence posts—pretty much everything stationary—although I still hadn't thrown a rope at a steer from a horse.

Every year, there was a professional rodeo in Skagit County, about twenty minutes from where I lived in Cornet Bay. I thought about what it would take to start my rodeo career in roping, and it didn't look too practical. I'd need a good rope horse, a saddle, and a truck and trailer to get to the events. All of that costs a lot of money, which was something I didn't have as a nineteen-year-old. The only way to get this rodeo career started was to enter the bull-riding event, since all I'd have to do was get a bull rigging. I was in luck because my new pals, Denny and Scotty, were also bull riders. Between them, I had all the coaching I needed to get under way.

The first time I felt the tension of a bull rope was about a week before the rodeo. Denny sat me down in a rocking chair on the porch of his house after he had wrapped the bull rigging around the bottom of the chair. Then he wrapped it around my left hand and cinched it down so tight I thought my fingers were going to pop off. He said the last thing I needed was to lose my handhold, so the tighter the better. Then he went to rockin' that chair every which way he could think of and telling me how the movement of my free hand was supposed to help me keep my balance. If I touched the bull with it, though, I'd be disqualified. It wasn't long before my schooling was over, and I was ready to ride.

That next Saturday, I didn't feel quite as ready. Actually, behind the chutes, putting on my spurs, I was scared to death. Then a dad and his son walked by, and I remember the boy saying, "Daddy, there's a cowboy puttin' on his spurs." Of course that lit my fire; in my mind I became the real deal. A few minutes later, Denny came over and said, "You can relax, Arn. They turned your bull out, and Wick is fighting it for the crowd."

That would be Wick Peth. Thank God for Wick, and I'm not the only one who has said that. Through the years, Wick has saved many a cowboy. For four decades he was a bullfighter the cowboys could always count on, and this rodeo was close to his home place, so he was well known in the area.

Now that the pressure was off for Saturday's performance, all I had to do was watch the rest of the show and think about the next day, which came pretty fast. Sunday morning I was up and at 'em, getting to the rodeo grounds early. I watched and studied every event, thinking, *I can do that. I can do that. I can learn to do that event too.* I was into it. Then it was Zero Hour, and once again I was behind the chutes putting on my spurs when a cowboy came up and asked if I'd be interested in trading bulls. His pal was ranked high in the standings, and the bull I'd drawn was a good one, which his wasn't. A ride on a good bull would help his score.

Well, that's the first I'd heard of a good bull or a bad one. All I knew was they were all big, and they'd try and eat you if you weren't careful. I had been told that trading bulls was against the Rodeo Cowboy Association rules and could hurt me down the road career-wise, so I said no.

And then I was up. I heard the announcer say my name, and I'll tell you, I was pumped. I had all kinds of help getting down on the bull, which had horns that looked as long as the chute was wide, and I sat down on his back just like I knew what I was doing. Unlike the rocking chair, Bull #20 didn't have a backrest, but I was ready.

Then, as Denny was pulling on the rigging to tighten it, the bull suddenly decided to climb out of the chute. I jumped clear and waited 'til he settled back down, then sat down on his back again. Denny pulled the rigging tight again, and I do mean tight.

A cowboy standing in the arena just outside the chute said, "Come on, cowboy, let's go," and I'm thinkin', *Hey, pal, let's not get in too big of a hurry here!*

Finally, I nodded, the gate opened, and there was an explosion. At least I think it was an explosion, but, then again, I don't remember much about it.

Eight seconds is a qualified ride, and some say I made it for about four. I couldn't tell you, because the next thing I knew I was looking at Denny's face and trying to grab my forehead. He said, "Don't touch that!" while he helped the medics lift me onto a stretcher and load me into an ambulance. I didn't wake up again until I was in the hospital.

I can't remember if I came home later that night or stayed the night and came home the next day, but I do remember I had a head that ached and lots of stitches in my forehead where the bull and I locked horns. Days later I paid a visit to Don and Barbara Hughes's house, and Don gave me a copy of the *Skagit Valley Herald* and told me I had made the front page. Sure enough, there I was, going off the back of that bull, knocked colder than a cucumber, and there was Wick with his hand right on top of the bull's head, making sure all 2,000 pounds of him was paying attention to Wick and not me, and watching me every inch of the way.

[Thanks, Wick]

That scene shows why Wick is an icon in the sport of rodeo. He's so good he's been inducted into the Pro Rodeo Hall of Fame and written up in *Life* magazine. He doubled for Glenn Ford in the movie Cowboy, and he's on the board of directors of the Pro Rodeo Cowboy Association. As for the awards he's received—well, I could go on and on, but I think the most important thing is that you can talk about Wick Peth to any cowboy, stock contractor, or anyone else in rodeo and what you hear is the utmost respect for Wick. He is the best.

Wick and I have had several visits since that day in May 1960, and not long ago we had another. Like he does with everybody, he met me with a handshake and a great big smile and made me as comfortable as anyone would ever want to be. I now have Wick's autograph on my copy of that newspaper, forty-nine years later. If he hadn't had his hand on that bull's head that day, it might have turned on me and we might not have had that wonderful visit.

Thanks again, Wick.

★ ★ ★ ★

Chapter Twenty

MY FUN TIMES IN THE MILITARY

In 1960, my friend Bill Roberts told me he was going to join the National Guard and he asked if I'd think about joining too. That way we could go through the six months of active duty together. I looked into it and it seemed like the thing to do, so in January of 1961 I found myself on a train headed to Fort Ord, California.

Things got interesting pretty quickly. On my third day, I tore the ligaments in my right ankle while double timing to the mess hall. I was quite a sight as I limped around. My hair had been cut off, and in addition to my Army cap and field jacket, I was wearing green civilian cord pants, a matching shirt—and loafers! Now, did I look like a soldier or what?

I lay in my bunk that night knowing I had a real problem. Because of my high school football days, I was used to sprained ankles. Sometimes I'd turn out on the practice field with my ankles wrapped so thickly in Ace bandages that I looked like a mummy. This felt more serious. My ankle had swollen big time, but I was convinced that if I could get my hands on some ice, I could get this problem under control.

Some of the guys managed to get me some ice the next morning and I did my best to get the swelling down, but even then, I had a tough time walking without help. My comrades suggested that I get it checked.

I hobbled out of the barracks and looked for someone with some authority so I could find out where to go to get looked at. I saw a sergeant—of course,

—★★★★—

When I got my walking cast on, they put me to work—in the maternity ward.

he could have been a general or an admiral, for all I knew, but at least someone above my rank had seen my problem. He pointed up the road and said, "Just up that hill and on the left is the hospital," and then he walked away. I was glad to know which direction to go, but now I had to figure out how on earth was I going to get there. I knew that standing around thinking about it wasn't getting me anywhere, so off I went up that hill, skipping, hobbling, resting, and then trying it all over again. After I had covered maybe a few hundred feet, which seemed to take forever, a taxi pulled up and stopped along side of me. The driver asked where I was headed and whether I wanted a ride. He didn't have to wait long for an answer.

"I'm trying to get to the hospital," I said, "and, yes, I'd love a ride, but I haven't got a whole lot of money."

That didn't seem to bother him. He showed mercy on me and drove me to the hospital—I don't think we went over a mile—for free. I thanked him and before I knew it I was sitting in front of a doctor who, I found out later, was a colonel. He examined me and said that as soon as the swelling went down enough, he'd put me in a cast, which he'd swap out later for a walking cast.

"You'll be in the hospital for about thirty days," he said.

"Whoa!" I said. "I'm not staying in this hospital for any thirty days! You just give me an Ace bandage and some ice and let me stay off it for a bit. I'll be back at it in no time."

I'll never forget that doctor. He leaned back in his chair and, with a very gentle smile, quietly said, "Son, you're in the Army now, and we'll take care of you." A nurse put me in a wheelchair and the next thing I knew, I was being taken care of.

I spent thirty days in a ward with a bunch of great soldiers who were also wearing casts, and after I saw what some of those guys were going through, I knew that my problem was nothing to complain about.

When I got my walking cast on, they put me to work—in the maternity ward. I held the hands of many ladies who were in labor and I folded a lot of diapers. It really wasn't bad, and an added bonus was working with another soldier who had been playing on the Denver Broncos football team.

Some of the guys in my ward found out that there was music in my blood and I was asked to be part of a Red Cross show scheduled for the hospital auditorium. I jumped at it. We had several meetings and after all that diaper folding, I felt like I was really part of something big. Along the way, I was learning how to tell a soldier's rank, something that helped me a lot when I realized that one of the nurses I'd made fun of after hearing her accent ("Ya'll eat that Arkansas corn?" I said) was a second lieutenant. You can bet I didn't ask her anything else.

When the curtain finally rose on the show, I was introduced and brought out on stage.

The place was packed. Like the rest of the guys, I was wearing loose-fitting hospital clothing, and my right leg was in a walking cast, but that didn't stop me from jumping in the air and clicking my heels together for a few laughs. (My doctor didn't laugh a whole lot but he did enjoy it.) When it came time for my song, I looked out over the audience and, lo and behold, there toward the back of the room was my buddy Bill, the one I had joined up with. I couldn't believe it! When he and I were still in high school, we would sit in his parents' kitchen nook and sing "Tijuana Jail" loud and long. Bill has a wonderful baritone voice and I thought, "This would be the perfect time to give that song a repeat performance."

Without a second thought, I introduced Bill, telling the audience a little bit of our story and inviting him to join me on stage. He didn't move. He did not want to get up there with me. I was dumbfounded. Several times I said, "Come on up here, Bill," and he just stood there. Before I knew it, some of the guys from my ward started chanting, "We want Bill! We want Bill!" and finally he came up and the audience went crazy, clapping, yelling, and having a wonderful time.

Now, the only problem was that Bill wasn't very happy about any of this. He was not having a good time. I had no idea that he wasn't comfortable in front of a large audience. In fact, he hated it, and as far as the song went—well, it was a train wreck. We couldn't get to first base with it and eventually he turned around and walked off the stage.

Bill had finished his basic training and was leaving the next day for Fort Bliss, Texas. He had come to the hospital to pay a visit and say "so long," but he couldn't find me. After asking around, he learned that I was in the auditorium doing a show, so he thought he'd just sneak in and be part of the audience. Boy, did he get a surprise!

Before I end this part of the story, I need to tell you that Bill overcame that fear and went on to become an outstanding schoolteacher and principal of a grade school in our home town of Oak Harbor. He later retired from teaching in the school system of Leavenworth, Washington, a beautiful town in the Cascade Mountains. He went into business for himself and later retired from that as well. These days, he and his wife Pat travel back and forth from Whidbey Island to Arizona, living life to the fullest. To this day, Bill and I enjoy laughing and reminiscing over our six years together in the Guard. We've had some great times together, and when the hospital story comes up, we both just fall apart. If I asked him today to jump up on stage with me, he'd do it in a heartbeat—at least I think he would!

My thirtieth day finally came around and it was time to move on; I was healed. I said my goodbyes and was recycled into a new company— Headquarters and Headquarters Company, 8th Battle Group, 3rd Brigade. I was just settling in when I ran into another schoolmate from Oak Harbor, this one named Dan Dillard. What a wonderful surprise! We ended up in the same platoon and even shared a bunk bed. Dan slept on the top bunk and I slept on the bottom.

After learning the ways of the Army, we began to shine and we both made squad leader, which gave us a little clout. Then, when we found out that if we could make the drill team we wouldn't have to do anymore KP, which meant no more peeling potatoes, and that we would also get weekend passes, we really set about diggin' in.

Jerry Sakoda, another squad leader in our platoon, had a lot of experience with a rifle from his ROTC days, and he became our coach. All three of us tried out for the 13-man team. Every chance we had, Dan and I would practice the 15-count Manual of Arms routine with the M1 rifle. As hunters, we were both familiar with rifles, but until this turnout, we'd never thrown one around; this was all new to us. But the three of us made the team—chrome helmets and the works! Our KP days were over.

We still did our normal basic training, marching, singing cadence and double timing for miles wearing full field gear in the Fort Ord sand. We'd visit the rifle range, throw hand grenades, and go through the gas house, as I called it, putting on our gas masks after they'd released the gas. Thank God they worked! Crawling in the mud under barbed wire and live ammunition (tracers overhead) was quite an experience and then there was the everyday P.T.— physical training. Thanks to those calisthenics, I was in the best shape of my life, weighing in at a taut 168 pounds. Then there were unexpected moments, like when Dan threw me a surprise birthday party, cake and all, and the time we had the barracks arm wrestling competition, when I proved I could hang in there with the best of 'em, until a snap in my right elbow ended my competition and made my normal routine somewhat of a problem.

★ ★ ★ ★

Crawling in the mud under barbed wire and live ammunition was quite an experience.

One day I was acting platoon sergeant, calling cadence during this long, hot, sandy march, and I came across a snake in the middle of the road. It had to be a sight watching our company do a column right, column left, and another column left and a final column right, but we didn't step on that snake. We did draw the attention of a 2nd Lieutenant, who came running up to me from behind shouting, "What in the @#%* are you doing?"

"Sir!" I said as we kept marching. "There's a snake in the middle of the road, Sir! I wouldn't walk over it, and I don't expect these men to, either, Sir!"

"Sergeant Deckwa! That snake is a black snake! And it's dead!"

"Sir, I didn't know that, Sir! But I still wouldn't have walked over it, Sir!"

My memories of my military days at Fort Ord are good ones, and it seems like we were looked after—especially the time three of us were seriously thinking about how great it would be to be airborne rangers. We decided to make a jump from an airplane at a local private airport to get the feel of it, and when the time came, we put on civilian clothes and headed for the bus stop. We were pumped! Then, while we were sitting on the bench waiting for the bus to take us to the airport, our platoon sergeant, Sergeant First Class Rivera, surprised us. He was a no-nonsense man who had heard of our plan and began hunting for us. Now, he could have ordered us to stand at attention and then chewed on us from one end to the other until we were all so scared we would have forgotten the jump altogether and hurried back to our barracks, but he didn't. It was the first time any of us had heard him talk quietly. We sat on that bench and listened as he explained to us the amount of money and time the Army invests in preparing just one soldier to jump from an airplane, and how going to a local airport and giving them $25 a piece, listening to their few minutes of instruction, and then letting them take us into the air and jumping out was not a very smart thing to do—and so we didn't. I'll never forget Sgt. Rivera. We learned that day just what a good heart he had, and he may have saved our lives.

After basic training, I was to go to Fort Bliss, Texas, and train on the 90 millimeter guns, but I ended up staying at Fort Ord and attending clerk/typist school, although typing was just the background for a few good adventures.

Right after I was assigned to the school, I went out for the evening and came back good and tired. I put my clothes in the locker and climbed into bed. It wasn't long, though, before I realized it wasn't mine. I was in the wrong barracks! Thank God the soldier who owned that bed had also gone out for the evening. It didn't take me long to get out of there.

I'll also never forget the time I spent a weekend visiting my cousins, Hugh and Bonnie Jonson, at their home in Oakland. Hugh was a lieutenant in the Navy Reserve and he had a meeting in Monterey that next Monday.

"There's no need for you to catch a bus back to the Fort," he said. "Just ride with me and I'll drop you off. Fort Ord is right on my way."

We arrived at my barracks late that Sunday night and I convinced him to spend the night in the vacant bunk above mine rather than find a motel. Early the next morning, I was awakened by the shouts of our sergeant, who had a great sense of self-importance and a desire to bear down on us as hard as he could.

He screamed for all of us to get out of bed.

"Who in the @#$%! does that car parked in front of these barracks belong to?!" And about that time he saw Hugh in the top bunk. As I jumped out of bed and stood at attention in my T-shirt and skivvies, this sergeant was just laying it on Hugh, who was not saying a word.

Finally and very slowly Hugh sat up in bed, rubbed his face, stretched out his arms and let himself down from the bunk. The whole time, the sergeant was yelling questions at him. Hugh paid absolutely no attention to him. He walked by, opened the locker door, took out his pants and proceeded to put them on. Then he put on his shirt and sat on the side of my bunk to put his shoes on. The sergeant still hadn't let up. Then he saw the brass on Hugh's coat and hat as he put them on. He snapped to attention and saluted Hugh, and I almost fell apart. Hugh, who wasn't paying him a lot of attention, simply saluted him back as he walked over to me, shook my hand and said, "See ya later, Arn." He went to his car and drove away, and from that time on I had no problem with that sergeant.

After graduating from school, I was sent to the reception station along with two other graduates to do paperwork in the main office. On our first day, we stood by a counter and watched an obviously stressed-out lad with huge stacks of paperwork on his desk sweating it out behind a typewriter. I figured out pretty quickly that I wanted nothing to do with this type of work and that the three of us had been sent to take his place.

The sergeant in charge walked over and asked, "Which one of you wants this job?" I never said a word, and finally one of the other guys said he'd take it. What a relief!

I don't know where the third guy ended up but I was sent to the testing building, where I finished my six months giving tests to recruits. I loved it. I stood behind a podium in front of a couple hundred soon-to-be soldiers, introduced myself, lightened things up a bit with a little entertainment, and then explained the tests they were about to take. The majority of them didn't know if I was a private or a general, and I had a ball.

I spent my first leave back home in Cornet Bay visiting my family. Then I drove my car, a beautiful 1952 Plymouth that had belonged to my grandfather Deckwa, back to Fort Ord. That car was great for adventure. My pal Mike Teel, who played high school football with me back in Oak Harbor and was now at Fort Ord, and I had all kinds of good times, many of them involving the beaches of Carmel.

When my six months was up, I left Fort Ord and reported to my home National Guard Armory in Anacortes, about ten miles from Cornet Bay, for six years of service that were a lot of fun. I especially enjoyed the yearly two weeks of active duty. Again, there were enough adventures for another book. There was the time my friend from Skagit County, Earl Peth, and I were checking out the Fort Lewis area and we came across some cattle in a pasture. I said "Earl, pull up alongside that steer and let's see if I can bulldog that sucker from this Jeep."

I don't know why it seemed like a good idea to jump from a moving vehicle to tangle with a steer, but it did. Earl did a great job of getting me close to it, but thank God it wasn't close enough, because that thing was runnin' full speed and we were flyin'; if I would have made the jump, I probably wouldn't be writing this book.

We were going to be heading home the next day, so Earl and I decided we ought to have a little fun. The company always had a party on the last night of the bivouac. It was a great morale builder and everyone had a wonderful time. Our company's tents and kitchen were sitting high on a plateau, about forty feet above some grazing range cattle, including one bull none of us wanted to get too close to. Wouldn't it be a hoot, we thought, if a bunch of cattle were to come running through the party? That would certainly liven things up a bit and give the guys something more to talk about. So, we collected a few other lads and, by the light of the moon, rounded up several head of cattle, pushed them gently toward the bottom of the hill, and then spooked 'em up and over the top. They ran over tents and through the kitchen and scattered guys all over the place.

★★★★

I don't know why it seemed like a good idea to jump from a moving vehicle to tangle with a steer, but it did.

We came up after it was over, acting like we'd had the fire scared out of us, too.

"Holy cow!," we said. "What in the #$%& was that all about!?!" On and on we went. Guys were comin' out of hiding places from all over, and nobody had been hurt. We had a good laugh and so did everybody else.

When everything had settled down to a mild roar I decided to call it a night and turn in, since it was going to be an early morning. I was one of the outpost guards and my pup tent was about a hundred yards from the company area. As I walked through the woods by moonlight to my tent, I heard a noise, and then a loud bellowing that sounded just like that bull, and I'm here to tell you it put the fear of God in me right down to my bones. With nothing but moonlight to see by, it was hard to know which way to run. And then I heard this laugh, which got louder and louder. It was my bud, Earl. He had left a little before me and circled around to get in front of me. Since he raised cattle, he knew exactly how to imitate a bull's bellowing. He did a great job and I've never forgotten that night—I still get chills thinkin' about it. He scared the wind and water out of me and we still have a good laugh about it when we get together.

I finished my six years with the rank of staff sergeant in a platoon whose job was to clear the way for our battalion. We compared it to the old TV show called Rat Patrol, but I loved it. After completing the Noncommissioned Officer Course, I was offered the rank of sergeant first class if I'd stay in, but it was time for me to move on. I very much enjoyed my six years in the National Guard and to this day I'm proud to have served.

[Team Roping—I'm the header]

★ ★ ★ ★

Chapter Twenty-one

◆◆◆◆◆◆◆◆◆◆◆◆◆◆◆◆◆◆◆◆◆◆◆

EDDY AND THE SPACE STATION

I was twenty years old when I bought my first house, the Grant Byhre place on Fort Nugent Road, about two miles west of Oak Harbor. More than once I spent the night in that house in the days when I was palling around with Dick Byhre. Dick's mom got a real kick out of me the first time I walked in because I told her that I liked the house and if she ever wanted to sell it, I'd like to buy it. Coming from the mouth of a fifteen-year-old, that statement really amused her, and we hit it off.

The Byhre home was always filled with music. Dick was a trumpet player and his dad played the fiddle and upright bass. I took my accordion there several times and played, and we always had fun.

One day I received a call from Mrs. Byhre, who said, "Honey, I know you've always wanted this house and I'm going to sell it. If you still want it, I'll hold the contract for you." I couldn't believe it! I was thrilled, and I said, "Yes, I still want it! Thank you for calling me!"

We got together, and after we finished the paperwork, I had a house and two acres, with eighteen more to use. I paid $12,500 for it, and she left it completely furnished—dishes, silverware, furniture—you name it, it was there. The beds were made, and there were even two pie crusts in the oven; she simply walked out of it. I went to work immediately on the two twenty-four-by-sixty-foot outbuildings. One I made into a barn with tack room, feed room, and two box stalls, and the other I packed full of hay. It wasn't long before I had a station wagon that pulled a horse in a single-horse trailer. I was set. My bull-riding career had ended in that arena back in May of 1960, but my career in roping was about to start. I entered rodeos in the area and was really active by the time a bunch of us pitched in to plan and build the North Whidbey Stampede rodeo grounds.

The rodeo brought a lot of excitement to the town of Oak Harbor and became one of the largest on the Northwest Rodeo Association circuit. It was held every July for seventeen years and drew cowboys from Idaho and Oregon, from across the border in Canada, and from as far south as California.

The rodeo grounds were built and maintained by members of other horse organizations around the area, such as the Island County Sheriff's Posse, 4-H, riding clubs and roping clubs, and other folks who just liked to be around horses and wanted to be part of the action. Picking the next president, chairman, arena director, and others was never tough, as we all saw each other almost every month at some meeting or other, and a lot of those folks, including me, took on new titles and responsibilities as the years went by.

Not long after I bought the Byhre place, I got married and started a family. Scott was born in 1964, and Laurie, who we call Sis, was born in 1966. My son Shawn would be born in 1974. That place was perfect for kids; they were raised around horses, cows, dogs, cats, and dirt bikes. They really took to the outdoor life and got involved in 4-H, Little League, water skiing, and in the Little Britches, Junior and NRA Rodeo programs, among other things, over the years.

I had fallen in love with that house as a teenager, and it was a great place to raise a family. We built a lot of great memories living there.

Around that time, I bought a horse off the track that could run a hole through the wind, and I just knew that with a little work I'd be throwin' a rope off him soon. I learned quick enough, though, that along with all that speed, Eddy had some buck in him. He wasn't a horse you could bring out of the pasture, saddle up, and kick out; he needed to be warmed up first, and he unloaded more than one cowboy who didn't believe that.

I was going to ride him into the arena at the opening of our annual rodeo that year. When the day came, I was really glad as arena director to see the place packed with people. The bleachers and the beer garden were full, and counting folks sitting and standing around, there were probably around three thousand.

★★★★

I knew he could buck, but this time it was like someone had put a stick of dynamite under him! That horse proceeded to run over me like a freight train.

I was a very busy guy making sure everything was going like clockwork and I asked my cousin Kendra to warm Eddy up for me. I hadn't learned yet just how much warm-up he needed, but apparently what she gave him wasn't quite enough. She brought him to me and I heard, over the loud speakers, "And now, ladies and gentlemen, your arena director, Arnie Deckwa."

"Jump off him, Hon," I said. "I gotta have him."

I jumped on him and away we went, runnin' wide open through the gate. I was standing up in the stirrups, waving my hat and smiling at the crowd as we crossed the arena in front of the bleachers. Then, all of a sudden Eddy jammed both feet into the ground, bogged his head and arched his back so high I thought I'd be helping the guys fix the space station. I knew he could buck, but this time it was like someone had put a stick of dynamite under him! One arm went under his neck and I got hold of some mane with the other, trying to hang on with my body hangin' off his left side. My left foot was still in the stirrup, but my right leg was flying around in the air, and that horse wasn't lettin' up.

I was trying with everything I had to get hold of a piece of leather, but by this time we'd made the turn at the other end of the arena and were in front of the roping chutes. Now, the only reason I know that is because that's where it all came to an end. Eddy snapped me down on the ground on my back and then proceeded to run over me like a freight train. One of his front feet clipped the right side of my head and it felt like it tore my ear loose, and then at one point he had both feet on my chest. How did I know that? I had a hold of 'em! It all happened so fast I don't know which came first, the ear or the chest. He seemed to know exactly what he was doing, though, and to this day I think he had radar in his hind legs because both his hind feet connected with the heels of my boots as I was rolling backward, and he really helped me along.

He left me lyin' in the dirt and bucked his way down to the other end of the arena. A couple of cowboy pals came runnin' out, and they leaned down over me. With grins so wide it's a wonder the tops of their heads stayed attached, they said, "How ya feel, Arn?" I looked up at them and said, "I feel like I just got run over by a horse. How in the blank do you *think* I feel?"

They helped me up, and I wiped most of the sand out of my mouth and tried to pull what was left of my shirt back around me. About that time Gary Erb, the stock contractor, had caught Eddy (I had a few other names for him about that time) and brought him to me. I'll never forget Gary leaning over his saddle horn while he held my horse and saying, "You wanna sell this horse, Arn? He can really buck!" All the guys standing around had a good laugh.

I took the reins, swallowed a bunch of pride, and got on him. As we rode out of the arena, we got a big round of applause from the crowd.

Outside, Jimmy Graves applied a little first aid and helped clean me up. After he wrapped my ribs good and tight with an elastic wrap and some tape, I borrowed a shirt from Ed Knutzen because I had an event to participate in. Joe Short and I were up first in the team roping that day. I was doing the heading (but not on Eddy) and Joe was heeling, and we placed and made some money.

After a lot of work, Eddy turned into a good rope horse, although he always had to be warmed up. After a few more incidents, I finally learned just how much.

★ ★ ★ ★

Chapter Twenty-two

POSSES AND CHARIOT RACES

Working with horses has given me a lot of satisfaction and more than my share of thrills over the years, and nothing packed more excitement than the annual collection of riding events known as the Washington State Sheriff's Posse Convention. It was a three-day horse and rider competition involving twenty or so posses, which were made up of volunteer assistants to county sheriff's departments. It was highly competitive—fierce would be a better word—and we just called it "The Meet." We were normal, forty-hour-a-week working guys who for those few days seemed to forget we had any responsibilities at all. Our Island County team always did really well, taking our share of first-place trophies in individual events and overall meets, but everybody gave it everything they had.

There were arena competitions, including individual and team pole and barrel racing, bareback relays and trailer races, and track events including

220-yard, 440-yard, and half-mile races. There were the flying baton relays, with four horses each running a quarter mile. You had 300 feet for the handoff, and you'd spend the first 200 getting your horses—one just starting, one finishing—running side by side and the next 100 making sure you got the handoff right. Grabbing that baton at full speed on a crowded track could be awfully tricky.

Then there was the six-man relay. You'd ride as fast as you could to someone waiting to catch your horse as you jumped off and ran to the next rider, who was waiting on his horse just beyond the second of two chalk lines for the baton. Now, the catcher was standing just in front of the first line, fifty feet from the other, watching you and your horse charging at him at full speed. He had to hold his composure and have a great deal of trust in you as a rider, since that horse had to be brought to a complete stop, or at least close enough so he could catch it and not let it go over the line. He'd grab the horse and hold it there while you ran to hand off to the next rider; if the horse stepped across the line, you were disqualified.

I'll never forget the time my father-in-law, a wonderful man named Jim Crewes, who I called Pa, was catching for me in a meet in Walla Walla. I was in the fifth spot, riding Pa's horse King, which I'd been working with. Pa didn't really know how good a stop the horse had learned, but I told him not to worry—no matter how hard and fast I was coming at him, King would stop. Pa said he wasn't worried and he wasn't about to let that horse go by him. I knew that to be a fact.

The time came, our fourth rider handed that baton to me, and we were off and running. That horse could fly, and before I knew it, we were coming around the turn, heading into the home stretch. I could see Pa waiting there, and when he saw I wasn't slowing down, his eyes got as big as car headlights— he told me later he didn't know if I was going to stop after all. I was almost on top of him, still wide open, when I began my dismount and King just dropped his tail to the ground and put on the brakes. I let go of the saddle horn and flew through the air for ten feet or so before I hit the ground. Pa caught King perfectly, and I ran the fifty feet between the lines and handed the baton to our last rider, who took it over the finish line well in front of the other teams. It was an absolute rush.

Every one of those relay horses knew what was happening; the closer a runner got, the more it wanted to run. It was no use expecting that horse to stand there, perfectly relaxed, until the runner made the pass; it just wasn't going to happen. Sometimes the rider had to pull with everything he had to keep his horse from rearing or running off before the exchange. If there were two runners coming toward two riders at the same time, it could get really crowded, although that never happened to me because Island County always did well in that race. By the time it came to the fifth pass, we were usually ahead.

Then there was the Pony Express. You'd ride as fast as you could to a horse being held by a team member, stop your horse, jump off and run to the next one, grab the saddle horn, lift your feet off the ground as the horse took off, and when it was running wide open, hit the ground with your feet and swing yourself up into the saddle. Then you'd ride to the next horse and do it again.

★★★★

What my horses didn't seem to understand was how to stop.

The ultimate eye-opener, though, was the Chariot Race. The "chariot" was the round bottom third of a fifty-five-gallon drum sitting on an axle connecting a couple of 90cc Honda motorcycle wheels. A tongue attached the axle to two horses whose job it was to haul you around that half-mile track as fast as their legs would carry them.

My horses were really good ones. Like everybody's, they had to run in several events, and they had a lot of speed and stamina. What my horses didn't seem to understand, though, when it came to chariot racing, was how to stop.

My experience with chariot racing started with practice sessions in Skinny Hassler's pasture, about three miles from where I grew up on Cornet Bay. Knight Smith, a legend in our county, had built a metal chariot that sat on an axle between two car tires. It was heavy, but he raced it. I climbed in, walked the horses around the pasture to get the feel of it, and thought it was great. I just knew the real thing was going to be a blast.

Not long after that, we met at a nearby racetrack for another practice run, this time in a new chariot, a bright red, sawed-off barrel on wheels. A couple of other riders were on the track as I stepped into the chariot, slid my goggles down over my eyes, and took hold of the reins. I did another slow walk around the track to make sure I had the hang of it. That went so well I decided to let the horses trot. They seemed to like that pretty much, because the next thing I knew they had kicked it up into a slow gallop. Now, these horses had never had a harness on before, and they sure hadn't been hooked up to a chariot, so we were all getting our feet wet at the same time. I'm not sure if they really liked it or if they thought this red piece of metal was after them, but in no time at all we were wide open and there wasn't a thing I could do about it. I was hanging on to two runaway horses that had no intention of stopping.

On the backstretch, I was leaning backward at a pretty good angle, my feet against the inside front of the barrel. I had my entire body weight pulling on those reins, and the horses weren't even slowing down. I pulled myself upright again, and as I went past Knight and Uncle Ralph, I yelled, "They won't stop!" and I heard them yell, "Go get 'em, Ben!" referring, of course, to Ben-Hur.

As we circled the track for a second time, a couple of riders came up alongside us and got in position to rescue me. In the middle of the backstretch, one grabbed the inside horse and the other grabbed the outside horse and all of us tried slowing them down. It wasn't happening. As we got closer to the turn, with all of us pulling, the horses were drifting toward the outside rail. *There's gonna be a collision,* I thought. Both riders let go of my horses, which shot across the track to the inside rail. I pulled hard on the right rein, and the chariot whipped around and tipped up on its left wheel, about to turn over. Luckily, it came back down on both wheels. As I was coming back out of the turn, the riders were waiting for me, and we gave it another go. This time, with all of us pulling, the horses decided they were tired enough that it might be a good idea to stop and rest some.

Uncle Ralph said he thought I'd done a good job and was proud of me, which made everybody laugh, since I hadn't done anything but ride it out. We inspected the chariot and saw that the left tire was flat—no wonder the thing had nearly tipped over. That brought on more laughs.

From that time on, whenever I finished a race, I had to be caught by a couple of team members who waited for me past the finish line. In fact, the announcer always made sure the crowd knew what was coming.

"Island County will be putting on an extra show at the end of the race," he'd say, and my horses always obliged. It was a big crowd-pleaser every time.

[With Randy Pepper]

★ ★ ★ ★

Chapter Twenty-three

ARNIE, RANDY, AND THE KILLER WHALE

My state trooper buddies included a guy named Randy Pepper. He was your normal trooper at the time—six feet four, 225 pounds. They all seemed to be that way. Randy was, in fact, a former Washington Huskies football player. Me, I'm five feet six and a half if I stretch, and I'm built kind of like a quarter horse, what my rodeo buddies call "pushed together and short to the ground." Our physical similarity ended with our badges. What we did have in common was that we were great hunting and fishing partners, and excitement never seemed too far from either of us. When we got together, that went double, although nothing we'd ever been through could have prepared us for what happened one beautiful summer afternoon in the early 1960s.

Randy and I decided to load up my twelve-foot aluminum boat and head for West Beach, about five miles from my place. It was the perfect day to land a nice-sized salmon, and we knew just the hot spot.

As I stopped the truck near the boat landing and yanked the parking brake, we were met by the cries of gulls and the rich smell of saltwater. Puget Sound was a placid blue-green, and the water lapping calmly at the shore was a welcome sight. This stretch of water can be downright nasty, and she's taken more than her share of boats down. Randy and I, looking like oddly matched bookends, carried the boat to the edge of the water. We tossed our gear in, hooked up my ten-horse Johnson, and pushed off. Randy, in the middle seat, rowed us out far enough for me to lower the motor. I jerked the cord once and away we went, bouncing over the swells at twenty-five or thirty miles an hour with the wind rippling our shirts and blowing across our faces as we drank Cokes and ate cheese crackers. What a life! The only thing that could have been better would have been a little smoked salmon instead of the crackers, and we'd be taking care of that momentarily.

We had a three-mile run to make Smith Island, and about halfway out, I leaned up and nudged Randy, pointing off the starboard side to one of the most beautiful sights on the sea—a blackfish cow and her calf, rolling and diving through the blue-green water. They're called killer whales, although the proper name is Orca, and they're twenty-five to thirty feet in length, jet black with basketball-sized white patches on each side and snowy white underbellies. As if that weren't thrill enough, we caught sight of a lone bull off the port side. His dorsal fin, standing high on his broad back, made him look like the king of the sea as he broke the surface and reentered the water with a loud slap of his huge tail. We were glad all three were a good distance away.

A moment later we spotted what must have been a hundred seagulls whirling in a tight circle on the breeze, taking turns diving into the water. I realized they had found a herring ball, a big school of small herring. The gulls dove and splashed, one after the other, pulling those shiny little fish from the water like they hadn't eaten in weeks.

"Have you ever dipped live herring?" I yelled to Randy over the roar of the engine and the rush of the wind.

"No," he yelled back.

"All right," I said, brushing a bit of salty sea spray from my lips. "Here's how we do it. Stand up and hold the dip net over the starboard side. I'll run up onto the school of herring and kill the engine. When I do, drop the net into the herring ball—quick, before they dive too deep—then lift it from the water gently and let the herring fall through the mesh 'til there are just a couple dozen left. Dump 'em in the boat and we'll have some nice fresh bait. Got it?"

"Got it!" he yelled, rising to his feet, his smile radiating anxious energy.

"Remember, now," I yelled, "brace yourself. When I kill the engine, the boat's gonna try to throw you forward."

"Okay," he yelled. He planted his boots firmly, and I had to laugh. Rising to his full height in that little twelve-foot boat, he looked like the Jolly Green Giant standing in a peanut shell. His crow-black hair and beard gave him the air of a larger-than-life pirate, except he was holding a dip net instead of a sword.

————— ★★★★ —————

Rising to his full height in that little twelve-foot boat, he looked like the Jolly Green Giant standing in a peanut shell.

"Whatever you do," I hollered, still laughing as we raced across the water, "don't fall out of the boat!"

As we got within fifty yards of the herring ball, the circle of seagulls broke up and flew off. At twenty-five yards we were still wide open, and Randy was steeling himself, his muscles taut, holding the dip net in the ready position. He was leaning forward just a little, ready to spring into action.

Suddenly, not more than twenty feet away, a huge black shadow rose right through the middle of that herring ball, breaking the surface directly in front of the boat. It was a killer whale cow, crossing from right to left, no doubt with her calf right beside her.

Yanking the engine toward me as fast as I could, I threw the boat into a hard left turn without slowing down at all. The boat flipped up onto its starboard side, and the propeller came out of the water, changing from its steady whine to the loudest, shrillest scream imaginable.

Randy was falling all over the boat, trying desperately to grab anything he could get his hands on. I jumped to the port side, trying to use my weight to keep it from tipping all the way over. For a moment, I was standing straight up as though the sides of the boat were rungs on a huge ladder sticking out of the ocean. In that instant, I could have scratched that whale's shiny black back without stretching.

Luckily, the starboard side of the boat acted as a brake and literally stopped us from taking a slide over that mountain of a back. The port side slapped back into the water, and the propeller flung us away from that whale like we'd come out of a slingshot. Coming up from the bottom of the boat, I reached as fast as I could to put the engine in neutral, then shut it off as I watched the whale and her calf dive in and swim away as though nothing had happened. In the silence, I rubbed my face with both hands, then looked at Randy, who was lying on his back amid all the tackle boxes and gear that had been flung around the boat. His head was at the bow, his size twelve boots practically in my lap. For all the tossing and rolling we'd done, we had both, by the grace of God, managed to stay aboard. He put a hand on each side of the boat and slowly pulled himself up onto the middle seat.

"Holy cow," he said, wide-eyed. "That was close!"

I realized that we had survived what could have been capsize and God-only-knows-what after that, and that for a moment it had been every man for himself. That's one reason I always liked hunting and fishing with Randy. I never had to worry about him.

We hadn't reached our original destination, but it seemed like touching land was something we both wanted to do, so we decided to head back. I restarted the motor, and, as we slowly gained speed, the salty sea breeze brushing across our faces, we'd look at each other now and then, shake our heads, and laugh, as if to say, *I'm sure glad we made it through that, old buddy.* And I looked up at the sky and said, simply, "Thanks."

[Going home in the fog, with Dave Milholland on the left]

★ ★ ★ ★

Chapter Twenty-four

A VETERINARIAN'S NIGHT OUT ON THE WATER

Back in those days, there were memorable friends on the cowboy side of my life too. There wasn't much, for instance, that my friend Kent Freer wouldn't tackle, and somehow he was able to get me involved in quite a bit of it. A cowboy-turned-veterinarian, Kent left his home in Wyoming to live on Whidbey Island, picking up a whole new outlook on life in the process.

I drove countless miles with Kent in his pickup truck, assisting him now and then in operations and foalings, although there were a few situations I wish I'd never been talked into.

"Everything's going to be okay," he'd say in his reassuring tone as I stood bracing myself behind this big white-faced bull, pushing his tail up over his back with all my might while Kent knelt on the ground between my legs and the bull's and made the bull into a steer.

"Whatever you do," I remember him saying with a big laugh, "don't let go of that tail."

We never knew when the radio would call us somewhere or exactly what we might be in for. It could be to doctor a horse or check a 4-H show animal, and then again it might be to deal with an out-of-sorts camel. It was like that—a new experience every time. There are so many stories that came out of trips to places like Image Lake, where we rode twenty-two miles into the hills with eighteen head of horses, or to Larch Lake on a "high hunt," riding five or six thousand feet up into the gorgeous Cascade Mountains, where the fishing is terrific and hunting with a camera offers a great shot every time you turn around.

Then there's the story of Kent's first commercial fishing trip with me. I was behind the wheel of a beautiful twenty-eight-foot boat, one of many my father had built. It was powered by a 440 Chrysler engine that could push it over the water at a good forty knots to the salmon fishing grounds in Puget Sound. This particular night was clear and cold, and we were sitting on calm water under a big, bright moon. We had eighteen hundred feet of net stretched out in a nice straight line, and my lantern jack was burning perfectly. David Milholland, a good friend of our family and an encyclopedia of fishing, was in his boat nearby; we were sitting near the end of his net. The hazards of fishing the Sound—rocks, reefs, high winds and big waves—were far from my mind.

Like my dad, David was one of those hard-working men I've always looked up to. Back in the early '50s he made his living beachcombing, towing logs to a holding area until he had 150 or so, then making the two- or three-day trip to Elliot Bay to make the sale. After my dad died in 1976 and I decided to go back and fish his boat for one more season, David pulled me out of messes on the water many times. This night, he was inside his cabin, sitting on the bunk, listening to election returns on his radio when out of nowhere he could see and hear a giant tugboat passing just a few feet from his cabin window. He knew if the tug had barely missed him, the barge it had to be towing wouldn't, and he and his boat would end up as splinters and toothpicks.

The tug had run out of the shipping channel and gotten into waters its skipper surely wished he wasn't in. Trying to tow a 200- or 300-foot barge through 30 or 40 drifting fishing boats, each with 1800-foot nets hooked to them, is a captain's nightmare. He had realized his mistake, tried to turn around, and almost clipped David's boat. David jumped up, started his engine, and cut the net loose, then roared away just as fast as that boat would go. He watched the barge run over the end of his net; a few seconds later, it would have run over him as well.

The tug's skipper, realizing what had happened, poured the coal to the engines and headed for the channel. David called me on the radio, although I think I could have heard him without it, and yelled, "Arnie! Arnie! Catch that tug and get her numbers."

————— ★★★★ —————

I turned hard and fast, barely missing a collision, which would have sunk us, and which the crew of the tug wouldn't even have noticed..

I'd seen what had happened and was moving already. I lit another lantern, tied it to the boat end of my net, and charged across the water. I was wide open, with only the moon and a spotlight to see by, trying to catch a tug that was a good distance away by now and moving fast.

For a moment in the excitement I had forgotten all about Kent. I looked up and he was standing outside, with the night air blowing against his jumper-type overalls. He had to be cold. He must have seen the look of concern on my face, and he said, "You do what you have to. Don't worry about me."

We caught up with the barge and I realized getting the tug's numbers was going to be difficult, since the skipper was shining his giant spotlight in my face, trying to keep me from seeing them. I pulled up so close that the tug's bumper tires, hanging from her port side, were actually above me. We could have touched her. As I was getting her numbers, five or six men came out of the galley and looked down on us. I got what I needed, pulled away, and headed back toward David's boat. Halfway there, still running at around thirty miles per hour, I thought of Kent, who was standing in the cold night air, now in just a pair of Wranglers and a T-shirt!

"Kent," I yelled, "what happened to your overalls?"

"Well, Arn," he said, "when you pulled up along side that big boat and all those guys came out on deck, I didn't figure we had much of a chance. But if you were going to board her, I was goin' with you, so I took 'em off to get freed up a bit."

Kent's a keeper.

He put his overalls back on, and we pulled up to David's boat to assess the damage. He'd lost quite a bit of net but was able to get what was left aboard. We all figured we'd had enough excitement for one night, so we decided to go to Bowman's Bay, unload our fish, and head home. I had the faster boat, so I followed David.

At the time, David was running a jet engine, which always kicks up a lot of steam, and with the fog setting in it was hard to see. After thirty minutes or so, as Kent and I followed about two hundred feet behind David's starboard stern, I noticed him turning hard left—almost a U-turn. In just a moment I saw why. Out of the fog, with no lights whatsoever, another tug towing a barge came into view. We were heading right between them, and the towing cable was about to decapitate Kent, me, and the cabin. I turned hard and fast, barely missing a collision, which would have sunk us, and which the crew of the tug wouldn't even have noticed.

The three of us waited for our hearts to settle back down out of our throats, then continued toward the bay as daylight started to lighten the eastern horizon. We ran about twenty more minutes, and except for the fact that the waves had come up a little, everything was looking okay until the gas sniffer began to beep. I shut down the engine and started to look for a gas leak. I could smell it, but I couldn't see it. By now there was enough of a chop on the water to toss the boat back and forth, and tearing into the carburetor was a real chore. We checked the entire engine, tightened every fitting, then started it up and headed slowly in.

"What happens if that beeper doesn't stop beeping?" Kent asked me.

"That's a good question. I can't seem to find any danger, but if she blows, I guess that means I didn't look hard enough."

"Well," he said, "with that reassuring answer, I feel a lot better now."

We had a good laugh, and it was nice to know we still had our sense of humor. We made it to the buyer and found David unloading his catch. We tied alongside and did the same. The water in the bay was much calmer, so I did a quick double-check for gas leaks. I still couldn't find any.

———— ★★★★ ————

I slammed my boat into reverse and poured the power to the engine.

David and I checked the tide book and realized we were going to be bucking a five-knot tide through Deception Pass to get home. That can get a little tricky, although it's easier going against the tide than going with it, especially in the fog.

That's right, the fog had moved in as thick as pea soup. *Lord*, I thought, *when are things going to let up?* I didn't get an immediate answer, so David and I went ahead and planned the attack. He felt we'd be all right if we headed straight for the beach on the Whidbey side and followed it up to the pass, then bucked her through. Because of his jet steam, I'd lead this time. So, with the utmost care and caution, Kent and I began cutting a path through the fog by compass, since neither David nor I had radar at the time. After this little tidbit coming, you won't be surprised to hear that it didn't take long for us to get radar installed.

In no time at all, we had lost David, and we were watching for him while we kept an eye out for rocks and debris. The wheel was outside on the starboard side, and since the net reel was to my immediate left, visibility was not good for me in that direction. Kent was watching on that side, and after about ten minutes, he yelled, "Watch out! David!" I revved the engine and turned hard right, as David, who had seen me about the same time, turned hard left, as I was looking at him. We avoided a catastrophic collision by just a few feet.

By that time my nerves were beginning to weaken. Kent must have noticed because in his usual dry way, he asked, "Everything going like you planned?" Then he laughed like thunder.

"You're cute," I told him. "Real cute." But he had gotten me laughing, which was just what I needed.

We finally came to the beach, a dark, dreary shore that was merely a shadow through the fog, but at least I knew exactly where we were. I had been along that beach hundreds of times as a boy, fishing with my dad, and many times it was in the fog at night. In those days, though, Dad was always at the wheel, and this time he wasn't.

Then I realized I had lost David again. We were in plenty of water, and I could feel the tide against us. The closer we approached the mouth of the pass, the harder it pushed. Slowly, I gave the engine a little more throttle, and we started making progress. I was nervously waiting to see rocks ahead so I could run alongside of them and gently turn us into the pass when out of nowhere came David's boat, broadside and directly in front of me. David, who couldn't see for the fog, had missed the mouth of the pass and was headed for the rocks.

I slammed my boat into reverse and poured the power to the engine—she sounded like she was going to come off her mounts. David did the same, and the back eddies began pulling us into the rocks. We were within five feet of them when I jammed the shifting lever into forward and gave her full throttle. We shot away from the rocks and into the mouth of the pass. From there, I just had to keep us going forward, bucking the tide, and passing two more islands before making a final turn into Cornet Bay, where we'd be home free.

There, bigger than life, on the port side off my bow, was Strawberry Island. I estimated the right turn I'd need, and sure enough, the blinking red light on Ben Ure Island was right where it was supposed to be. I followed the island and turned finally into Cornet Bay. What a wonderful sight! The marina's lights looked like a Christmas display through the fog. As we entered the harbor, I was surprised to see David right behind me. I was so happy when we tied up to the dock that I wanted to kiss it. David walked over to my boat and said, "You did good, Arnie."

That statement, coming from one of the greatest fishermen who ever lived, who had fished for years and years with my father, made me feel for just a moment like a man who could handle anything. And then I realized that I never wanted to go through that again.

As David walked up the dock, I looked at Kent, who was gathering his belongings from the boat.

"Well, pard," I said, "if the night would have been normal, we might have caught a bunch of fish. Things just didn't go like I planned."

"You're kidding," he said. "I thought every night with you fishermen was like the one we just went through." And then he laughed and laughed.

As we walked up the dock, Kent said, "You guys are a tough breed. Swing by the place when you get a chance, and I'll pour you a cup of coffee. I enjoyed the night; we'll have to do it again soon." He said it like it was just a normal night of work until he sat in his truck and rolled his window down.

"Arn," he said, "next time can you make it not quite so exciting?"

[Uncle Ralph West]

★ ★ ★ ★

Chapter Twenty-five

THE ALBERTA MOOSE HUNT

Although hunting has put a great deal of food in the freezer and on the table throughout my life, there is much more to it than that. Hunting gave me a special connection with my father and grandfather, the way it has connected fathers and sons, brothers and uncles, grandparents and friends for millennia. Hunting let me renew ties with my buds, some of whom I only saw once a year or so, as we'd sit around a campfire telling stories, reliving old adventures and plotting new ones.

I've hunted with more people than I could count, beginning when I was big enough to hold a rifle. Two of the most memorable, other than my dad, are my Uncle Ralph and Arnie Freund, both of whom have been kicking me in the fanny since I was knee-high to a grasshopper. Both of them are real characters and as I write this, Uncle Ralph is 87 and Arnie, who was our sheriff, is 92.

When I was in my 20s and they were in their 40s, the three of us went to hunt moose near Whitecourt, Alberta. We towed a seventeen-foot camp trailer, which served as our campground and headquarters, to a fairground outside of town. From there we would drive north, past the area's oil wells, to Swan Hills, where we'd keep our eyes peeled. Finally, one afternoon as we drove past a pond, we spotted a moose cow and her calf, maybe forty yards off the road to our left. I was in the middle of the front seat, with Uncle Ralph on the driver's side and Arnie on my right. When we stopped, neither one was getting out fast enough to suit me, and I nearly went right through Arnie. He and I went around to the back of the truck, where he raised his rifle, got a good bead and pulled the trigger. A cold metallic "click" was all we heard.

"My gun's jammed," he whispered.

I had a borrowed rifle that I put to my shoulder and aimed, ready to get us a moose.

"Click."

By that time, the moose had spooked and run off, and there we stood. I looked at my rifle. The bolt had slid up over the top of the shell, which didn't slide into the chamber. From here on out, I would only be getting one shot at a time.

We got back in the truck, good and depressed. It was deadly silent as we rolled down the road. Finally, Uncle Ralph spoke up.

"Well, boys," he said, "you had your chance."

I couldn't believe what had happened. And Uncle Ralph was right. We'd had a great chance. Then it dawned on me.

"Uncle Ralph," I said, "if you're going to give us a hard time, you've got a question to answer. You were closer to the moose than either of us. Why didn't you shoot?"

There was another long pause.

"I couldn't," he said. "I dropped my clip on the ground."

Arnie and I laughed like crazy.

For the next couple of days, we beat the bush and drove those roads trying to get some meat for the table. One day Uncle Ralph and I had been riding in the truck for quite a while when all of a sudden this huge, and I do mean huge, bull moose walked out onto the road and stopped up ahead of us. Uncle Ralph slammed on the brakes and we jumped out.

I killed my first deer when I was about seven years old and I had seen and shot a lot of animals through the years, but nothing had ever impressed me like this. That moose started walking again and I raised my rifle and looked through the scope. "Good Lord," I said. "Look at the size of that rack." Talk about buck fever! I had contracted a big case of it. I lowered my rifle and simply watched in amazement. The moose took two more steps and disappeared into the brush.

That happened in the '60s, and to this day, Uncle Ralph and Arnie haven't let me forget it.

"Why didn't you shoot it?" they say.

Fortunately, just after that old bull got away, a two-year-old moose walked onto the road and Uncle Ralph dropped it. It might have been smaller, but it was still a big, big animal, and that's when I learned you don't dress out a moose the way you do a deer. We had some real work ahead of us. As luck would have it, this moose was right along the side of the road. We weren't so lucky with the second one, which we ran across the next day. We had split up and I was about a quarter of a mile from the road when I heard the shots. I knew it was Uncle Ralph. Arnie knew it too, and he showed up at the site just when I did.

This moose was a lot bigger than the one we'd bagged the day before, although not nearly as big as the one I let get away. The three of us just stood there for a bit and talked about the sheer size of the thing. I took a couple of pictures and then we all agreed we'd better get at it.

The three of us tipped that moose up on its back and did the best we could to get the hindquarters sloping downhill from the head. Arnie, who is 6'3" or 6'4", had a hold of one leg, and the knee was at about the level of his face—I still couldn't believe how big it was. Uncle Ralph and I—we're both about 5'6" on a good day—were pulling as hard as we could to get that moose gutted and we weren't having any success. Finally, it dawned on one of us geniuses that someone should get inside and push.

When you hunt, the kid of the bunch is the one that does the tough, dirty or unpleasant jobs, from changing flat tires in the mud and rain to, well, cleaning out a moose. They were both twenty years older than I was, so without further ado, I got inside the thing, stationing myself in the ribcage and trying to get everything pushed out.

"You can do this, Arn," they said, smiling ear to ear. "You can do it."

Finally, with me pushing and them pulling, we got that moose gutted. At first, we were going to quarter it, but then Uncle Ralph and I decided just to split it down the middle, hook ropes to the halves and drag them one at a time through the snow to the truck, which was only about fifty yards away. Arnie heard that and started laughing, but Uncle Ralph and I weren't phased. We got the rope attached and started pulling. And pulling. And pulling some more. We might have moved that moose about an inch, although I think that may be stretching it a bit.

We knew what we had to do. We started cutting it into quarters and dragging them one by one to the truck, where we had to lift them up onto the bed, a process that took us the rest of the day. That left the head, which I wanted to haul out so we could tie it on top of the canopy. I wanted everyone to see just how magnificent that rack was.

"I'm gonna carry that head out," I said.

Uncle Ralph and Arnie laughed and laughed.

"You can't carry that out, Deckie," Arnie said.

Well, we may not have been able to drag the carcass out a half at a time, but I was young and strong and stubborn enough to figure I could get the head out, big as it was.

I got under it and, with a great deal of contortion and grunting and exertion, got it pretty much onto my shoulders. I started staggering toward that truck, got maybe ten feet and collapsed. I had to concede this just wasn't gonna work. We went about separating the rack from the head, and we got that onto the truck.

As we climbed inside, we knew we had a freezer's worth of meat, a good-sized rack, and a great tale to tell. It had been a good day.

[Larch Lake, in the Cascade Mountains]

★ ★ ★ ★

Chapter Twenty-six

HUNTING THE ROCKY MOUNTAIN GOAT WITH A BOW

It's one thing to hunt with rifles. It's quite another to use a bow and arrow. I knew when I got into bowhunting that I'd have to take it very, very seriously. I bought a recurve bow from Herter's, the great outdoor catalog, and I made my own arrows and even a few bowstrings. I was going to need plenty of practice before I'd ever consider going on a hunt, so I set up targets in the back yard. Every night after work I'd shoot at least sixty shafts. Then I set up a real challenge. The kids had a tire hanging from a rope over the sandbox, and I put a target behind it. I'd start the tire spinning slowly and I'd back up and try to shoot an arrow through the hole and into a balloon on the target. I broke plenty of shafts trying to get the hang of it, but I knew that given perseverance and practice, I could get it done, and finally I got to where I could get an arrow through that tire and break a balloon. Even so, my dad wasn't impressed.

"What are you going to do with a stick and a piece of string?" he said. "Won't you miss that 'bang'?"

But then after visiting with his friend Bill Johnson and getting an invitation to go on a bowhunt in Bill's part of the country, Cortez, Colorado, Dad finally broke down and got a bow for himself. We had a great hunt in gorgeous territory we'd never seen before and we brought back a deer.

Once I'd gotten proficient at bowhunting, I put in for a goat hunt that was drawn by lottery. Some friends of mine had been applying every year without success, but the first time I entered they pulled my name for a hunt in September and October of 1969. My friends didn't believe it and I didn't either.

The permit allowed me to take a buddy, so I asked Chuck Jaeger, my son Shawn's godfather, to go with me. We'd grown up together and had hunted and fished together since we were kids. We loaded up the truck and headed east down I-90, over the summit of Snoqualmie Pass toward our destination—Davis Mountain, in the Cascades outside Cle Elum. We got where we were going late at night and slept on the ground at the head of the trail.

Now, we didn't know anything about Davis Mountain other than what the guy in the last town had told us when we stopped for lunch.

"You may want to think about going up that mountain, boys," he said. "There's an old brown hanging around up there."

We knew he meant a brown bear, but we thought their range was a lot farther north. There might be black bears, and maybe cougars, we figured, but not browns. Chuck and I talked about how seriously we should take this guy. Remembering what my dad had said about the fact that we were carrying sticks and pieces of string, I decided at least to keep the warning in mind.

The next morning, we put on packs loaded with 48 pounds of stuff. The only food we had was dehydrated, and we realized after hiking a good way and not seeing any creeks that there wasn't going to be water available on this trail. All we'd have is what we started out with.

This was definitely craggy, hilly goat country. It seemed like it took us all day to get to the top of the mountain, where we ran into two guys who had been hunting up there. They had camp caches, little tents made of a round piece of tubular plastic Visqueen sheeting. Not far from their camp, we picked out the flattest spot we could find and cut a ridgepole, used Visqueen as a cover for ourselves and our gear and called it a night. It wasn't a spot where you would want to walk in your sleep, as there was a cliff that must have dropped five hundred feet on the other side of our beds. This was definitely goat country. The good news was that the guys we'd run across had water they'd gathered in a makeshift Visqueen catch basin when it rained, and they shared it with us.

The next morning, Chuck decided he'd go west, toward Terence Lake, to fish, while I went north to hunt goats.

"If I'm not back tonight, don't worry about it," I told him. "It means I've gotten into some goats. But if I'm not back by midmorning tomorrow, come looking for me."

This country was definitely a challenge. Everything was steep. I realized how foolish I'd been when it came to footwear. I was wearing Army boots, which were slick as ice up there. They made for a few bits of fun, where I'd squat down, lay my bow across my lap and slide down a hill, but they also made for some nerve-wracking steps now and then.

★★★★

The rocks and dirt let loose, and my feet went right out from under me. I was heading straight out into the wild blue yonder.

After quite a while I came into some jack pines and ran across what must have been forty goats. One scrawny little kid walked right by me, not five feet away. As they moved up the hillside I got ready to take a shot. I moved out along Opal Lake and glanced up at a goat standing on the ridge not forty yards away. Here's where all that practice was going to pay off. I drew back and let one fly—and missed! Then another came into view and I missed again. All the stuffing went out of me. I was so deflated it was unreal. I decided to head back toward where we were camping.

I didn't want to go back the same way I'd come, knowing how long it would take. I decided to circle around and take a shortcut. Not too far along, though, I came upon a cliff-edge with a huge drop-off. There was nothing but blue sky below me. I looked out and could see our campsite, two ridges over. To my right, the cliff wasn't as steep, and at the bottom there was a goat trail that led in the direction I wanted to go. If I could get down there, I'd have it made.

As I headed that way, I was reminded again that I was wearing the wrong boots. I wasn't getting any traction at all. I started down, the rocks and dirt let loose, and my feet went right out from under me. I was heading straight out into the wild blue yonder. Instinctively, my right hand grabbed for a limb jutting out from some roots on the cliff face. I caught enough to let me get my left hand up there as well, and my body weight swung me around to where I slammed full-body into the rock face. I was hanging on with both hands, scared to death, my bow and quiver on my back. I honestly figured God was about to take me home. Slowly, one reach and one step at a time, I managed to inch over and down to that skinny little goat trail, and from there, I made my way around and over those ridges. As I was walking through a section strewn with 15-foot boulders, I looked up and, a few hundred feet away at the top of the ridge, Chuck and those two guys were standing with a spotting scope, watching me come back. I was really glad to see them.

"Well, Little Buddy," Chuck said when I got there, "I thought we were going to lose you." They had been watching me for some time.

The next day, the two guys left and gave us their camp caches. It was raining like crazy, so we slid our sleeping bags into them. That night and the next, we could hear something nosing around, rattling the plastic at our old campsite, where we'd left some of our provisions covered up. I started thinking about the brown that guy had been talking about at lunch.

"You hear something, Chuck?" I said.

"Yeah," he said.

The next night, our last, it was still pouring down rain. We were inside those caches, hoping nothing was going to leak, and somewhere around 1:00 or 2:00 in the morning, I had to go to the bathroom—really bad. I was lying on my left side in the fetal position, trying to convince myself I didn't really need to get up. I'd drift halfway off and then the discomfort would wake me. I'd shift a little and drift again and the pain would come back. Finally, it was so bad I knew I was going to have to get up. At that instant, like an explosion, something huge poked itself into my right shoulder socket hard enough to flip me over. Dark as it was, I knew it was a bear. I screamed so loud I should have woken people in L.A. and I came out of that cache like I'd been shot out of a cannon. I could hear it running off—I must have scared it as much as it scared me. I stood there in the pouring rain, and I guess the rain was loud enough and Chuck was far enough away that he didn't hear any of it. The next morning, as we packed up in the rain, I said, "I got rolled over by a bear last night." He looked at me as if to say, "Yeah, right."

I couldn't believe it! I had spent the night wet and petrified and he looked like he didn't believe me.

We walked on down that mountain. I was as depressed as I could be from missing the goats and still a little shaky from my encounter with the bear, and at one point we stopped to take a break. Chuck looked at me.

"You know, Arn," he said. "I heard some noise. You didn't know it, but I brought in a .22 pistol." I laughed like crazy, both because a .22 pistol wouldn't do anything but annoy a bear, and because Chuck always packs in a tiny little pillow wherever he goes. I could just see that pistol under that little thing. He got to laughing too.

We got back to the truck, changed into clean, dry clothes we'd left there, and headed back.

I told the story to Uncle Ralph back home and he looked at me just like Chuck did when I talked about the bear rolling me over in my sleeping bag.

"Arnie," he said, "that was no bear. That was a Shesquatch, a female Sasquatch. She'd gotten tired of her husband and was out looking for a new guy. She was just trying to get into that bag with you."

Somehow, it was the perfect capper for the trip.

[With Randy Pepper after a successful trip]

★ ★ ★ ★

Chapter Twenty-seven

RANDY, ARNIE AND A WORLD-CLASS GOAT

As disappointed as I was by that unsuccessful hunt, I knew I had a little more time left on the permit, so I decided to go back and try it once more. My buddy Randy Pepper agreed to go with me back to the same area.

He and I drove past the trail that went up to Davis Mountain and followed the road all twenty-two miles to its end. We were going to backpack in eleven miles to the Michaels Lake area, below the mountain. We had hiked in about three miles by the time it got dark, and made camp under a big tree. We woke to three inches of snow, but when it warmed up, I realized I had brought in too many clothes, so I stored some in a bag under a log and we took off hiking.

Compared to the crags and cliffs I dealt with the last time, it was like we were on interstate highways. I'd been here on horseback several times before, and either way, it was beautiful territory. We hiked the eight miles to where we wanted to camp and found a spot. We cut our ridgepole, made our Visqueen tents to get our gear under cover, and built a fireplace with a high back wall of rocks to reflect heat out at us. We still had some daylight, so I said, "Let's grab the bows and hike a ways to see how close we are to Davis Mountain."

Randy had a Herter's recurve too. They're beautiful bows with rosewood grips—his a 72-inch, mine a 66-inch. In fact, we still have them. I'm not sure they'd be the bow of choice for most hunters today, but they seemed to work just fine then.

――――★★★★――――

It didn't take us long to figure out that when a great big guy and a little stubby guy are carrying a goat on a pole down a mountainside, you want the big guy in the front.

We took off and saw the high ridges looming to our east. In fact, we could make out the area where I'd been the month before. As we got to a meadow by Michaels Lake, we looked up and on the ridge above us and to our left was a big white spot. Between the last hunt and this one, I'd been reading a lot, and I'd learned that the big billy goats were loners; most of the time, they weren't with the herd. Here was my proof, perched well above us. We got out the binoculars and soon realized he was huge.

Randy and I knew that when you hunt goats, you want to get around and above them, since they're generally looking down. When they're spooked, they tend to go higher. Randy went left and I circled down to the right to find a spot to start my climb. This particular hill was rocky and steep, but it was nothing like what I'd experienced the month before. It was still quite a hike, however, and it was a good while before I decided that surely I was above that goat. It was getting late in the day, and I headed off to my left, looking down to see if I could spot him from above. Then, about thirty yards in front of me, there was the goat, grazing and moving in my direction. He hadn't seen me yet, so I squatted down in a crevice.

"This is perfect," I thought. I may have missed the two shots I'd had on the other hunt, but anyone who could put an arrow through a spinning tire and into a two-inch balloon had to hit one out of three.

He looked up at me and I pulled the bowstring back and let that arrow fly. It zipped toward him—and passed within an inch of his right side. I had missed! If he had turned his head or moved his backside I'd have had him—it was that close—but he hadn't. He spun around and ran down and around a hill and went out of sight. I was dumbfounded—and down another shaft.

I slowly walked down the hill he had run around, thinking maybe I'd see him again. Man, I was discouraged. I could hear Uncle Ralph saying, "Boys, you had your chance." I was stumbling down the hillside just below where he had run when all of a sudden there he was again, not twelve feet in front of me on the trail. He scared me to death. This was his country, not mine, and I didn't know what he'd do if he decided he didn't like me there.

As it turned out, I scared him as much as he scared me, because as quick as we looked each other in the eye, he spun around and ran back up the same trail. I was on fire with adrenaline and I turned around and ran up the trail I had just come down, putting an arrow on the string as I ran in hopes of seeing him again. He came out into the open at the same instant I did and I let the shaft fly. He was on a dead run and that arrow went in and under his right ribcage and into his heart—a perfect shot—and down he went. I couldn't believe it. He was huge.

Any hunter knows the real work starts after the game is down, and here we were high on a hill with some steep country to descend and night falling.

As we field dressed the goat, I saw that Randy had placed an arrow in him too and said, "Hey, Randy, you didn't miss!" Then the real work began. We cut a ridgepole and with the twine we had in our pockets we tied the legs to the pole. We started carrying it down the hill and it didn't take us long to figure out that when a great big guy and a little stubby guy are carrying a goat on a pole down a mountainside, you want the big guy in the front so the little guy doesn't have the goat sliding down onto his back.

We reached the bottom of the hill just before it was too dark to see. We decided to skin the goat and hang it in a tree, then come back in the morning, bone it out, pack up and go home. We had no flashlights and could only see the trail by the path cuts in the trees. There was snow on the ground, so we knew it was cold enough that the meat would be fine until morning; more than once I had left a deer hanging in cold weather, taking care of it the next day.

We packed the head and hide back to camp, built a fire, got cleaned up and climbed into our sleeping bags. The next morning, we got up early and went back to get the rest of the goat and it was gone—plain old gone. We were devastated. Something—a bear, a cougar—got our kill and the only consolation was that at least it didn't go to waste. We went back to camp, packed everything up and hiked back to the truck, where we had a fresh change of clothes and headed home. It was getting late by the time we reached Mount Vernon, about twenty miles from my house, and I had a brainstorm.

"Randy," I said, "I'm gonna call Bud Peck. He's an avid bowhunter who raises horses and sells horse trailers. He and I used to ride cutting horses together, and I know he's going to want to see this goat."

I told Bud that Randy and I were on the way with a good-sized goat I'd taken with a bow and arrow. When we got there, he went bananas.

"We're going to call a friend of mine who owns Jack's Sports Shop in Mount Vernon," he said. "I want him to see this. He can measure those horns and tell you where you're at with it."

Jack was as excited as Bud was. He said, "Arnie, you've got a record goat here." We hadn't gone after a record; this was just the goat we saw up there. I knew it had a nice set of horns, but the thought of a record never crossed my mind.

He measured it and said, "You need to get the official measurement taken by the Jonas Brothers in Bellingham. They'll mount it for you, too."

We went home and showed it off to some of the guys and to Chuck, who I'd hunted with the month before, and then I took it to the Jonas Brothers. The green measurement—the one you take when it's still fresh—placed it in a tie for second in the world for a goat taken with a bow. Later, when they took the dry measurements, it wound up eighth on the list in Pope and Young's record book, and that ain't bad.

★ ★ ★ ★

Chapter Twenty-eight

ONE FOR THE GIPPER

I was always an active guy, so it was never hard convincing me to take on a physical challenge. A few years after high school, my friend Bernie Lang talked me and a bunch of other guys into a memorable one.

I had known Bernie's family all my life—in fact, I was working for his dad when I was seventeen and bought the '57 Chevy I loved so much. Bernie was a class act. He also had what they call "game." He pulled together a bunch of us has-been athletes for a Junior Chamber of Commerce game against a semi-pro football team called the Cavaliers. These were big, tough guys my age and a little older who didn't quite make the big leagues, although that didn't make them any smaller. Bernie, who must have been in his forties at the time, was going to be the coach. We borrowed pads from the high school and suited up against them.

We played them close, and then, in the second half, Bernie, who promised his wife he wouldn't play, couldn't stand it anymore and decided to pitch in. He was a sight charging across the field on those old bow legs. He was an absolute riot, and he got a good butt-chewing for going back on his promise.

I played linebacker, and there was a play that sent a monster of a running back around the left end of the line straight toward me. It was November and everything was wet, and I charged across that field toward him. We were out in the open, just the two of us, and I decided this would be his last hurrah. I was going to flatten him. I closed in on him, and all I could see was his determined grimace and his white shining teeth, when all of a sudden this blocker came out of nowhere and ran right through me. I went up in the air and back down again, hit the ground, and slid on my belly across the out-of-bounds stripe and onto the sidelines.

I came to a stop next to this pair of big shoes, and as I was getting up slowly, I saw this red-and-black plaid jacket, which was what my dad always wore. I shook my head and looked again. It was my dad, who was the last person on earth I expected to see. Even during my high school football days, he was always out fishing in the fall when we played. It turned out he had decided to come and see me play in this game, and there I was, sliding to a stop at his feet. I couldn't have done that again if I'd rehearsed for a month.

He had picked a good game to watch, though, because as tough as those guys were, we lost by only a few points. And I'll never forget him standing there, just looking down at me with his hands in his coat pockets, shaking his head with a smile that seemed to say, *You are something else.*

There is no money that could have bought the feeling he gave me by being there. Like he had so many times, that night my dad proved he was a real keeper.

[On stage in Hawaii]

★ ★ ★ ★

Chapter Twenty-nine

MUSIC: THE GOOD, THE BAD, AND THE MARRIED

Playing music professionally is kind of like sandpaper—there's a smooth side and a rough side, and through the years I've experienced my share of both. On the rough side, first is just getting it together. Finding, auditioning, and rehearsing musicians, keeping the good ones happy, letting the bad ones go, and keeping everybody straight and motivated all present challenges. You might get an idea of just how challenging it can be when I tell you I've worked with more than a hundred different people in bands over the years. There were guys with attitude problems, drinking problems, the inability to show up at rehearsals or gigs on time, and a whole host of other maladies. Sometimes it took patience and determination just to keep things together from one gig to the next.

On the other hand, there's nothing as magical as rocking along on a tune with musicians who really click with you, whether you're in a living room in front of a handful of friends or on a big stage in front of thousands of people. I've been very fortunate along the way. There have been plenty of good gigs and a lot of wonderful memories. I've made friends I'll keep for a lifetime. I've played with the same bands and musicians as some of the Grand Ole Opry greats and shared stages and dressing rooms with musical legends. There aren't many things as enjoyable or rewarding as music when it's going well.

I started putting bands together when I was in my early thirties. Some of the early ones were pretty ragged, but we were trying, and eventually we got more serious and began growing musically. I had been in love with music ever since I was a kid admiring those singing cowboys. As an adult, I had paid bills as a deputy sheriff and a commercial fisherman. When I was 28 and left the sheriff's department, I built houses for a while. I formed Peterson and Deckwa Construction with a friend, and then Deckwa Construction on my own, building houses and developing land. Then there were my rodeo days, which cost me more money than what came in. But through it all I knew I wanted music to be the way I made my living. I figured once you discover what you're passionate about, you need to be doing it, since you get only one shot at life.

The music I loved came from all over the map, and my band could handle a lot of different styles. I've told you about the Big Band, cowboy, and country music, particularly the Sons of the Pioneers and my dad's favorite, Eddy Arnold. By the time the '60s started and I was out of my teens, I'd also been influenced by the blues and jazz greats, including Ella Fitzgerald. I liked the Kingston Trio and the Brothers Four, the Everly Brothers and the Platters—I can't tell you how many times I danced to songs like "Smoke Gets in Your Eyes"—but rock 'n' roll really put me on the dance floor. That beat would just take hold of me, the way it did with millions of kids in the '50s. I suppose the biggest influence was Elvis, but Carl Perkins's "Blue Suede Shoes" always got my attention, and Little Richard sure let me know he was around. Then, as far as entertainers went, Sammy Davis Jr. could get this cowboy's blood running. Down deep inside I would have loved to tap dance and do what Sammy did. I loved to watch him and great dancers like Gene Kelly, Ray Bolger, and Fred Astaire. I love to see that kind of energy on stage, and when someone like that can really sing as well, as was the case with Sammy, man, what a show!

The first honest-to-goodness professional band I put together was called Arnie Deckwa and the Sunshine Express. It felt like family—even more so when my son Scott, who was fourteen at the time, got involved. Scott inherited my love of music early on. We practiced at the house, so he could see what a good time we were having, and it didn't take long for him to come aboard playing bass. Soon we were playing weekend gigs all around the area. I had been writing songs since I was fourteen or fifteen, and now I was able to play them in public, along with Waylon and Willie songs and other current hits.

The house was an eighteen-hundred-square-foot log home I had built in the middle of our property on Fort Nugent Road west of Oak Harbor. We had started with 20 acres, and when the 20 next door became available, I bought them and started building. There were five tons of rock in the fireplace, and horses and cattle in the pastures. As a single dad following a divorce, I can tell you that when *Kramer vs. Kramer* and *Mr. Mom* came out, the writers left a bunch out of the scripts. It was a very interesting time in my life.

The band and I rehearsed all the time, and any one of those rehearsals could turn into a big gathering. The living area was huge, and plenty of friends would come by, which was great for me because a lot of them were ladies. I fell for one of them, and about a year later I married her. I sold the log house, and the kids and I set up housekeeping in her home on the south end of Whidbey Island. I later built four new bedrooms on the house and a twenty-four-by-forty-foot studio with a stage where the band and I could rehearse our shows.

Around this time, several other opportunities came up. I was offered the chance to run for sheriff and county commissioner, and then to take the county building inspector's job. I'd had enough of full-time careers, though. I was focused on music, and I turned them all down. That didn't sit too well with my wife, although she'd known about and supported my music from the beginning. She knew the life I led and the life I was hoping to lead, but the thing that attracted her to me apparently wasn't working for her anymore. When you're on stage singing and playing guitar, it's exciting. She loved that part of it, but she didn't understand all the sacrifice and uncertainty behind it.

To make some extra money, I went into the wood business. A good friend of mine, John Richards, helped me put a new hoist under the bed of an old Chevy dump truck I bought, and then I converted a hay loader to help load the wood onto the truck. Through the bank, I was able to pick up a mammoth splitter that would split each piece of wood into five pieces; there was only one other in the state like it. I would go out and cut a few cords of wood, sell them, and make a couple hundred bucks. I'd come home and get washed up, and the band and I would rehearse until 11:00 or midnight, until finally we had that show down solid. When we went out to play, we were tight.

We performed around the Northwest, then got the chance to go to the Far East. I jumped on it. We could play good music for big crowds and explore another part of the world. For several reasons, my band members couldn't get away long enough to make the trip, so I had to put yet another band together. Once I did, five of us, under the auspices of the Air Force and military bases in the Far East, took off. We went to Honolulu, then Tokyo, traveled all over South Korea, went to the Philippines, then back to Korea and Japan. The last stop was Okinawa. By that point, the band was really cooking, and I was asked if I would add a gig to the tour. The military wanted to fly us to Misawa, Japan, to do one more show. It was a fast trip, but one I will never forget.

Traveling with five guys all the time can take its toll if you don't get some space, and after we landed and got set up for the show, we split up to have a look around. Come dinnertime, I decided to eat alone in the officers' mess hall. It was a beautiful place, and as I walked in, about twenty feet in front of me, a young man got up and said, "Hi, Arnie." I couldn't believe it. There, standing in front of me, was Bob Hallberg, a friend I had gone to school with in Oak Harbor. It's such a small world. He was in the Reserves, and he was there doing his part. We had a wonderful visit, and later on he took in what turned out to be a great show. I had him come up on stage, introduced him, and put my guitar and a hat on him for some pictures.

Afterward, I was visiting with some folks there when this young soldier, dressed in his greens, walked up and said, "Arnie Deckwa?" I said, "Yes," and he said, "You know my dad. His name is Pete Borgman." I like to have fallen over backward. Pete went to school on Whidbey and I knew him well. He and I had also run into each other while we were stationed at Fort Ord, California.

Then, this older gentleman shook my hand and said, "Arnie, you're gonna make the big time. You've got the personality, and the way you took that stage . . ." If my hat wasn't tight then, it was getting there. I thanked him, then looked him in the eyes and said, "I hope I make the big time, 'cause if I don't, it's gonna be mighty hot down there. The big time to me is eternal life in the kingdom of heaven with the almighty Father, and if we all haven't got that figured out, we need to be workin' on it." He smiled and then went on his way.

We spent three months on that tour and had a wonderful time. Three months, though, was plenty of time for my wife to give some serious thought to the state of our relationship. I didn't fare too well. When I got back, my belongings were all boxed up and sitting in the back room. After five years of marriage, she had finally had enough of the music, and I was out of there.

[Scott Deckwa, Doug Glein and yours truly]

★ ★ ★ ★

Chapter Thirty

BULLDOZER BLUES

There are two ways to approach a marital break-up like that. You can get mad and do something terrible and end up in jail—which plenty of people have done—or you can get some rest, regroup, and make plans to rise above it. That's what I decided to do.

My friend Dick Francisco offered to put me up. He was a wonderful guy, the owner of the fifty-acre M-Bar-C horse ranch. He was the kind of guy who'd bring kids or older folks from rest homes down to his place and take them for rides or put on parades of llamas. There was always something going on out there. He said, "Arnie, why don't you stay in my trailer here on the place until you can get things worked out?" The kids were with their mother, so I stayed in his twenty-eight-foot house trailer and started thinking about my next step. It wasn't an eighteen-hundred-square-foot log house, but it would be home for a while and I was grateful for the chance to stay there. When I wasn't working, I'd go up to the local coffee shop and visit with friends. Every now and then some of the band members would show up. In general, they were sympathetic, but being guys, they couldn't let it go without getting in a dig or two at me.

"What are you going to do with those four bedrooms you put on that house?" they'd ask.

"I'm gonna get me a TD24 cat and 'doze 'em off," I'd say, kidding right back with a reference to bulldozing the place.

The line, "Hey, Arn, have you taken those bedrooms off yet?" became a standing joke, something to lighten the mood as I reentered the community as a single man.

Then one day a friend sent me a copy of *People* magazine that had on its cover a woman standing in what was left of a house. As I read the piece, I saw that it was in Enumclaw, Washington, less than two hours from my place. The woman's husband was in the construction business with his father, and he owned the house, a nice place complete with antiques. His situation was a lot like mine. He came home one day, and his wife handed him divorce papers, telling him, "I keep the house. You can have the bills."

He got a demolition permit, and nobody thought anything about it, what with him being in the construction business. He went down to his shop and loaded up a bulldozer, took it out to the house, and proceeded to flatten that sucker. Before he finished, the city was there. The police came in, but they couldn't do a thing about it. He owned the house outright, and he had a permit. He pretty much said to his wife, "There. Now you've got your house."

I got such a charge out of it, I wrote a song. I was not the kind of guy who could ever get behind the controls of a Cat, crank it up and demolish her house, and I knew I couldn't even harbor hard feelings if I was going to stay happy and productive. Still, I needed an outlet for the emotions I was going through, so I turned them into humor, which would keep everything from getting to me. The result was a song called "Bulldozer Blues."

A fellow I knew named Vern Conrad, a drummer for a group called the Island City Jazz Band, heard about the song through the band's trumpet player. Vern had a tavern near where the Seahawks trained, and some of the players were among his customers. He was a hoot of a guy, and the Island City Jazz Band, made up of retired folks from all walks of life, played Dixieland. He called and said, "Arnie, what have you got going with this thing?"

I played him what I had, and he said, "I really like this. Would you mind if I wrote a little on it?" I told him to have at it. He wrote another great verse.

BULLDOZER BLUES

I've been on the road workin' all the time
Tryin' to make a dollar so I could end up with a dime,
When I came home to see my little wife,
She handed me some papers and they cut me like a knife.

She said I'll take the house, you can have the bills,
My mind was overcome with some liberated thrills,
I'll get a permit, and a D9 Cat
And I'll open up the throttle and smash the house flat.

Chorus:
The bulldozer blues, the bulldozer blues,
I'll end up in trouble but I'm doin' what I choose,
Do what you feel is right, you'll either win or lose,
But you'll never have to live with the bulldozer blues.

I did what I wanted, it's what I had to do
It seems to me that all us guys need liberatin' too,
Do what you feel is right, you'll either win or lose
But you'll never have to live with the bulldozer blues.

Chorus:
The bulldozer blues, the bulldozer blues,
I'll end up in trouble but I'm doin' what I choose,
Do what you feel is right, you'll either win or lose,
But you'll never have to live with the bulldozer blues
But you'll never have to live with the bulldozer blues
But you'll never have to live with the bulldozer blues

"Come to Seattle," he said, "and we'll record this thing." So we recorded it with that Dixieland jazz band, with their lead singer, Lynda Travis, joining me on the vocals, and it turned out to be hot. We pressed up some 45s, and before you knew it, I had it on twenty-two radio stations. Then, just as it was taking off, I got a call from some women's groups, including some that dealt with abuse and domestic violence, saying, "Why are you doing this?"

"Ma'am," I'd say, "I'm not trying to hurt anybody. It's just a decision I've made about the way I'm going to walk through life. I've had this situation happen to me, and I know you can either get above this kind of thing and find some humor in it and get on with life, or let it take you down. And I'm not that kind of guy."

Some of them, though, said, "We don't think it's very funny," so not long afterward, I quit pushing it and kind of let it fall. It had had its day, and I had one more interesting experience to look back on.

[Rusty Richards, Casey Tibbs and me]

★ ★ ★ ★

Chapter Thirty-one

REGROUPING

For a while after the divorce, things were tough for me financially. I didn't panic, but I knew I had to get my head clear, so I put in a call to Charlie Boone, a friend in Arizona, and asked if I could come down and visit. He said, "Sure," and I got things squared away.

My airline ticket and expenses were coming out of the last $500 I had, but I knew this trip was just what I needed to keep from going loco. I decided to stay for a week.

It was damp and cold in the Northwest as I left, and I bundled up for the trip. Not thinking, I guess, I figured it would be about like that in Arizona, a place I'd never visited. Well, I got off the airplane and walked out of the airport into an oven. The heat was just excruciating. Now, you're dealing with a man who had never lived with air conditioning—there was just no need for it.

The first night there, we decided to go to Scottsdale and have dinner. Along with air conditioning, I was a stranger to Mexican food, which is what we had that night. It was wonderful, and Charlie also used the occasion to introduce me to my first pitcher of margaritas. Naturally, given my dire circumstances and this renewal of our friendship, we had to drink the whole thing. We got to talking, and Charlie said he was training for a 5K race. I was running three and sometimes five miles a day, so I told him I'd join him the next day on his training run. We got pretty happy and had a lot of fun that night.

We got up at six the next morning, and between the margaritas and the peppers in the Mexican food, I can't say I was at my best. We were on horses at eight, cutting cows right off the bat. Cutting, for those of you unfamiliar with it, involves riding a specially trained horse that separates, or "cuts," a cow from the rest of the herd so it can be moved or branded or whatever needs to be done.

We did pretty well for an hour or two, and then that desert heat kicked in and just kept getting hotter and hotter. When we finally knocked off, it was like being in a pizza oven, but I had told him I was going to run with him. When he changed into running clothes, so did I.

We were going to do laps around a cotton field, and it was about a mile a lap. I made it around once, and I was frazzled, sweaty, and ready to flop down under the nearest shade tree, which is just what I did. It's a testament either to Charlie's fitness or to his willingness to endure pain in order to look good that he ran around that thing six times. I can still see him laughing at me.

Divorce causes all kinds of changes, and many of mine were financial. Banks I'd dealt with all my adult life were throwing up red flags, and what I had left of that $500 wasn't going to do much toward the several hundred thousand I had to come up with.

The trick was not to panic. I had learned that from Uncle Ralph, who used to say, "They're not gonna come out of the walls with axes and chop you up in little pieces." He taught me not to get too excited, but to figure out the right thing to do and then do it. That little getaway to Charlie's had helped clear the cobwebs so I could get that done.

Before I left Arizona, I did what I could to get the wheels turning again. I called a neighbor on Whidbey, and he agreed to sell me twenty acres and let me turn them into two-and-a-half-acre tracts and pay him as they sold. What a relief! I was back in the game.

Putting my financial house in order was never easy, and sometimes it was downright nerve-wracking. Luckily, I had music to keep me going. The band was still performing, and with the checkbook finally stabilized, I decided we needed a van. I looked around and found quite a few in the $12,000 to $15,000 range. I kept after it, and finally I found a much cheaper one in Freeland, on Whidbey Island. It had something like 100,000 miles on it, and let me tell you, they showed. There were three rock-hard benches, which held nine people altogether. It wasn't very comfortable, especially for the guys in the back, but at a thousand bucks I could afford it, and that made it close enough to perfect for me.

We had a real chance to break it in when I was invited to do a week-long engagement at a major get-together in Santa Barbara, California. A group called Rancheros Vistadores holds an annual horseback ride for two thousand people from all over the world on the Janeway Ranch, adjacent to the late President Reagan's place. They are a cross-section, from horse-shoers to presidents, coming together in a great brotherhood, united by their love of the cowboy life, horses, and the Old West. The group has included heavyweight officeholders, contributors, party friends, and loyalists from all over the country, including entertainment titans like Roy Rogers and Walt Disney. I was really excited and honored to be invited to perform.

During the long drive down, I threw in a cassette so I could point out harmony and guitar parts to the new guys. That's when I discovered the van's sound system wasn't all that much better than its suspension.

That year's attendees included Rusty Richards, the Sons of the Pioneers tenor who had also done work in the movies and as a horse trainer and rodeo cowboy, and who recently penned a book titled *Casey Tibbs: Born to Ride* (www.rustyrichards.com) and the subject of that book, nine-time world champion cowboy Casey Tibbs. There were even rumors that President Reagan, a longtime member of the group while he was governor of California, just might show up. I was in heaven. It just couldn't get any better than that. I was sitting around with a bunch of guys chewin' the fat, and one of 'em said to me, "Arnie, what are you going to do if the president comes and starts up a conversation with you after you're done playing?" Everybody got kind of quiet and looked my way. I pondered for a bit and said, "I'll tell him, 'Mr. President, it's an honor to meet you. Can you hook me up with Slim Pickens?'" They all just about fell out.

It turned out the president couldn't come after all, so I never got the opportunity, but from what I know about the kind of guy he was, I'm sure he would have laughed and laughed. He did call us, though, and talked to us through loudspeakers, saying, "I didn't realize when I took this job, I would have to take so many people along when I went anywhere, so I'm not going to be able to visit you." He talked for quite some time from his ranch, and it was hard to believe I was lying in the grass with a lot of other cowboys listening to the president of the United States talk to us. It was a wonderful experience.

We played every night and then took a long trail ride to a site where we did the last night's concert. We shared a bill with country legend Rex Allen Sr. and Casey Tibbs, a wonderful and fun guy who did a show that included a mock fight. I remember that show well because the fight ended up on our stage just before our performance, and most of our mikes were knocked over. Casey was something else—one of a kind. I have a picture of him riding a saddled-up Texas longhorn into an arena, but that's another story.

Our set went really well, and we finished with my version of "Ghost Riders in the Sky." They introduced Rex, and he came up and took the microphone. Then slowly he turned and looked at me and said, "Now that you've finished with my opening song, what am I supposed to do?" I like to fell through my socks. Though my stomach was rollin' like I was about to come out of a chute on a two-thousand-pound Brahma bull, I held my composure—never let 'em see you sweat. I turned around and looked at the band, and then at all those cowboys out in the audience. Everything got very quiet, and I said, "I don't know, Rex. Do you know any other songs?"

He loved it. He laughed and the crowd laughed, and they launched into their show. Rex, of course, had a repertoire of songs that could last a lifetime, and to this day, that gathering remains one of the biggest highlights of my life.

The van got us back home again, but that trip proved it didn't have any real comfort to speak of, let alone luxury. Starting with the band, people quickly convinced me the thing needed an overhaul, and not long after we got back, I rebuilt the engine and replaced a few other odds and ends up front. Then I gutted it, taking out all the seats and stripping the coverings off the walls and inside roof. I put three-and-a-half-inch insulation on the floor and in the walls and then covered the floor with three-quarter-inch plywood. I made the wall and roof coverings from quarter-inch plywood and had a fabric company cover them with a beautiful dark maroon velour.

After trimming out the edges with walnut-stained fir, I put a beautiful, short-napped mauve rug on the floor. I took an old couch from my grandmother's house and cut it to fit in the back. It folded out into a bed, so

I cut the mechanisms to fit as well. I had that reupholstered along with four captain's chairs, all in a matching mauve color. In the rear, I built a closet you could only get into by opening the back doors of the van. Soon the whole thing looked like a piece of furniture. It was absolutely gorgeous all the way around. Sometimes I'd just sit there with a guitar and marvel at it.

Then there was the new sound system, with speakers in the top of the closet in the back and in all the doors and the sides. When you put a tape in that stereo, you could hear a guitarist's finger positions change, and there was no guessing from then on about a harmony or a chord. I loved that old van, and it was the one I would eventually drive to Nashville.

★ ★ ★ ★

Chapter Thirty-two

CHRIST AND CHOCOLATE CHIP COOKIES

It was somewhere during this stretch of time that I got my act together as a Christian. I had drifted away from regular church attendance as a boy, although I always believed in God and in Christ as the pathway to the Father.

There were people who'd planted seeds in my heart along the way. One, of course, was my mother, whose faith was always strong and whose influence was always profound. She and my father said more with the way they lived than they ever could with words. Another was Ron Murphy, a junior high classmate. He moved away when his dad, a Navy man, was transferred, and some time later I got a letter from him telling me how he'd found Christ. I was still a teenager and I remember showing it to Ann Miller, a friend of my parents' who was visiting.

"This reads like a priest wrote it," she said. Here was this guy who had been right there with me with the D.A. haircut and the pegged jeans and white

T-shirts and now he was immersed in Christ. It let me see how powerful faith could be and it helped those seeds take root. He would visit now and then—still does—and seeing him and hearing him talk about a life in ministry that has now stretched over 40 years is always cool rain to my spirit.

Then, once in the mid-'70s, just after I'd left the sheriff's department, I was sick in bed in my log house and another schoolmate named Gary Shepherd came to visit me. He was a missionary who had endured all kinds of hardships to spread the gospel all over the globe. He brought photos of some of the places he'd been and the people he'd met—among many other accomplishments, he had translated the New Testament into the Magar language for the people of Nepal—but more importantly he brought me a Bible and said, "I want you to read the gospel of John." I did, and that visit stayed with me, helping that seed to sprout and begin to grow.

By the early '80s, I was playing music regularly around the region, with a lot of gigs in our local American Legion. During that period my songwriting branched out from country to country-gospel. The part of me that was reaching for a real grounding in my faith needed expression, and the words and music started coming.

It was then that I ran into Jeff Alexander, a conductor, composer and arranger who had worked with Elvis and Frank Sinatra and composed scores for films including *Jailhouse Rock* and *Support Your Local Sheriff.* I knew he lived in the area and some of my friends used to kid about how I should go introduce myself. "Right," I said, "I'm playing at the American Legion and I'm going to say, 'Mr. Alexander, I'd like to write music with you.'"

Well, one day I was in a restaurant parking lot when a man got out of a chartreuse Porsche. He walked up and said, "You're Arnie Deckwa."

"Yes, sir, I am."

"My name's Jeff Alexander. I'd like to visit about your music. Why don't you to come to my house?"

I like to fell over. I took my guitar and played him a song he wanted to hear—one of mine called "It's O.K. to Pray"—and that started a friendship and collaboration that extended for several years. Here was a man who had worked with the greats—he called Sinatra once while we were together and wished him happy birthday—and his love for Christ and the desire to do something to further the kingdom was so strong he was spending his time with me, which was so flattering, writing gospel songs. I found out after he died that he was battling cancer the entire time we worked together, and the level of his commitment affected me that much more. It was a lesson in conviction and faith in action that still touches me deeply.

I was going to church now and then, but I wasn't a regular until a friend invited me to St. Stephen's Episcopal Church in Oak Harbor. Now, I had been baptized in a Methodist church, went to Sunday school in a Lutheran church and had gotten married in a Catholic church, so I could get comfortable wherever I was, but this time, something really clicked. That seed had become a flower and, let me tell you, it was blooming. I went to services three times a week. I got involved in the Cursillo movement, which is aimed at letting Christianity fully flower in a person, and I took the next step with my songwriting. I hooked up with a singer/songwriter named Jock Heverling. He and I sang together in church and began writing songs together. We started doing programs, playing gospel music for school and youth groups, including for kids with various handicaps, just sharing the gospel message.

Soon I became the church's youth director. Then I got involved in the Kairos prison ministry, part of a national group aimed at bringing a message of love and forgiveness to prisoners, their families and those who work with them, and assisting them in the process of becoming productive citizens. Ours was the first Kairos ministry in the state of Washington. We had a team of almost sixty people. About forty of us went into the prison, each as the sponsor of a "candidate," which is what the program called the inmates who participated. A team of cooks prepared homemade meals for the candidates every day, and we brought in 10,000 dozen cookies sent to us from all over the country, enough for a dozen for everybody in the place every time we walked in the door.

★★★★

We brought 10,000 dozen cookies sent to us from all over the country into that prison.

I don't mind telling you that at first I resisted becoming part of Kairos. My mind was focused on going to Nashville by this time, and I didn't need anything else on my plate, especially something that committed me for a time.

I was pulling every string, shaking every tree, doing my best to set up my move to Nashville, and it was all rolling along pretty well when the guys from Kairos asked me to be part of the team. They figured that between my outgoing personality and my musical abilities I might be a good addition to what they were doing.

"Can't do it," I told them. "I have too much going on. Besides, the last thing I need is to be an ex-sheriff's deputy going into a prison with people I helped put there. I'm not going to do this."

"Arnie," they said. "God wants you on this team with us."

"Maybe he does, but this cowboy doesn't need to go into that prison."

It was the strangest thing. Right then, all my promotional skills, all my abilities at setting things up, began failing me. It was like somebody put a cage around me. I couldn't get anything going. I've proven I'm a pretty good promoter and marketing guy, but right then nobody was buying what I was selling. My Kairos friends just laughed.

"Arnie," they said, "God wants you on the team."

It didn't take a rocket scientist to see that things were lining up to support their point of view.

"Look," I said, when I finally gave in, "I don't want anybody knowing I'm an ex-deputy."

We were scheduled to spend three days in the prison. On the first day, two law enforcement officers attached to the program from inside the prison said, "Arnie, we'd like you to go down below with us and help hand out cookies."

"That'd be fine," I said. We got to the tower that led to all the cell blocks, and the guards there stopped us cold and said, "We don't need any cookies." What they really didn't want was any change in the routine. Finally we convinced them we had approval all the way to the top and we were able to go through the blocks, among the prisoners, and hand out those bags of cookies. Of course, the guards got some too. The second day was much easier and by the third, they were saying, "Arnie, good to see you! Come on in." That, my friend, is the power of Christ and chocolate chip cookies.

———— ★★★★ ————

We'd sing, we'd talk, we'd share the power of Christ in our lives.

The rest of those days involved programs with the candidates. We'd sing, we'd talk, we'd share the power of Christ in our lives. My candidate, John Anderson, was a very intelligent man who looked like Indiana Jones. On the second day, one of the enforcement officers found out I'd been a deputy sheriff and asked me if I knew just who my candidate was, and what he was in for.

"No, I don't," I said. "We're not supposed to know. As far as I'm concerned, he's here for joyriding."

He said, "He's really well known. He's serving three consecutive life sentences for murder."

As a deputy, I'd been on high-speed chases and looked down the barrel of a shotgun, but somehow this scared me—a lot. That night, those of us from Kairos met at a church for a communion service. At one point I stood on a chair—I was one of the shortest guys in the room—and poured my heart out about my candidate and my ability to do what I needed inside that prison. I felt intimidated. I felt inadequate. What was I going to say if he started talking about who he was and what he'd done? I needed guidance.

★★★★

He said, "He's really well known. He's serving three consecutive life sentences for murder."

The guys talked to me about faith, and about the fact that God won't give you more than you can handle. Finally, I resolved that I'd just let Him work through me the best I could.

Sure enough, the next day John said, "Arnie, I'm in here for murder." He was really emotional about it. I looked at him and the words just came. "What you did may have been wrong, but you know there is forgiveness in Christ and you could be a soldier in his army. People in here look up to you. They respect you. You could use that for good or for evil. Do you know how wonderful it would be if you were able to guide some of the young kids who come in here?" It was as though the right things to say were just there, waiting for him to make that statement and for me to open my mouth.

John ultimately latched onto Kairos with everything he had. He became the inside lay director and there's no telling how many lives he influenced for good. Kairos changed both John's life and mine for the better. It was a time neither he nor I will ever forget.

One day after I'd moved to Nashville, he called me from prison. He said, "Arnie, I know you'll find this hard to understand, but my life has never been better than it is now. When you're working for Christ, your life feels good, and all of a sudden I've come to realize that there are a few guys in my life who are at the top of the list when it comes to what they mean to me, and you're right there. I love you, brother, and I just had to say thanks."

I bawled for a week and I can still get emotional just thinking about it. It was confirmation that Kairos was indeed God's call to me, that it was something I needed to do before I moved to Nashville. And by the time my service in Kairos had come to an end, I knew my faith was a garden that had bloomed fully, and I knew it would be a lovely and vital part of every day I lived from then on.

John and I still visit now and then and he is as strong for Christ today as he was when his involvement with Kairos began. He is still filled with hope that the army of soldiers for Christ will keep growing and spreading the good Word, and he and I are both happy that he's part of this book.

[With Barbara Mandrell]

★ ★ ★ ★

Chapter Thirty-three

GETTING MY ACT TOGETHER

As a single dad spending more and more time and energy on music, I was in a great position to get things rolling. The people around me knew I was poised to move it all up a notch as well, and they approached me with an idea. In 1985, some friends and I talked about forming a small corporation to put a little financial muscle behind my music. These were people who had been behind me as my reputation grew regionally, and they wanted to be part of an effort to go national. A local attorney thought it was a great idea, and he dotted the i's and crossed the t's. We talked it all out, and I made it clear this should be money they could afford to lose—it was all a big roll of the dice. Still, no one was more sincere about making it work than I was.

A final hurdle was dealing with the uncertainties that go with relying on other musicians. I'd be moving to Nashville on my own, but I'd be working with musicians both there and back home. Remember, I had worked with well over a hundred people in various bands. One night after an especially bad rehearsal, I thought about bagging the whole idea of going to Nashville, and I said so. My son Scott, who was then 18, had been in bands with me ever since he was just a little guy. I remember him trying to hide behind me on stage when he was just starting out. Eventually, as he grew taller—he's a lot taller than me now—his confidence and ability grew as well. He was a fixture with me, and as both my son and my long-time bass player, he knew me really well.

"Dad," he said, "you know this is something you've always wanted to do. If you let it stop, you're crazy."

I didn't have to think for more than a second to realize he was right, and that little pep talk helped me kick it back in gear.

I had recorded my first album in Washington. Now that there was a little money to work with, it seemed like the time to consider doing a second album in Nashville.

Jimmy Gray, a writer/photographer friend I met through Vern from the Island City Jazz Band, was a voice from Nashville urging me to give it a try, and he finally pushed it over the top. I had only dealt with him by telephone, and it would be almost a year before I'd meet him in person. In that sense, Jimmy was a lot like Charlie on *Charlie's Angels*, someone who directs a lot of great activity from the other end of a phone line. Actually, the angel part fits him too, because he was the closest thing to an angel I'd met up to that time. It was my future wife, Joanne, who inspired me to write the song "Please Send Me an Angel," but I always kid that it could have been written about Jimmy. I've never seen him without a shirt on, so he may just have wings for all I know. He's a precious friend.

Jimmy looked a little like a shriveled-up Bob Hope. Besides working as a photographer and having several photos appear in *Life* magazine, he had formed a company with Barbara Mandrell's father called Mandrell and Gray. He gave me more education about the music business than I could have hoped for. At the time, he was working in a tape business on Music Row and traveling all over the country, visiting recording studios and dealing with clients. Even over the phone it didn't take long for us to get into the project that would become my second album. "Why don't you just record down here and see what you can get done?" he said.

I knew it was finally time to go to Nashville. Rusty Richards of the Sons of the Pioneers had recorded an album at Gene Breeden's recording studio, and I decided that's where I'd cut mine. Jimmy said he would line everything up.

As I planned the trip, I decided it would be wonderful to take my mother.

"You're the one who put that accordion in my hand," I said when I brought up the subject with her. "Why don't you come with me? You'll get a kick out of it." Of course, she jumped at the invite. A country-music-loving friend of hers—"Auntie Audrey," we called her—wanted to come along, and I thought it was a great idea. She could keep Mom company while I was in the studio. Soon these two wonderful ladies, both in their seventies, and I were on a plane bound for Nashville.

★★★★

Watching Mom visit with Barbara Mandrell was unexplainably good medicine for me.

Once we arrived and I got into the swing of things, I came into contact with other people who had Opry ties. One of the engineers, David Signs, was Johnny Russell's keyboard player, and through him and Dennis McCall, who was with the great Opry backup group the Carol Lee Singers and whom I met through Jimmy Gray, we were able to go backstage at the Opry and meet people I'd only read about. Mom and Auntie Audrey were having a ball. Watching Mom visit with Barbara Mandrell and her husband, Ken Dudney, who had been stationed at Whidbey Island Naval Air Station, was unexplainably good medicine for me. This little Russian lady of a mother, who was never afraid to pick up a shovel or dress up and dance to the Big Band sound, was rubbing shoulders with some of the greatest country stars ever.

We planned to do an introductory video while at the studio working on my song, "World's Champion Daddy," which we would be releasing as a single. It would include an interview of me by Dennis McCall, and Jimmy lined that up as well. The trick was, he still wasn't there. He'd been traveling, and I hadn't yet met him face-to-face. One night the phone rang at my motel. It was Jimmy.

"Where are you?" I said.

"I'm in Chicago. I've got it all set up for you." He gave me a number and told me to say he was the one who told me to call. "I'll call you back and find out how it all went," he said.

Sure enough, he had everything set up and running smoothly, and we spent the day in the studio with all the video people. That night, back at the motel, the phone rang again.

"It's Jimmy. I'm in Boston. Did it all go well? . . . No, I won't be coming there. . . . You're doing fine. Everything's going to be great. Don't worry."

I couldn't believe this guy. We got ready to head back to Washington with the finished masters, and I still hadn't met him.

Back home, I took a page out of Loretta Lynn's career. I went to one radio station after another all over Washington and Oregon. I did my own promotion, marketing, press kits—everything I could think of to let people know about the record. I literally did exactly what the old-timers did; I know that routine like the back of my hands. I stood on the same stages and put in the same kind of sweat that a lot of Hall of Fame artists did, but no one was guiding me at the time. I could sing and I could entertain a crowd, but I never did get that big hit record.

★★★★

Back home, I took a page out of Loretta Lynn's career. I went to one radio station after another all over Washington and Oregon.

When it was all over, I had $1,500 left. I've heard of reincarnation, but I've never talked to anybody who's been there and back, so I decided I needed to use that money to move to Nashville and give it a real go. Every trip into the studio had taught me more about music, about recording, and about myself as an artist. Now it was time to try to put it all together. I had a three-month plan where I'd go to Nashville, put a band together, and do everything I could to try to hook up with a publishing company and all the rest. I didn't know many people—Jimmy, Dennis, and Brent Burkett of the Four Guys were about it, and at that time they were just acquaintances—but I'd been packing a five-piece band all over the country and had handled three months of touring in Southeast Asia. I knew now was the time.

[With Garth Brooks]

★ ★ ★ ★

Chapter Thirty-four

OFF TO NASHVILLE

In January 1987 I hooked a trailer to my refurbished '73 Dodge van, filled both with clothes and musical equipment, and headed for Nashville. My goal was to try to make it in country and country/gospel music. It felt like my entire life had led up to that trip. All those dreams, all those days marching with my accordion, all the bands, all the triumphs and heartaches were rolled up into this journey down 2,600 miles of life's highway. I was one excited cowboy.

My youngest son Shawn and my good friend Frank Erickson, whom I'd known most of my life, shared the ride with me, then flew back home after we got there. Shawn was just twelve, and he passed up an elk-hunting trip with his grandfather to go on the road with his dad. I was carrying the good wishes of a whole lot of friends back home and a $1,500 cashier's check to get me started.

I could write another book on that trip alone. So many incidents stood out. Two that come to mind immediately had to do with running low on gas. I hadn't yet developed a feel for exactly how far I could go on a tank in this one-ton rig. It held a lot of gas, but seeing that needle on empty out in no-man's-land got a little worrisome.

It happened first at one or two o'clock in the morning as we drove through Twin Falls, Idaho. Frank and Shawn had dropped the couch down and were taking a rest. I was on the CB, carrying on a conversation with a driver who called herself Brown Eyes. She said she had passed me a while back in her red eighteen-wheeler and asked where I was headed. I told her the story, and she said, "Nashville! You sing?" I said, "Yes," and she jokingly said, "Sing me a song." I sang some of "World's Champion Daddy." She got a big kick out of that and asked if I had an album. I told her I did, and she said she wanted one.

As we talked and laughed, I glanced down and checked the fuel gauge. Sure enough, we were on empty; we needed to find some gas quick. I told Brown Eyes the situation and asked if she knew of any gas stations nearby. At that moment, we sped right by one. I asked if she knew of a nearby spot wide enough for me to turn around and get back to the station, and she said she didn't. As luck would have it, though, another trucker came on the radio and told me there was a spot just up the road. He said he had been listening to our conversation and was right behind me. He told me he would pass and pull in front of me. Then I was to pull up as close to the back of his trailer as I could without hitting him. He said the wind between his rig and mine would act like a suction cup, and I'd save some gas. He passed us, and I did exactly as he said. He was right—it was almost like being towed. Brown Eyes came back on the radio and said she wanted us to stop at the turnaround so she could have an album. The other trucker said he wanted one too.

Frank and Shawn had been listening to everything, and they came up front and watched as we all pulled over to the side of the road. Shawn asked if he could give them the albums, and I said, "Sure." We all stepped outside in the cold wind and had a short but great visit with Brown Eyes and the other driver as Shawn gave them each an album. We all shook hands and said so long, then hustled back into our warm rigs.

What a kick! I realized that more than likely never again in my life would I have an experience like that—two big ol' eighteen-wheelers pulling off the road at the same time to get one of my albums. We got turned around, and as we were pulling into the service station, the van began to cough. We had just made it.

Another time, around midday, we were in the middle of nowhere, driving through Wyoming. Shawn was in the passenger's seat and Frank was relaxing in the seat behind me when I looked down at the gas gauge. It was on empty. "Oh, no," I said. "We have a problem."

"What?" Shawn asked me.

"Well, pal, we're out in no-man's-land and soon to be out of gas."

"What are we going to do?" he asked.

I looked around at a whole lot of nothin', just Wyoming's cold, bare January hills, and said, "The only thing I know to do now, son, is pray," and that's what we did.

We hadn't driven five more miles when around the next curve, off to the left, was the most beautiful sight we'd ever seen—a Little America Truck Stop with big trees and green grass all over. It looked like an oasis. We couldn't believe it. I had written a song called "It's O.K. to Pray," and to this day I believe our prayers pulled us through.

It took us about fifty-four hours of driving stretched over three days, with two nights in motels along the way, to get to Nashville. One of the first things we did when we got there was to meet Jimmy Gray at a Cracker Barrel restaurant. It was a pleasure after all that time to be able to put a face and body with the voice I'd only heard on the telephone. At fifty-six, Jimmy was as generous with his time, energy, and seemingly endless knowledge as I could have hoped for. We caught up about a lot of things and talked about the music business; I felt like we were in the presence of Nashville's one-man welcoming committee. He's proven himself over and over through the years to be a great, upbeat kind of guy with a big heart and a contagious sense of excitement.

My first order of business was to find a place to stay. Now, I didn't think I was the apartment type—up to this point I had never even stayed in an apartment—but I reasoned that starting out, that would probably be the way to go. A house like I'd want would be out in the country, complete with chores and more expenses than I could afford. It wasn't hard to picture myself spending so much time and money on a house that my career would suffer.

I was thinking about apartments in some areas geared toward tourists, but Dennis McCall of the Carol Lee Singers said those could be a little rough around the edges and steered me toward another area of town. It turned out to be great advice. My buddy Frank, who knew all about the city, got a newspaper and found me the perfect place.

They were called the Warren House Apartments, and the husband and wife who ran them were really sweet people who had been Kansas farmers.

You could pay by the week or by the month, and there was no big, long lease to sign. It was perfect for musicians, and there were plenty, including names like Steve Wariner, who had stayed there over the years. All I needed was to cash that cashier's check and move in.

The trouble was, nobody would cash it. I'd never heard of such a thing. That was the reason you got a cashier's check in the first place, as far as I was concerned—anybody'd cash it. It turned out I was wrong. One place after another turned me down. Finally, Jerry Hutchinson, a friend of Jimmy's who owned the National Tape Corporation, where Jimmy worked, and who had been Buddy Holly's drummer at one point in his long career, took it from me, wrote me a check for the amount, and got it cashed. So, finally, after three or four days in motels, I moved into #35-A at the Warren House Apartments.

————★★★★————

I desperately needed to learn how to survive cheaply and Jimmy was just the guide I needed.

I would be paying $343 a month in rent, and believe me, that looked like a good chunk of change at the time. I desperately needed to learn how to survive cheaply as I started pursuing music, and Jimmy, who had a world of savvy, was just the guide I needed. He was incredible. He would call up and say, "Have you eaten yet? No? Come and meet me at the Music City Sheraton." He'd explain how to get there, and I'd meet him. The Sheraton was a classy place with a big lobby with chandeliers that looked like they were fifteen feet in diameter. It was beautiful. We'd grab a table in the bar; Jimmy'd have his glass of red wine and I'd have a tonic water and Rose's Lime, a nonalcoholic drink I really liked that only cost a buck. Then, because I'd bought that one drink, I could help myself to the free, all-you-could-eat buffet all through Happy Hour. Along an entire wall they had vegetables, and then they had a table of sandwiches. One night they rolled a canoe in there full of oysters and shrimp. The chef was in between the vegetable and sandwich tables cutting beef, and I got to eat all that for a buck!

Jimmy also took me to a Mexican place that had a similar Happy Hour. They featured all the tacos, rice, and beans you could eat, also for a buck. Then there was an Italian place—same kind of deal. The guy really knew how to get by in that town, and he was just the tour guide for someone trying to get established on a limited budget.

To this day, Jimmy, who is now in his late seventies, is full of excitement and adventure. We stay in touch, and he always has something cooking. His phone calls can be real adventures. One time when I was in Nashville, I got a call from him.

"Arnie, this is Jimmy."

"Where are you?"

"You'll never guess."

"Well, let me give it a try."

I guessed and I was wrong. Turned out he had just walked out of the Cornet Bay Marina, where my mother was working, like she had for thirty-five years. He had heard so much about our lifestyle that, on a trip to Seattle for the National Tape Corporation, he decided he just had to meet my mom. She was elated. She took him into her heart as readily as I had, and he became a part of the family. When Joanne and I got married, on June 17, 1989, he was the photographer, and I'm not talking a guy who's an interested amateur. As I said, he's taken pictures for *Life* magazine, and he's done photos and text for displays at the Shiloh Civil War battlefield museum near his home in Savannah, Tennessee. He's one of a kind.

[Son Shawn Deckwa, heading up a construction job]

★ ★ ★ ★

Chapter Thirty-five

MY COOKING SCHOOL

All my life I've enjoyed good food. It's true whether I'm eating someone else's cooking or my own. Since Nashville is where my cooking career got its start, it's time I talk about how I learned to cook in the first place.

It started aboard my dad's fishing boat when I was about eight years old. The first thing I remember making is hash, something Dad really liked, on a little Coleman stove on the *Charlotte D.* As we took longer trips, say up to the Point Roberts/Blaine fishing area by the Canadian border, Dad had me cook bigger breakfasts. I'd make eggs and fried potatoes along with hash for us and Uncle Bill, our fishing partner, and for anyone else who came aboard.

From there, my interest in cooking grew and grew because I really enjoyed doing it. Mom was always getting me involved in putting together our meals. It was nothing elaborate—I mean, I'm not talking pheasant under glass or Cornish game hens—but it was good, basic fare. We had venison and elk from the freezer; in fact, it was 1973 or so before I ever had beef in my freezer. There was an incredible array of seafood, including salmon, clams, crabs, and shrimp, which we baked, boiled, fried, or stewed—there were a lot of ways to go about it. The thing was, you became part of the cooking process because you were part of the family, and the family was a real team. That was important to all of us.

I liked to create things. I still do. I'd give the recipe a quick once-over, but I'd never stick to it. I was always trying something else. Of course, I messed up a lot of recipes because for a long time I didn't even know what the spices were. I'd think, *Hmm, that ought to be pretty good*, and I'd throw in a spice that had no business in the dish I was making. I just sort of learned as I went along, having a great time at it.

————— ★★★★ —————

We'd cook salmon and oysters and boil up some crabs. We'd have a live band, and people would just keep dropping by all day.

I'd look for places to cook. Those six months active and six years total in the National Guard gave me plenty of opportunities. I'd go to the mess hall, and things wouldn't be moving fast enough back in the kitchen. I'd say, "You guys need some help?" "Well, yeah." So I'd throw on an apron and jump in and start scrambling eggs and frying bacon. They had these big, beautiful grills, and the more guys, the better. A lot of what made it so good was the interaction, cutting up with the other cooks, joking with the guys in the line as you'd slap it on their plates. That was the fun part.

When I returned to Whidbey Island and got on my own, I'd have people come over to the house, and we'd have these big feeds with spaghetti or venison chili, or I'd cook some salmon on the grill out back. Good Lord, we had fun, and it was never just a few of us. They were real feasts with at least twenty people or so. We had a great big grill made out of concrete blocks, with diamond steel tops, and we'd cook salmon and oysters and boil up some crabs. We'd have a live band, and people would just keep dropping by all day.

Then, when I was president of the Skagit Island Law Enforcement Council, we'd have the nearby city, county, and state police departments get together every year for a salmon barbecue. I'd end up helping to cook for 150 people, and I'd just keep it coming and everybody would be happy.

I think that's why when I came to Nashville and was asked to help cook one of my favorite dishes, smoked salmon fettuccini, for the Nashville Chefs' Association, it didn't seem to be a big deal. A friend who owned a restaurant named Giuseppe's was a member of the association, and he and I had done cooking shows together. It was his turn to cook at the meeting, so I wasn't completely on my own, and at the time it was just a fun thing to do.

People around me would say, "My gosh, Arnie, the Nashville Chefs' Association!" But then, I never really zoomed in on a chef as a chef. I just plowed right in as if it were another cookout like the Law Enforcement Council barbecues and said, "Yeah, I'll cook it." I mean, here's a guy with a white outfit on and me with a pair of Wranglers. What's the big deal? Everybody loves to eat; that was the attitude I went in with. I cooked it up and everybody loved it. Now I look back and think, *Good Lord, these guys were some of the greatest chefs in Nashville!* I suppose if I had to go back and do it now, I'd probably be nervous, but everything turned out great. They taught me I can cook for anybody and we'll have a ball, and I think as long as I can hang onto that attitude, I'll always enjoy cooking.

[With Brent Burkett of the Four Guys]

★ ★ ★ ★

Chapter Thirty-six

"YOU NEED TO DO SOMETHING WITH THIS!"

Because I was hanging out with Dennis McCall of the Carol Lee Singers, I got to spend time backstage at the Grand Ole Opry—in fact, I'd practically live back there for the next ten years, although I wouldn't have dreamed that at the time. Carol Lee is Carol Lee Cooper, the very talented daughter of Opry stalwarts Wilma Lee and Stoney Cooper. Singing with them, she became the youngest member of the Opry in history on January 12, 1957, a distinction she holds to this day. She has recorded with a Who's Who of artists, including Johnny Cash, Loretta Lynn, Porter Wagoner and Glen Campbell, and sang on many classic records, including Conway Twitty's "Hello Darlin'," "I've Never Been This Far Before" and "Linda On My Mind." She formed the Carol Lee Singers 37 years ago and has been a regular on the Opry and a mainstay of country music since those days. She has performed for four presidents and with Dolly Parton at the United Nations. She quickly became one of many people at the Opry who were free with time, advice, friendship, and good wishes. Dennis was the only one I knew when I first got there, and he was the first to see how impressed I was with my new life. One Friday after the Opry, I said, "Can I walk out on that stage?" Everybody was gone, and he said, "Sure."

I couldn't believe it. Here's this kid who was raised in a commercial fishing family, who used to listen to his dad play Eddy Arnold on an old 1947 tube radio on a gill net boat, standing on the stage of the Grand Ole Opry, which we couldn't even get on that radio back home. I was thrilled!

I walked out onto that stage and stood in the middle of the circle where Roy Acuff, Hank Williams and so many others had stood, and I sang one of my songs with all the gusto I could muster to 4,500 empty chairs. I loved it. When I went home, I called my mother and said, "Mom, I just sang at the Opry."

The next night, of course, following that great adventure, the juices were really flowing. Dennis introduced me to more artists—Little Jimmy Dickens, Charlie Walker, Minnie Pearl, Roy Acuff—and that was the night Brent Burkett of the Four Guys, the terrific quartet, came into my life. He was a 285-pound giant of a man in a tuxedo, which the Four Guys always wore, and he was an especially treasured part of the big Opry family that was accepting me on its own turf. He was also the guy who put the first key in the lock that opened the door to an entirely new and unexpected career for me.

My mother could smoke salmon better than anyone I have ever known, and every now and then she would send me some. That was wonderful on a couple of levels. First, I was operating on a very tight budget, so a little extra protein was nothing to sneeze at. Second, it was a touch of home I deeply appreciated. Nashville was wonderful, but it was hundreds of miles from the nearest body of water with salt in it, and a couple of thousand from the Whidbey Island dead-end road that had formed and shaped every aspect of my life.

One night, I carried some of that salmon to the Opry and gave Brent a piece. I'd learned he was an enthusiastic fisherman, and I figured he would really appreciate it.

This was a man who knew how to enjoy good food and how to express appreciation. In the hallway between the green room and Roy Acuff's dressing room, Brent bent over, so as not to stain his tuxedo, and took a bite. He stopped, shook his head, looked up at me, and said, "I know you want to sing, cowboy, but you need to do something with this."

I said, "Do what with it?"

"Sell it!" he said.

"Sell it? To who?"

"To Kroger!"

"Who's Kroger?" I asked him.

Kroger, it turned out, was Nashville's big grocery chain. Actually, it's a national firm headquartered in Cincinnati, with stores in thirty-one states. At the time, it was the largest grocery chain in the nation and these days only Wal-Mart sells more groceries. I laughed it off as a lighthearted compliment and went on to the next thing, but week after week, I realized people really did like this stuff, and since we were so far from an ocean, it was not a treat they ran across often. Something big was happening, although I didn't know quite what it was yet. Charlie Walker started saying, "Here comes the singin' salmon man. He's gonna own this place one day." Or I'd be in Roy Acuff's dressing room with a smoked salmon cheese ball. God bless that man; he loved those things. I'd kneel down beside him and he'd eat while I handed him eight-by-ten photos of him and me to autograph for friends back home. He was so supportive, as was Little Jimmy Dickens, who became a good friend. I'll never forget him looking up at me and saying, "You've got yourself involved in quite a few things, don't you?"

Charlie Walker started saying, "Here comes the singin' salmon man. He's gonna own this place one day."

"I've just gotta keep this going," I told him.

The next step in keeping it going was bringing Arnie's Country Cookies into the fold. That expanded my repertoire, pleased the Opry stars' taste buds from another angle, and helped assure my easy access to the proceedings. Normally, getting into the Opry's backstage area took an act of Congress, especially when it came to getting past Mr. Roy Van Dame, the security guard. So once I started baking the cookies—usually chocolate chip or white chocolate almond—I took a big cardboard box and took a black-tip Sharpie Fine Point marker and wrote "Arnie's Country Cookies" on it. I'd make several dozen cookies, break them into hundreds of pieces, and put them in the box to take backstage. Mr. Van Dame would dip his big hand in there first, and he was always glad to see me coming with them. "Arnie's here!" he'd yell. Then all the entertainers and folks who passed his desk would partake of them as well—long before the Opry was over for the night, that box would be empty, and I do mean empty.

Plenty of wonderful and instructive conversations happened over a plate of salmon or a box of cookies. Those singers told me about the ups and downs, the triumphs and tragedies they'd had in the music business, and I quickly realized they were speaking about universal subjects. Whether you're a commercial fisherman or a mill worker or a parent or anything, really, you're going to have great times and really tough times. These folks had just been able to have a lot of them in the public eye, working in a business that compressed dreams and heartaches into three-minute slices of life that fed the dreams of other people, including me. All of us had to learn to look at each new challenge as just another bump in the road. I can't tell you how great it felt to be backstage, hearing those stories, dreaming big dreams with people who'd lived them.

Minnie Pearl was especially sweet to me. She was a mother to a lot of people who came through Nashville at one time or another. I remember her grabbing my son Shawn and just hugging him. She was so pure and so honest and, like many of the stars, so enthusiastic for me. I can still feel her finger in my chest, saying, "You save your money!" She'd lived so much and had seen so many people get a chart hit or two, have six figures in the bank, buy the big house, the boat, the plane, and then, when the hits dried up, lose everything. It's like that with plenty of people in business, too.

[The Carol Lee Singers--Dennis McCall, Norah Lee Allen, Carol Lee Cooper and Rod Fletcher]

★ ★ ★ ★

Chapter Thirty-seven

"HEY, COWBOY, YOU WANNA DANCE?"

Talking backstage with legends is wonderful, but of course you don't put any money in the bank that way, so I started going out and doing shows. I pulled musicians together from among my new friends at the Opry and worked up a show that combined music with a message about not using drugs and alcohol, aimed at kids in grade school, junior high, and high school. I'd seen enough damage from drug and alcohol abuse as a sheriff's deputy—and I knew too much from my own experience, including that awful car wreck— that I felt it was the perfect way to put even more passion on stage when I went out to sing. I'd be making something positive out of the tragedies I'd witnessed.

I decided to take shows to the schools themselves and, in conjunction with the American Legion or other groups, to theaters and community buildings in the area. I'd call potential sponsors or administrators, tell them about the show, and say, "I'll come into your town and do interviews with the newspapers and radio stations. I'll make up the tickets. You sell them. You keep the first thousand dollars we make, I keep the second thousand, and we split the rest. These will be top-notch Nashville musicians, and it'll be a great show. I'll come to the grade school, the junior high, and the high school and do a whole hour show at each."

There's nothing like good music in service to a great cause, and that's what I felt like I had with these shows. The "Just Say No" approach to the subject had been worn out at the time, so that wasn't the tack I took. I would be talking about turning peer pressure from negative to positive. It was something I knew from experience. Back in the days when I was trying to figure out who I was, there were plenty of people telling me that smoking and cutting class were cool. Precious few talked about hard work and big dreams. I wanted to make sure these kids got to see the difference and how important it was to offer each other the support I wished I'd had. The world had enough people who were stealing other people's dreams.

One of the best of all of those shows—and one of the most memorable experiences of my life—was a pep assembly in a junior high school gymnasium outside Nashville.

I talked with the principal before the show to set it up. I told him, "I want two very athletic girls I can teach to dance in about fifteen minutes." He picked them and sent them down to the gym for rehearsal.

One of them, Sally, was a cheerleader. I told her, "I want you to be on top of the bleachers, way up high. After we've been playing a while, when I give you the cue, run down the bleachers and out into the middle of the center line and yell, 'Hey, cowboy, you wanna dance?' I'll throw my hat in one direction, and we're gonna dance the jitterbug to old rock 'n' roll. I'll throw you down between my legs, over my back, and that sort of thing. Can you do that?"

"Yes, sir, I can."

So we practiced a few moves, and she turned out to be a natural. I knew this was going to be dynamite.

Then I turned to Debbie. "You'll be sitting in the bleachers close to the band in the front row, and after Sally's danced with me, one of my musicians is going to call over the microphone, 'Arnie, Debbie wants to dance.' I'll say, 'Come on, Debbie.' You won't come and you won't come until Sally gets on one side of the auditorium floor and I'm on the other, and we're leading all eight hundred kids in chanting, 'We want Debbie. We want Debbie.' When I come back to that center floor and look at you and say, 'Come on, Debbie,' I want you to hesitate for one last moment, and then I want you to run and jump in my arms. We'll start jitterbugging, the band will be playing like crazy, and the crowd is just going to go nuts.'

"All right, kids," I said, "We're going to do this show."

Well, the students poured into the gym and filled the place to the rafters. The band was at one end and I had a podium near the center court. Off to one side of it was an empty wine bottle.

I kicked the band into gear. Everybody likes 1950s music, and that's what we gave them—"Rock Around the Clock," "Hound Dog," a lot of the classics. The guys were in great form, and they were just rocking.

All of a sudden, Sally was up on her feet at the top of the bleachers, yelling, "Come on, cowboy, you wanna dance?" She ran down the bleachers and out onto the middle of the basketball court and yelled it again. I purposely hesitated, and then the band members said into their microphones, "Dance with her, Arn!" Sally yelled one more time, "Come on, cowboy, you wanna dance?" By that time, the crowd was getting into it. Then to the beat of the music, I threw my hat and jacket to one side and ran to the middle of the gym. The band jumped into "Blue Suede Shoes," and Sally and I tore it up, jitterbugging with gusto. I lifted her by the waist, and then down through my legs she'd go, then back up in the air and over my back.

The song ended, and then the band was pointing at Debbie and saying how she wants to dance. Everything went like clockwork. Sally was working one side of the gym, and I was working the other. The kids were screaming bloody murder, "We want Debbie! We want Debbie." It was just so much fun. Finally, I went out to the center line and nodded, and Debbie came running like a track star and jumped up in my arms. The crowd went nuts. She went down through the legs and then over my back, just like Sally. The song ended, and then they both went back to the bleachers. As the crowd settled down, I walked slowly out to that podium in the middle of the floor. I took the microphone off the stand and took a few steps. It had a hundred-foot cord, so I could walk the whole floor while I talked. The crowd got really quiet. I was at the far end by the time I was ready to start talking.

I said a few words, and all at once a guy in the bleachers yelled, "What are you going to do? Lecture us now? Tell us stupid stories? We don't want you to tell any stupid stories."

"Why don't you go back where you came from?" yelled another guy behind him. Then he yelled it again. The other guy started up again, and pretty soon both were yelling to the point where the kids around them started saying, "Shut up! Leave him alone." They started calling these two guys names.

Well, the two guys doing the heckling were two other plants. I'd recruited them, too, and they both could have gotten Academy Awards. Finally, I quieted everything down. I walked over and picked up the empty wine bottle that had been sitting there the whole time. I said, "You have just screamed at the top of your lungs from fun. Everybody's been having a great time, and it didn't take this to get it done. Nobody can accomplish anything with alcohol and drugs. And look what you're doing to yourselves right now. When these guys were telling me not to tell stupid stories, on your own you started telling them to shut up.

"Look at how quickly something so wonderful can turn into something so negative. In just a matter of seconds, one or two people, in a crowd of eight hundred, can do that. And that's what can happen to you and your good times and your plans and dreams with the influence of somebody negative."

From that point, I was able to tell those kids about all the things my kids got into at home— rodeos, 4-H, Little League, softball, football, basketball, snowboarding, water skiing, snow skiing, photography, and more.

I asked them, "How much do you do with your mom and dad? What do you do with your friends? Do you just hang out, or do you try to do things, to accomplish something?

> ★★★★
>
> *"Don't let them steal your dreams,"* I said. *"Surround yourself with positive people."*

"Don't let them steal your dreams," I said as I started to wrap it all up. "If you're talking to the star athlete and he's talking down your dreams, urging you in the wrong direction, ignore him. He's not the guy you want to hang around with. He's just out to steal your dreams. Now, say you're also talking to a guy who's not in a glamour position. Maybe he's a second-stringer. But if he's supportive and can help you move in the right direction, he's the one to pal around with. He's got something life-affirming.

"Surround yourself with positive people, keep Christ in the center of your life, and go after your dreams. Do that and you're going to have a wonderful time and a wonderful life."

I still get emotional looking back on that day and that show. I couldn't believe how well it went. It was one of the sweetest, most wonderful times I've ever had. The kids were coming up after the show, telling me how fortunate I was to be running a commercial fishing boat at fourteen and to have had all the other experiences I'd had.

Then they were talking to me about their own interests. One mentioned that she thought a lot about photography, and I suggested she find a way to get a camera. We talked about developing creativity, about sticking with it, about sharing it with others. Kids asked about guitars and music, and that led us into more conversations about dreams and staying focused.

I did that show many, many times, sharing my life and dreams and viewpoints with kids at an age when they're so vulnerable and so impressionable. It's something I'll always be glad I got to be a part of.

[With David Long at the Bellevue, Tennessee, Kroger]

★ ★ ★ ★

Chapter Thirty-eight

◆◆◆◆◆◆◆◆◆◆◆◆◆◆◆◆◆◆◆◆◆◆◆

THE MAGNIFICENT SEVEN

◆◆◆◆◆◆◆◆◆◆◆◆◆◆◆◆◆◆◆◆◆◆◆

I took Brent Burkett's advice and started getting smoked salmon into a few Kroger stores. I brought it in from back home, and since I couldn't smoke two hundred pounds of salmon myself in Nashville, I used a commercial smoked salmon company that shipped it to me. I got started in the Kroger store in Brentwood, a suburb south of Nashville, and eventually seven seafood clerks brought me in to seven Kroger stores. They were Buddy Hayes in Brentwood, Glenda McClurkan in Green Hills, Tim Woodard in Belle Meade, David Long in Bellevue, Paul Long in Goodlettsville, Natalie Birdsong in Gallatin, and Buddy Perrin at Williamson Square in Franklin. I started calling them the Magnificent Seven, and I still think of them that way.

At first, selling smoked salmon in and around Nashville, Tennessee, was painfully slow. These were people two thousand miles from the waters that produced it, and they had no idea what to do with it. It was the South, home of deep-fried everything, meat-and-three restaurants, and barbecue. I was facing a real uphill battle. The initial thrill I'd felt at lining up seven stores was quickly replaced with a deepening gloom as I realized how slowly the salmon was selling. I had a wonderful, nutritious, great-tasting product, and people just didn't get it.

I decided to show people what to do with it. I'd make dip and let people taste it. They'd love it, they'd buy the salmon, and they'd take it home and make the dip.

I was set up in the Green Hills market one day, making dip, giving it to people on crackers, chatting and telling stories, and cutting up with people the way I always did, when a lady with a long cigarette holder came barging through the crowd. She was dressed in a fur hat and coat, and she looked like she had just stepped out of a Rolls-Royce. She grabbed one of those Ritz crackers and got herself a big scoop of dip. In a minute she charged through and did it again. Then she stormed off. She came back later, and I thought, Oh, here we go. This time, she walked right up to me and got in my face. "Young man," she said with a stern voice, "I don't see your dip anywhere. Where do I buy it?"

★★★★

She said, "I don't want to make it. I want to buy it!" and she charged off. That's when the flashbulb went off.

I said, "Ma'am, you don't buy it. You buy the smoked salmon and you make it. I've got the recipe right here."

She said, "I don't want to make it. I want to buy it!" and she charged off again. That's when the flashbulb went off. It was one of those moments that changes your life. I went from being annoyed to being a man with a mission. I went back to the Brentwood Kroger and said to Buddy Hayes, "Let's make this smoked salmon into a dip. Everybody knows what to do with a dip."
That's exactly what we did, and it started selling. That sour lady had put me onto something.

I did the same thing in the Bellevue store. Then Tim Woodard in the Belle Meade store found out about it, so he and I started turning the smoked salmon there into a dip. Then I did the same thing with Paul Long and Natalie Birdsong. Pretty soon I was doing it in all of the Magnificent Seven's stores. In fact, once we got started, they wouldn't let me quit, which was a good thing, because the frustrations were many. It was wonderful being in seven stores, but still, it was only seven stores, and that's not exactly big-volume business. Making Arnie's Smoked Salmon Dip was a slow process—slicing and dicing and mixing, and then labeling everything. It was all done by hand, and it seemed to take forever.

I remember David in Bellevue helping me through a long session of making dip behind his seafood counter. We worked well into the evening, when Ralph Emery happened to come in. Ralph had a morning television show, and I really wanted to get on it. I talked to him for the longest time, and I gave him my card. It almost happened, but the program was cancelled before my appearance date.

★★★★

"Maybe I just need to go home and start building houses again," I told him. "I'm tired of being broke."

David and I probably made more than thirty pounds of dip that night, cutting and dicing and putting it in containers and on crackers and talking to people. He was a great help and he had become a great friend, but I was as discouraged by the end of the night as I could be. When I got ready to walk out of the store that night, it was after nine o'clock. David was still behind the counter. I had worked hard all day long and had a pretty bum attitude. David could see in my face how worn out I was.

"Remember, Arnie," he said, "don't you give up."

"Yeah, right," I told him. "We just made over thirty pounds of dip, Dave, and I ain't makin' a dime. All I'm trying to do is get this smoked salmon moving out of the stores. I'm tired. Maybe I just need to go home and start building houses again and make some money. I'm tired of being broke."

He said, "Arnie, you're dealing with a multi-, multi-billion-dollar company, and you're making things work. It may not feel like it right now, cowboy, but you're making real progress."

I started making circles with my index fingers in mock jubilation as I walked away from his counter. I was heading for the door. I could hardly afford enough gas to get back to my apartment.

"I'll see ya later, Dave," I said.

"I want you to rent the movie *Baby Boom* with Diane Keaton," he said. "She's a small-town businesswoman making it work against big odds."

"I don't even have a VCR," I told him.

He said, "Arnie, get one. It'll be a great training film for you."

As I look back on it, his encouragement and that of a few others really kept me going.

I didn't take his advice then, but I did later and he was right on. *Baby Boom* was terrific. It reminded me just how much he and the rest of the Magnificent Seven, the people at the Opry, and friends like Jimmy Gray cared, and how much they meant to me and to my dream.

Nobody does anything by himself. You've always got someone helping you out some way, somehow, even if it's just being there and listening now and then. And I have never forgotten the Magnificent Seven.

[Allen Shamblin]

★ ★ ★ ★

Chapter Thirty-nine

"YOU MUST BE STRIPPED! STRIPPED!"

Back when I was doing those shows and getting started at Kroger, I was spending a lot of time with Allen Shamblin, another struggling songwriter who lived at the Warren House Apartments. He had an efficiency down at the other end of the apartment building. We were both trying to write songs and do whatever it took to pay the bills. He was a big inspiration—a guy with a degree in marketing who was out chasing his dream. He was parking cars in a hospital parking lot at the time. I'd sit in his apartment and tell him about my day peddling songs, doing those grade school and high school shows, or making and selling dips, barely scraping by. He'd tell me about doing different things to get songs heard. Then we'd write a gospel song together.

I was always blowing and going at eight thousand miles an hour, and he could hear my boots clomping down the hall toward his apartment well before I got there. He'd be yelling, "Go away! Go away!" and I'd just walk on through his door and we'd laugh and carry on. Then later I'd hear his footsteps coming to my door. He got to hear the good things, the excitement, the dreams, and the bad things, the discouragement, the woe-is-me stuff.

I was down in the mouth one time, watching this little black and white television I had taken out of my van. I was thinking, *All my buds are having a great time at home. They're rodeoing, fishing, hanging out. I'm down here trying to make something happen in this business, making and selling this dip. If I really want to make some money, I should start building houses here. People need houses in Nashville just like they do in Washington. But then, I might just as well go home and do that. I'm so tired of being broke. That $1,500 sure didn't go very far.* And on and on like that.

Then Allen came waltzing into my apartment. He's a little guy, and I remember him walking back and forth, back and forth. He looked at me and never said a word. Then he walked to the chair, turned and looked at me, and said, "You're going home, aren't you, Cowboy?"

I just looked at my TV. I didn't know what I was going to do, but I knew I was going to have to do something. Man, I was discouraged. He walked into my bedroom. When he came back out again, he had my hat on, pulled way down over his face so that his ears stuck out. He had my Bible, and he opened it. He started walking back and forth again between me and the TV, only this time, with big, long, "Mother, may I?" steps, preaching in this booming voice.

"And the Lord says one must be stripped—I mean stripped! Down to nothing so that when the slightest little good happens, you will appreciate it." He got just a few sentences into it, and I was laughing my head off. He kept preaching and preaching. It helped me to snap me out of it and gave me enough fuel to make it another day, another week, another month.

It was a time when that kind of moral support was just what I needed. I was 2,600 miles from a home I'd just built, risking everything. I'd call my mother and say, "Mom, I've done some pretty dumb things, but this has gotta be the stupidest thing I've ever done in my life." A week later I'd be calling sky high over some little piece of good news. And in between, Allen was often the medicine that kept me going. We'd be up until all hours writing, together or alone. I'd get a call at two in the morning. "Wanna go for a walk?" he'd say. "Yes," I'd reply, and I'd pull on my boots and join him. So many times it was a great way to come down from everything we were doing, just to decompress and talk about things. We'd get an ice cream sundae or something, and talk over our day. We kept each other there, and he became like a brother.

One day I came stomping down the hall toward his place, blowing and going like I usually was. This time, though, I didn't hear "Go away!" I didn't hear anything. I knew something was wrong. I knocked on his door, and finally, he opened it. This wasn't the same Allen. He was in the kind of mood I'd been in when he walked in my door a few months earlier. So I pulled my hat down and opened his Bible, and I went to marching. "One must be stripped! Stripped! I mean stripped! Down to nothing, so that when the slightest little good happens, you will appreciate it!" It was his turn to break up and get that little boost that gave him another week.

Then I walked into his apartment one night. "Arnie, I want you to hear this song," he said. We were always kicking something back and forth. He started to play. He played a terrific verse, then another, then another one. He got done and gave me a look and said, "Well, what do you think?" I thought about it for a minute and then said, "Man, that's a hit song." Still, I kept thinking something wasn't quite where it needed to be. After a while, I left. By the time I had walked to the end of the building and up the stairs to my apartment, right next to the stairway, and grabbed hold of my door, the phone was ringing.

"What didn't you like about that song?" he said.

By then I knew. "Man, it needed a chorus."

That night, by himself, he wrote the chorus to that song.

The next day Joanne, whom I'd just started dating, came over to the apartment for a visit. We were kicking back, and all of a sudden there was a knock on the door. It was Allen with his guitar, and he was excited. He said, "I want to play you my new song," which he had titled "He Walked on Water." Listening to that song and knowing it had come from his heart was an awesome and emotional experience. It was a little piece of heaven.

Then Allen went through the whole process of trying to get that thing cut. It wasn't easy, but he stayed in the middle of it and kept pushing. Finally Randy Travis cut it, and it went to #1 and turned into a dynamite video. It got Allen started on an awesome songwriting career.

Allen is a great guy, and another example of how when you want something bad enough, you need to stay at it until you make it happen. Joanne and I watched as on November 10, 2010, Allen's "The House That Built Me," co-written with Tom Douglas and sung by Miranda Lambert, was named the CMA's Song of the Year. To this day, we feel pretty special knowing we were the first two people to hear his breakthrough song. We're very proud of him.

[With Joanne and Buddy Hayes at the Brentwood, Tennessee, Kroger]

★ ★ ★ ★

Chapter Forty

MOVING UP

The encouragement I'd gotten from David at the Bellevue Kroger and a few others had kept me going, but I still needed a break. Finally, someone at Kroger decided the company was going to carry my dips on a larger scale. The seafood buyer called my apartment.

"Arnie," he said, "we're gonna put your dips in the stores and in the warehouse. I want you to make an appointment with me and come up to our headquarters and show this product."

For the life of me, I couldn't see why on earth I had to come to his office and show the dips to him. I had been making them out in the stores for what seemed like forever, and he'd been looking at them for months. Still, I knew this could be the break I'd been looking for, although getting a break and knowing what to do with it are two different things. I was really green on two levels. First, I had never even been in a grocery store seafood shop in my life before I started marketing this smoked salmon to Kroger. Growing up, if you wanted fish, it was there in Cornet Bay, right in front of the house. Second, I'd never dealt on a business level with any grocery chain. I had a lot to learn on both counts.

I got advice from those Magnificent Seven head seafood clerks, then went down to the Brentwood Kroger and met with Buddy Hayes to make sure I had this thing nailed down. David always said that big displays and excitement sell product, so I got two of the big containers their catfish came in. They were about three inches tall by about fourteen inches long and twelve inches wide. I washed and sterilized them and made up some regular smoked salmon dip and some Cajun-style smoked salmon dip, got some crackers, and waltzed on into the Kroger offices on Elm Hill Pike in Nashville, just like I knew what I was doin'. I set these two containers on the buyer's desk and pulled the lids off.

I know now that he was expecting to see a case packed with twelve labeled, seven-ounce containers of dips, but I sure didn't know it then. With my normal enthusiasm, I said, "Here's some crackers. Give it a try." I could see from his expression that he was probably thinking, *This cowboy makes great dips, but he knows nothing about the retail food world,* and if that was his thought, he was absolutely right. But he did take the time to give me some good advice, and my first headquarters call was over. Now the work was really going to begin.

★★★★

Being accepted by Kroger put me at the bottom of a brand-new and much steeper learning curve. Now I had to manufacture dip in quantity.

Being accepted by Kroger put me at the bottom of a brand-new and much steeper learning curve. It left me with a thousand things to learn. I had been doing this by the seat of my pants, at home or in the seafood shops, turning to whoever happened to be nearby for help. Now I had to manufacture dip in quantity. I had to get labels. I had to find lots of containers. And I had no idea how to do any of that stuff.

That's when I learned I was getting involved in a very serious business. It's also when I began to learn again about the basic goodness of people. I called the Health Department, and a woman there turned me on to George J. Haines Jr., who oversaw seafood labeling for the federal government. Finding him was like finding gold. He showed me the way to list ingredients and nutritional information, and told me everything else that went on a label. As the other aspects of the process started falling into place, I was off and running.

During a visit to a food brokerage office, I was introduced to a man named Jimmy Nelson. As it turned out, he owned a company called Granny's Salad Dressings not far from where I lived. We talked, and I told him the whole story about the path that led to my smoked salmon dips. "Arnie," he said, "why don't you just come down to my manufacturing plant and see if you can work with it? Maybe there's something we can do. Show up at 3:30 tomorrow."

I went down there the next day for what I figured would be a tour and a discussion. Instead, he just threw me his keys; he was leaving.

I said, "Where are you going?"

He said, "We start pretty early. You wanna make your dip? Go ahead. Just wash everything down when you're done and lock the door when you leave." Then he walked out. Here's his office and a manufacturing plant with stainless steel counters and great equipment, I suppose fifteen hundred square feet altogether, and it was mine to use. I hardly even knew this man!

I shook my head at my good fortune and his generosity, and then rolled up my sleeves and went to work, and that's where I made the dips for a while. It was quite a change.

I ended up leasing the space next to his—about twelve hundred square feet for $600 a month, with the water and power included. It was in rough shape when I first saw it, with concrete walls and floors and exposed ductwork overhead, but I could picture it after a lot of work, so I took it and was off on the next great adventure.

★ ★ ★ ★

Chapter Forty-one

◆◆◆◆◆◆◆◆◆◆◆◆◆◆◆◆◆◆◆◆◆◆◆◆◆◆◆

WADING THE PINEY RIVER

◆◆◆◆◆◆◆◆◆◆◆◆◆◆◆◆◆◆◆◆◆◆◆◆◆◆◆

Visiting Buddy Hayes's store in Brentwood was always a treat, and most of the time I would try to plan a visit when we could go to lunch, where we'd talk about our families and, of course, the food business. Buddy was a good listener and a great talker—it was always fun to hear the way he'd tell a story with that laid-back Tennessee accent of his.

One day Bud decided he and I needed a break.

"Arn," he said, "you and I need to fish the Piney River. It's close to where you live, and once you get geared up and we leave, we can be there in an hour."

"What are we fishin' for?" I asked.

"Oh," he said, "nothin' big like you're used to in your part of the country. This is Tennessee style. We'll catch some little ol' sunfish and maybe a bass or two. Who knows? The main thing is just to wade the Piney. You'll like it."

"Okay," I said. "Sounds like fun."

"I know y'all are used to wearin' waders and bringin' along a lot of fishin' gear," he added, "but all you need for this trip is just a pair of shorts, a shirt, a short pole, and somethin' to wear around your waist to hold a little tackle in. That's it—oh, and tennis shoes."

When the day came, we met and headed for the Piney. Once we got there, I looked around a little nervously. The river is smack dab in the middle of the woods, and those woods have all kinds of critters in them, most of which crawl and bite—and they're poisonous. I'd heard all the stories about snakes falling out of the trees into boats, and the water moccasins swimming by while guys were fishing, and the ones about the rattlers and copperheads. In fact, I'd heard so many stories that for a while, every time I went near any woods I just knew there were millions of them waiting for me.

Even with my fear of running into something deadly, I wasn't going to let my good ol' pard think I was a wuss, so we geared up and down into the river we went. It wasn't real wide—probably about thirty feet in places and maybe forty in others. In no time, we were knee deep and all was well. We were casting over to the left against a high bank, catching little sunfish and turning them loose. Then we waded down a little farther until we reached a big hole. Now, this presented a problem for me, because off to my right was a three-foot bank with high brush growing on top of it and a large undercut beneath it. Both, I was sure, held very big snakes and their families. To the left was a rock bluff about thirty feet high. Plenty of tall trees were growing up and over the river, and I told Buddy it looked like we were right in the middle of *National Geographic* country.

It was plain to see the only way downriver was to keep wading. I followed Buddy as the water got deeper in a hurry. There was no way to fish at this point, and when he held his pole above his head, I did the same. The water rose to Buddy's chest, and it was touching the bottom of my chin when all of a sudden, I stepped on something round.

"Buddy," I said, "do the snakes in these waters lie on the bottom where a guy could step on one?"

With that slow drawl of his, Buddy said, "Oh, I don't think you'd step on one, Arn. If anything, you'd step on a herd of 'em!" And that's when this old cowboy shifted gears. If you know what the unlimited hydroplane named *Miss Budweiser* looks like going through the water at full throttle, you've got some idea what I looked like, 'cause I was getting out of that water!

I headed as fast as I could to the short bank on the right, reached up, grabbed some grass and pulled myself up. At the same time, my legs went under the undercut and against the bank, which I knew for sure by now had to be occupied by a large family of snakes. Up and out of the water I came. Buddy followed, but he was laughing so hard, he had a worse time getting out of the water than I did.

We hiked through the woods until the water became shallow again, then waded back in and walked to a dry gravel bed. Standing there drying off, I told Bud I wasn't going back to where we started by means of water. I was going through the woods because I knew the road was up there somewhere, and I was gonna find it. I was talking away when all of a sudden I heard this shrill, fire-alarm-loud scream right by my leg as something hit my calf. I jumped so high it's a wonder I didn't knock myself out on a tree limb. When I landed and looked around, there was my good ol' pard, laughing so hard I thought he was going to pass out. It turned out I was standing by a locust, and when it let out its scream, Buddy reached over and popped me one on the leg with his fishing pole.

You can bet it was an experience I'll never forget. Buddy, of course, had a great day, and even I have to admit the country was gorgeous and I did have quite the time.

[With Joanne, my beautiful wife]

★ ★ ★ ★

Chapter Forty-two

LOVE HAPPENS

At a time when the thought of going back home was still coming to mind now and then, I met the woman who would complete me and make me a happily married man. Of course, I didn't know that at the time.

When I met Joanne, I had around $6.50 in cash to my name. You can find out pretty quickly whether someone likes you for who you are when that's the kind of bankroll you've got. She made a big impression on me, and it probably helped that I met her at church. My faith was key to my life at this point and I was particular about the church I wanted. I visited eleven before I found one that felt like home—Grassland Baptist Church—and that's where I met Joanne.

I remember very well our first date, which needed to be entertaining and inexpensive. Whatever that may sound like, it wasn't because I was a cheapskate. I was frugal because I was just plain broke. We went to the

Stagedoor Lounge at the Opryland Hotel, and I couldn't wait to get there. It felt so good to be able to take her to a nice, classy place where we'd be entertained without spending a fortune. The Four Guys played there every night, and Brent Burkett, my buddy from the group, knew I had come to Nashville on nothing but hope and prayers. To help me avoid the cover charge, he made sure I could slip in upstairs through the side door—he actually took a glass ashtray and blocked it open, and we went upstairs where we could look down on the stage. Nobody'd hound you to buy drinks up there either. It was a great show, and we had a wonderful time.

On our second date, I took Joanne to the Opry. I was really in my element; taking her backstage made me feel pretty darned special. I was having a ball introducing her to all my friends. Then she started introducing me to some of the folks who were working there, and finally she introduced me to the manager of the Opry. I looked at her and asked, "What exactly do you do?"

She said, "I'm the manager of wage and benefits for Gaylord, and they own the Opry." I was introducing her to the stars, and she was introducing me to the people they worked for! We had a great time, and that was the first of many. I can't count the times we visited the Opryland theme park, the trips we took on the General Jackson sternwheeler, or the parties and dinners related to Gaylord and the Opry. I quickly learned she was a very well-liked lady.

As we dated, Joanne learned all about my musical dreams and about the opportunity in the food business that had popped up in conjunction with those dreams. She turned into a big supporter of both, and it's a testament to how special a lady she is that eventually she helped me buy what I needed to refurbish the space that would become my new manufacturing plant. She helped me redo the place and helped me make dip when she wasn't working at Gaylord—with her family pitching in to boot.

Now, I didn't know anything about building a licensed, commercial manufacturing plant, but I knew the building trade and I knew how to work. Joanne pitched right in, and let me tell you, she was wonderful. We went to Sears and bought inexpensive tools, got some lumber, and put every spare minute into it. I gutted that place, removing all the big ceiling vents that used to suck up the sawdust when it was used for building cabinets. Then I got a big pressure washer and washed down those concrete walls, ceiling, and floor. I put my experience as a building contractor to work, drawing up a set of plans for the office and the wall that would separate the manufacturing area from the warehouse. I redid the bathroom, built my office, and did the thousand

and one other things you need to do to turn nothing into something.

We installed stainless steel sinks and counters and brought in a little cooler. There was nothing big and elaborate, and everything we bought was used. We went to an old restaurant supply house and got a Hobart mixer that could handle one hundred pounds of food at a time.

——— ★★★★ ———

I could see the faith Joanne had in me and in my dreams, and how much she wanted to be part of them.

As it was all coming together, I realized how much I appreciated Joanne. I could see the faith she had in me and in my dreams and how much she wanted to be part of them. I realized I'd found someone who saw me for what I really was. She had said, "Let's go build this thing," and before long, Joanne and her daughter, Karen, who was ten at the time, her fourteen-year-old son, Alan, and her parents, Jimmy and Milbry Jenkins, who were retired, were all jumping in to help out with what soon became a big, fun family project. Then it was time to call the Health Department, where I dealt with Rick Heimlich.

"Rick, this is Arnie Deckwa." I told him. "I'm putting together a plant to make smoked salmon dip, and I want you to come down and look at this. I don't want to go much further unless you say it's all right." He came and looked the place over, studied the plans, and made a few minor suggestions, like putting Mylar on the walls behind the sink.

When it was finished, we started making smoked salmon dip. I'd go out and get the orders. Joanne's mother put this big apron on, set the salmon in a big bowl on her lap, and removed the skin and bones. Her dad peeled onions and put boxes together, taking a break now and then in a lawn chair he brought just for that purpose. I'd run the salmon through a food processor called a Buffalo Chopper and put in the onion, mayonnaise, and other ingredients. We had a little filler machine that put the finished product in containers, eight ounces at a time, which was a step up from the old system, where we filled them with spoons and set them on a little scale to weigh them, taking some out or putting some in to hit eight ounces exactly.

I had never done anything like this in my life, and neither had they, so the fact that we were doing it at all led me to believe we were doing great. We'd make a hundred pounds at a time and empty it into five-gallon buckets, put it into eight-ounce containers, attach the labels, and then box it up, twelve containers to a case. It was big-time, buddy, let me tell you. I'd refrigerate it overnight in the cooler and the next day deliver it to the Kroger warehouse on Elm Hill Pike, where, once again, I found I had a world of support. I'd back my minivan up to the dock in between all those big eighteen-wheelers, and the guys would walk out from the warehouse and yell, "Come on in, Arn." These were guys who were used to loading and unloading pallets with up to 150 cases on them, but they'd get all excited with me as they set my ten cases on a pallet. "Go get 'em, cowboy," they'd tell me.

They were lighthearted in their encouragement of this little guy between these big rigs, but it was big-time to me. I had just gotten past the point of taking orders from each store and carrying two pounds to the other side of Nashville, three more pounds fifty miles down the road toward Tullahoma, and five pounds someplace else—and those two or three or five pounds would be in a huge five-gallon bucket. Sometimes I'd actually have ten or twenty pounds in one, which would look a lot less ridiculous. I'd start my deliveries in the morning and stay on the road until nine at night. Later I realized that during those days I was attending my own food college—Arnie University— and to this day I look back on that time with great joy and satisfaction.

When Joanne and I were dating, I met Tommy Coats at the Grassland Baptist Church in Franklin. Tommy was tied into the Meadows Ranch, a horse ranch on Franklin Road owned by Jerry and Sherry Meadows. Tommy knew I could throw a rope, and that was a skill his son Jeff, who worked at the ranch, wanted to learn, so he asked if I'd help out. Let me tell you, it was a lot different from the ranches back home. This looked like a plantation, and the barn was nicer than some of the houses I'd lived in—well, not quite, but we're talking class. That ranch became my babysitter during the times I wasn't making or selling dip. I worked horses, broke some colts, and taught what I could, while working with Hilda Hadley, who worked at a veterinary office and also managed the cows and horses on the Meadows Ranch.

That magnificent ranch was the setting for one of the big lessons I've carried with me since, a lesson that came in the form of a tornado that roared through Franklin in 1988. The Nashville area has had quite a few tornadoes over the years, and this one danced right up through the Meadows's place, cutting off the end of the house, blasting through fences, breaking the windows out of all the box stalls, sucking a beautiful two-wheel oak cart from one end of the barn to the other and out the door, and lifting a three-horse trailer all the way over a paddock fence. If that wasn't enough to get someone's attention, the giant earth mover being used on a nearby highway construction site was literally picked up and tossed onto its side.

Now, I know there's a lot we can do. We can design and build rockets and fly to the moon, and we can come up with the fanciest computerized devices in the world. But even here, in the greatest nation in the world, we can't control a tornado or stop an earthquake.

You can sell dip 'til the cows come home, you can have the richest men and women—multibillionaires—on your board of directors, and when that final day comes, you aren't gonna get any more of a chance than if you didn't have a dime. Like I said early on, the big-time is eternal life in the kingdom of heaven with the almighty Father, and if you haven't got that figured out, you'd better be working on it. Otherwise, you're spittin' in the wind. That's the only knowledge, the only surety, that has pulled me through all these ups and downs I've been through, and there have been plenty. We all have to work hard and stay focused to make a dime, but if you're hanging onto what this earthly world has got to give you, you're hanging onto the wrong thing.

I also learned that life goes on no matter what nature is doing. On the day of that tornado, I was in my rig, delivering dip to stores. It was dark and gloomy, and at one point I had to pull over and stop under a bridge to get out of the rain, which was coming down so hard the windshield wipers just wouldn't take care of it. In many places there were several inches of water on the road, and roads were being closed just after I had traveled on them. It was hardto believe what was going on. Sure, we had plenty of rain in the Northwest, but we didn't have tornadoes or the systems that spawned them. As I learned just how extensive the damage was, it hit me just how small we really are.

[Our daughter Karen, her husband Craig and our grandson Carter]

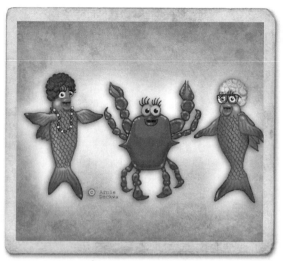

[The Cornet Bay Dipettes]

★ ★ ★ ★

Chapter Forty-three

"YOU GET A LINE, I'LL GET A POLE"

Success in most anything involves a series of connections between people. One day my songwriting friend and supporter Allen Shamblin said, "You need to go to ASCAP and see Tom Long." ASCAP is the American Society of Composers, Authors, and Publishers, an organization that collects royalties for songwriters and publishers. Tom worked there at the time, and he was one of the friendliest and most knowledgeable guys on the Row. He quickly became a close friend, somebody who helped me make connections and helped me stay sane at the same time. Whenever he was part of a Music Row event, it seemed like he'd find a way to include me.

He set up an introduction that led to one of the most fun bits of public relations I've ever been part of. He hooked me up with Joe Zanger at TNN, and the next thing I knew, they were willing to come anywhere to tape me making and selling dip for their *Cookin' USA* show. They wanted to do a before-and-after story, showing how I'd come from backstage at the Opry to having my own business, with my dips in a growing number of stores.

We went into Buddy Hayes's store in Brentwood to show how we'd done it in the old days, with Buddy and me mixing it up behind the seafood counter under a huge banner you could see from clear across the store. It had the caricature of me as a cowboy and said, "Smoked salmon dip—Take a dip with Arnie." Buddy was always supporting me, telling me, "You're gonna make this thing fly," and for the taping he combined his enthusiasm with his natural showmanship. We got behind the counter that day and made dip for the cameras, singing as we went. Buddy, with his big beard, would be closing his eyes and belting out, "You get a line, I'll get a pole, honey." He was great.

Then we filmed in the plant, making dip the modern way, with all that gleaming stainless steel around us. After that, they talked about going backstage at the Opry. I knew the policy there, and I said, "Joe, they don't like TV cameras backstage at the Opry."

"Arnie," he said, shaking his head, "we're TNN."

"Oh, yeah," I said.

So we went there, and I happened to bump into Porter Wagoner in the hallway. I said, "Porter, I've got TNN doing some filming of me in the green room. Would you walk around to the other door and walk in on camera and talk to me?"

He said, "Sure."

So he came in and said, "Hey, Arnie, what have you got going here?" They filmed Porter and me eating smoked salmon dip, and then they filmed us with the country cookies. Like Tom Long, Porter was always glad to help out.

Finally, the whole thing got put together in a package that opened with a big voiceover by Joe Zanger. "Many people have come to Nashville to try to make it in the music business," he said. "Then there's Arnie Deckwa." It turned into a great *Cookin' USA* show that aired on national television four different times.

[Amanda Christian, Elizabeth Nixon, me, Jennifer Styers, Karen Sullivan]

★ ★ ★ ★

Chapter Forty-four

ARNIE'S SMOKIN' SALMONS

We added another store, and then another, and pretty soon we were in twelve, then seventeen, then twenty. Now we had printed labels on the containers with a caricature of me, combining the cowboy and salmon elements. The exposure on Music Row was increasing, since whenever there was a #1 party or gold album party at ASCAP, Tom Long would make sure I was there with the dips. I met a lot more people in the music business that way, and word about the dips continued to spread.

As the dip business got bigger, so did our promotional ideas. The trouble was, we were still up against small budgets. I knew we needed to advertise, but there was just no way to afford it, so I went to one of the executives at the Nashville Kroger office with an idea. I said, "How about a trade? Come Labor Day, I'll do a Northwest-style salmon barbecue with all the trimmings in front of your store if you'll give me an ad in your weekly store paper."

"Deal," he said, and I went to work. I built a four-by-eight-foot grill out of concrete blocks and welded up some grates. With the help of Buddy Hayes, Joanne, and the kids, we set up in front of the Brentwood Kroger store for a salmon barbecue blowout.

It was hot anyway, and we had this big fire going in the pit, so we hung fans to blow cool air on us. I was used to having alder to barbecue salmon, but in Tennessee I was introduced to the southern tradition of using hickory. We barbecued six hundred pounds of salmon in front of that store and sold every bit over a two-day period. It was delicious, and the weekend was a big success.

Around that time, we also did a show with Arnie's Smokin' Salmons, a group I put together in front of Joanne's condo on Boxwood Drive in Franklin, Tennessee. Joanne's daughter, Karen, along with seven of her friends, ranging in age from nine to thirteen, worked up a dance routine that went with a rap song I had written—"Take a dip with Arn—You'll love it." It started out, "Hi, we're Arnie's Smokin' Salmons and we're here to tell/You a story about a product that tastes so well . . ." Watching the kids create their own dance routine out in front of the condo was an absolute hoot, and the rehearsals drew quite a crowd from among the neighbors.

A friend and keyboard player named Joe Loesch had a little studio nearby where we recorded some tail-kicking tracks to go behind this thing. I took Karen and three of the other girls to the studio to do the vocals. They'd grab those microphones and start rapping, and it was a sight to behold—and something they haven't forgotten to this day.

When it was all put together, the president of Kroger's Nashville Division, two vice-presidents, buyers, and everyone else I could get hold of came to the Brentwood store. As soon as they arrived and were in place, I waltzed all these kids out in front of those cash registers, wearing shirts that said, "Arnie's Smokin' Salmons." The place was just filled with customers who were lined up behind every cash register, wondering, *What on earth is going on here?* I hit that boom box button and the kids went into it, reciting and dancing for all they were worth. It was really something watching all those lines of customers clapping and seeing the smiles on everyone's face. It was a great promotional gimmick, and we had them do it again out in front, where we were cooking all that salmon.

Karen later worked for us full-time for over two years before leaving with her husband for California. The Smokin' Salmons provided a really good training ground!

[The Singin' Salmon Man]

★ ★ ★ ★

Chapter Forty-five

◆◆◆◆◆◆◆◆◆◆◆◆◆◆◆◆◆◆◆◆◆◆◆◆

"THE FIRST AND ONLY COWBOY..."

◆◆◆◆◆◆◆◆◆◆◆◆◆◆◆◆◆◆◆◆◆◆◆◆

There is more than one way to grow a business, and as we expanded the number of stores we were in, we began to think about expanding our product line as well. I got the idea for a Cajun-style smoked salmon dip, which would involve spicing the original recipe just the right way. I tried various combinations, but the spices I was using at first just weren't working well for me. Now, if I'd have been a huge start-up business, I'd have hired somebody with expertise in spices and tapped into that knowledge. But this was a shoestring operation, and I had to become an expert the only way I knew how—trial and error. So, gaining what confidence I could from the fact that we were actually running at all, I started creating my own. Now that was a process. I'd work up a batch and have Joanne take it to work at Gaylord to get her coworkers to try it. I was looking for a Cajun spice that would perk up the salmon dip without burning your mouth. The process took eight full months.

I'll never forget when I put the spice I'd just developed into a container of what was about to be the first batch of Cajun-style smoked salmon dip destined for paying customers. I'll tell you what—it took a lot of intestinal fortitude. Yes, I had tried several test batches, but this was going to be the big one. I looked at that one hundred pounds of dip and saw dollar signs flying out the window if it didn't work like I figured it would. Everybody was watching; the only thing missing was a drum roll. I took a big, deep breath, poured it in, and stirred it up. I took a spoon, dipped it in, and brought it to my mouth. It tasted wonderful! It was a great and satisfying moment. So I gave the spice the name "All Around Hot Seasoning," and today it sells from the shelves in grocery stores.

★ ★ ★ ★

"I never have seen a cowboy come in from an island and ride into the history of country music on smoked salmon."

Not long afterward, we took another big step that wasn't my idea at all—it came about because of John Nutter, who worked for Oscar Mayer. One day he brought a big case of imitation crabmeat into the shop and threw it onto the stainless steel table.

"Here's some crab," he said. "If you can make smoked salmon dip, you can make crab dip."

I hadn't thought about it, but I realized right away he was right. There was one small problem, though.

"I can't pay you for it," I told him. In those days I was always between a rock and a hard place when it came to finances.

He looked at me. "You need a new product out there," he said. "Just take this and start making it."

That began another new adventure—learning how to formulate a new product. I'd get a batch of crab dip made and start carrying it around, getting people to taste it, gauging the texture, and then I'd work up my nerve and go for the big batch.

With the new products, we were a truly diversified operation. Of course, we still had a long way to go, and the people who had believed in us from the beginning were still more than willing to help spread the word. Jimmy Gray called me one day and said, "A bunch of us are going to have lunch at Tavern on the Row. I want you to meet some people." I met him there and he introduced me to friends of his from several record labels. They were great people, and lunch was really enjoyable.

And then at one point he popped up and said, "How does it feel to be first?"

I said, "First? What do you mean?"

He said, "I have seen every phase of humanity come to Nashville and leave, but I never in all my days have seen a cowboy come in from an island and ride into the history of country music on smoked salmon. How does it feel to be the first?"

I couldn't get that off my mind for a couple of weeks. We'd visit and talk about different things, and we'd come back to that phrase of his. Finally, we tweaked it until it became, "the first and only cowboy ever to ride into the history of Nashville's country music on smoked salmon." It fit me like it had been waiting for me all along, like all those careers were stepping stones to get me to Nashville and have my dreams meet my realities. It became my handle. That phrase has gotten me write-ups in newspapers and magazines all over and has planted an idea of who and what I am in the minds of new friends, old associates, businesspeople, music people, and a host of others. It's a description that doesn't fit anybody else in the world, but it sure felt like it fit this cowboy like a second skin the minute it came out of old Jimmy's mouth.

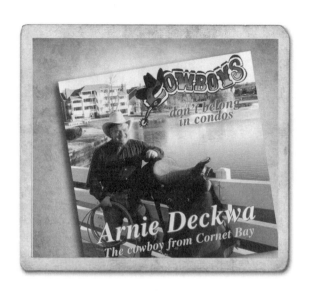

★ ★ ★ ★

Chapter Forty-six

◆◆◆◆◆◆◆◆◆◆◆◆◆◆◆◆◆◆◆◆◆◆◆

COWBOYS DON'T BELONG IN CONDOS

◆◆◆◆◆◆◆◆◆◆◆◆◆◆◆◆◆◆◆◆◆◆◆

When Joanne and I got married, I moved into her condo on Boxwood Drive in Franklin, Tennessee. Now, you wouldn't think moving into a condo would kick off a whole new series of adventures, but by now you know that no matter what the circumstances, this cowboy's life is never dull. It didn't take long for things to get interesting.

Yes, I'd lived in an apartment in Nashville, but I was used to a house and land, and I like to stretch out a bit around a place. The condo didn't have a shop for me to work in, so I was always building something out in the driveway in front of the garage. That's normal when you've got a stand-alone house and property, but some of my new neighbors didn't appreciate my driveway carpentry. They were also likely to complain when they saw something extra parked in the condo parking lot—say, my band equipment trailer or a boat.

The condo association had plenty of rules about what you could or couldn't do, and it was clear pretty quickly we weren't going to see eye-to-eye on some of them. It also seemed that quite a few neighbors had nothing more to do than make phone calls to keep it all stirred up.

The project that really got the association president's phone ringing was the one where I started moving our backyard fence out to make the patio larger. That patio was the size of a postage stamp, and I at least wanted a bigger stamp. I had gotten verbal approval from the president and a couple of board members, and it was all on my property, but when the first post went in the ground, it all hit the fan. I got a call that told me to stop working and to come to the next board meeting to show everybody exactly what I was planning to do.

I drew up plans and went to the meeting, and you could tell the president was impressed with the drawings—he studied them like they were blueprints for a skyscraper. He said, "I certainly didn't expect you to spend money having professional plans drawn up." I guess he figured I was going to scratch some lines on a piece of paper to show them what I had in mind.

"I didn't spend a dime on this," I said. "I drew 'em up myself."

The room got as quiet as a Monday morning church.

"I thought you were a musician," someone said.

"I am," I said, "but I've done a few other things in my life."

Some of them seemed pretty impressed that I wasn't a one-trick pony. If I'd have been anybody else, I'm guessing my stock would have risen at that point, but then it started. A lady said she was worried I might be planning to park a boat inside that new expanded fence.

I scratched my head. "Ma'am, if you can't see the boat when you drive by, what's the worry?"

Score one for the cowboy.

Then a lady who was on the board was worried that if I moved my fence out a little, other people might want to do the same.

"Well," I said, "once I expand mine, it'll be the same distance from the curb as yours, so what's the problem with that?"

That one slid by too. I assured them I was perfectly capable of building this fence. I told them when I was finished, I would plant a few rows of flowers between the fence and the curb, and somehow I convinced them. By the way, all that fuss, all the phone calls, all the planning, and all the work made the patio exactly seven feet wider. Then, while I was planting the flowers, my neighbor came over to check out my work. He was a good guy in his eighties with a lot of stories of his own, but he could get all worked up about nothing. He was also a big part of the rumor mill that seemed to swirl around me like a swarm of bees. I had my rows laid out between the curb and the fence, and I was even lining them up with string so they'd be perfectly straight.

We talked for a minute—he commented on how he'd never seen anyone use string to lay out flowers before—and then he started talking about the place across the street. "What would you think," he said, "if our neighbor over there wanted to extend his fence to the same five-foot distance from the curb as yours? That would make his patio more than thirty feet deep!"

I got up and brushed the dirt off my knees. "You know, I've been thinking about that," I said, "and I think it would be great if everyone had the opportunity to enlarge their patios. In fact, there are some other changes I'd like to see made here on Boxwood Drive, and so I'm planning to run for the condo presidency to see if I can't get 'em done."

I walked him toward the gable that protruded a couple of feet over the patio off the kitchen.

"Look at that," I said. "I'd like to extend that gable all the way over my patio and make that upper level into a studio. That way, I could work on my music up there and have a cover for my patio!"

He got this mildly troubled look on his face, like something he'd eaten wasn't sitting quite right. I turned and faced the double driveway, which we shared.

"I think folks should have the right to build a carport over their half of the driveway," I said. "Now, you wouldn't have to build one on yours, of course, but I'd be able to put one on my side. It'd be great! Then when I was working out here, I could at least be out of the hot sun or the rain."

By now the look had a bit of panic to it, and I could tell the conversation was over. He straightened up, pushed out his chest some, and headed down to the end of the road. I watched as he went into one widow's house and then into another's, spreading the news about what that crazy cowboy up the street had in mind.

Now, as funny as these situations could be, all the rules and rumors were beginning to wear on me, and I could feel the Russian disposition I'd inherited from my mother being pushed a little over the edge. I had to come up with an idea that would let me blow off steam and not get me thrown in jail. I decided to write an album in cowboy poetry style detailing some of the experiences I had while living there, emphasizing the humor and maybe embellishing just a little. The fence turned into a poem called "Cowboy Condo Life, Neighbors and Fences." The rumor mill turned into "Cowboy Condo Life and the Rumor Express Condo Hot Line."

Then there was the time my friend Benny Day and his wife Alice came to visit. Besides being great at making saddles, reins and other tack, Benny is a trader—the biggest this side of the Mississippi. His company's called Western Specialties, and he's always on the lookout for anything Western, from saddles to wagon wheels, from blankets to buffalo heads. He's got a warehouse back home and every weekend you can find him at an auction or an arena, selling the treasures he's come across. I've known Benny for more than 40 years. We rodeoed together. Well, he arrived at our place while Joanne was away and he couldn't believe a guy like me, who'd always loved plenty of room and cowboy atmosphere, was living in a cramped-up condo with showroom furniture. His reaction became another bit of cowboy poetry I wrote for the album:

Cowboy Condo Life and My Country Friend Ben

When I come home from a business trip
after coverin' lotsa towns,
It's never a surprise to see that my wife
has changed all the furniture around.

Then I hear, "Well, how do you like it?"
and about all the work she does,
and I'm thinkin', She must be bored to do all of this
'cause the furniture was fine just the way it was.

[Benny Day in his shop]

Well, it doesn't take long for a cowboy to grow restless
cooped up in a condo lifestyle,
so while she was gone, on a weeklong trip,
I decided to change things to my way for a while.

As I started to move things from one room to the next,
I heard a familiar voice yell, "Anyone around?"
And fillin' the opening of my front door,
was Benny Day, from my hometown.

Now Ben's a character, a good friend with a travelin' degree
In road, horse tradin', swappin' and life.
And for 35 years keepin' him straight
Is Alice, his wonderful wife.

He works a lotta leather, makin' saddles n' such,
and travels to sell his wares,
Three thousand miles from his place to mine,
hard to believe he was standin' there.

Two days he stayed and ol' times we shared,
then he said, "Son, your new style's a shame,
looks like condo life's not only addin' weight,
but you ain't talkin' 'n' actin' the same.

Tell ya what, I'll send you ol' Blackie,
that steer head's got a five-foot spread,
and he'll put excitement to your den wall
and it needs it, cause that den really looks dead.

I'll send you moose 'n' elk horns, ol' saws, spurs and guns,
you can hang 'em all over your place,
why it'll tickle that Southern belle of yours,
put smiles all over her face.

And you need to change that chandelier,
you know, the one by that cherry china hutch,
I got a lighted wagon wheel
That'll give that room a good Western touch.

And in that formal living room, Pardner,
a different rug needs to be in there,
and I got a dandy out in my truck,
It's a ten-foot grizzly bear."

Well, it didn't take long for Ben to do what he said,
'cause right away it all came in the mail,
and before my wife got home the inside of our condo
looked like a tradin' post on the Chisholm Trail.

Needless to say when she finally arrived
the shock was almost more than she could take,
why, I was stunned, at her being confused,
to either bury me alive or burn me at a stake!

I said, "Now honey, that cherry dining room table
made that whole room feel stuffy,
and those high back chairs that came from England,
none of it's country, and there's no need in you gettin' so huffy!

"The picnic table goes
with the wagon wheel light
And my ol' spurs 'n' that bridle hangin' on that cherry hutch,
makes it real purty, it's a good-lookin' sight.

"Now, doggone it, Honey,
ya gotta' settle down,
unfold your arms
and quit stompin' the ground.

"We've got the only condo
with a buffalo head by the head of the stairs."
And that's when she lost it …
and she started tearin' up the air.

Swingin' 'n' kickin'
'n' yellin' at me,
I said, "Easy girl … Whooooa honey,
it'll be OK, you just wait 'n' see."

Well, we're eatin' again at a cherry dining room table,
And when I talk of changin' things around, her looks say no,
Ya know, it's not easy for a cowboy,
to live inside a condo.

As far as Blackie and that ol' buffalo head,
they have new homes, and so does the rest of my stuff,
and my sweet Southern belle wife, wants to meet my country friend, Ben,
She says, "That man ain't never seen tough!"

Before long, I had enough for an album, and I went in and recorded it.

About the time that album, *Cowboys Don't Belong in Condos*, came out, my pal Randy Pepper pulled into the condo lot in a half-size school bus to visit us. He had retired from the Washington State Patrol and decided to scratch another item off his "bucket list"—the things you'd like to do before you kick the bucket. He jumped on his motorcycle and rode the better part of three thousand miles from his place in Anacortes, Washington, to Fort Valley, Georgia, where he often picked up buses from the Blue Bird company to deliver back home. He picked up a bus, put his bike in the back, and headed toward Washington, stopping by our place on the way. When he did, the neighborhood kids really got excited about this bright yellow bus parked in our driveway.

"Arnie," they asked, "is that your school bus?"

"Sure is," I said.

"Wow! Can we ride in it?"

"Sure can," I said.

Kids are one thing. Their parents and grandparents are another. I knew it wouldn't be long before I got a call. Sure enough, after about twenty minutes, the condo president was on the phone.

"Arnie," he said, with his slow and very low voice, "tell me you haven't got a school bus parked in your driveway."

"I don't have a school bus parked in my driveway," I said. "I've got it parked in the next-door neighbor's part of the driveway."

There was a long pause, and then he said, "Son, you sure like to keep it stirred, don't you?"

I told him the story and said my neighbor was on vacation and wouldn't be back for some time, so I didn't think it would hurt anything to park it there for a while. He got a kick out of the situation but then asked if I'd move the bus down to the public parking lot a few hundred feet down the road. So all of us, including the kids, jumped in with Randy as he drove it to the lot.

When we got out, I told Randy I'd have to tell the lady who lived across the street why we'd parked the bus there. Randy, who had no way of knowing what had been going on, asked why. "Because she thinks she needs to know," I said. I knocked on her door and there we stood: Randy is six feet four, I'm five feet six and a half at a stretch, and the kids came up to my waist; we were like a set of those containers that come one inside the other.

When the lady came to the door, she looked a bit ruffled. I began telling her why the bus was parked across the street.

"How long will it be there?" she asked.

"About three months," I said.

Randy shook his head and said, "I'm leaving tomorrow."

I laughed and we began walking away.

"Arnie," she said.

"Yes, ma'am?"

"You're funning with me, aren't you?"

I said, "Yes, ma'am, I am."

She said, "I listened to your album the other night."

This ought to be good, I thought.

"Did you now?" I said.

"Yes, and I have a question to ask you. I want to know, am I one of those old ladies that drink the beer?"

I laughed and said, "I don't know, Hon, do you drink beer?" and we all broke into laughter.

She said, "No, I don't, but any time you want to come down for bourbon and water, you come on. And I loved your album."

I found out later that the condo manager had played it and really got a kick out of it too. In fact, most of the folks on Condo Range, as I called it, had heard it and loved it. I was later asked to come to a board meeting and recite some of the stories, but my better judgment told me to decline. I was even asked if I would consider the position of the condo presidency. I thanked them for the offer and told them if we weren't going to be moving home soon, I would take the job with pleasure. I later thought how wonderful it is to see what humor can do. It's great medicine, and that album, which is still available, proved it to me once again.

[Little Red's farewell to friends at Anne Murray's publishing company]

★ ★ ★ ★

Chapter Forty-seven

DRIVING THROUGH AMERICA IN YESTERDAY, LOOKING AT TODAY

It was great to have something to show for my Condo Range experience, but now that *Cowboys Don't Belong in Condos* was out, I knew it needed a little push. I decided to combine a trip home to Cornet Bay with a promotional tour.

I'd be driving my 1954 half-ton Chevy pickup, a 100 percent stock vehicle with a little rust and plenty of heart. I got it checked over to make sure it could handle a three-thousand-mile jaunt, and it came through with flying colors. I did install electric windshield wipers, since I knew the old vacuum wipers that stopped when you gave the rig some gas weren't going to be much good in a snow storm. Then I had to build a box that would fit in the truck bed and hold my suitcases and tools, along with the blankets, paper, and kindling I'd be taking—after all, we were well into the fall.

As I built that box, the kids started gathering around to watch, and I got to feeling like Noah must have felt when he built the ark. The box was long and narrow, and lying in the bed of that truck, it looked kind of like a casket. It was closing in on Halloween, so I told the kids that's what it was. Their eyes got so big it was like having a bunch of owls looking at me.

"A casket?" they said, their mouths open as they stood on their tiptoes to peer at it.

"Yep. My buddy told me with his last, dying breath that he wanted to be buried at home in Washington State. 'Take me there, Arnie,' he said, and just before he died, I told him I would."

"Wow!" they said. "That's scary!"

Having those kids around was a real hoot, and it sure made the work easier.

I filled all the holes in the truck's firewall with silicone to keep the cold air out, put more padding under the driver's seat to give me a lift, and installed a CB and an AM/FM radio.

Then there were the promotional touches. I had some nine-inch oak rails painted to say "Arnie—Cowboys Don't Belong in Condos," and put them on either side of the truck bed. A company called U.S. Internet loaned me a laptop, and a guy who worked for them ran a web site for me. He would handle all my e-mails and send them to me every night on the road. My pal Buddy Hayes accompanied me to the library to help lay out a media plan—I'd be stopping at newspapers all along the route we plotted across the country. I also planned to do interviews of my own with interesting people I found—the kind Charles Kuralt used to find for his "On the Road" segments—sending the best ones back for the web site, along with photos of that old '54 in every interesting place I could find. I'd be promoting the album and having a blast at the same time.

On October 21, I had the black box in the back filled with what I needed for the trip. On the front seat I had a laptop computer, a camcorder, and a 35-millimeter camera. I gave Joanne a kiss, said, "I'll call you sometime tonight," and left Condo Range with an adventurer's spirit and a gas gauge that didn't work.

My first stop was Music Row. Tom Long was managing Anne Murray's publishing company, Balmur Music, on Seventeenth Avenue, and he suggested I start with pictures of me and the truck in front of their building. He brought the whole staff out, and I had Bill Kimmins, a terrific photographer, take photos of all of us.

Then it was down the road. After a stop in a tobacco field in Dickson,

Tennessee, where I got some great shots, I headed north into Kentucky. I had my first real cause for concern as I crossed the state line. I was driving forty-five or fifty miles an hour when I heard the loud sound of jake brakes coming up behind me. It really got my attention—here I was, putt-puttin' along in a seventy-mile-an-hour zone, and those brakes were telling me at least one trucker felt like I was in his way.

The driver eased the truck down to my speed, then pulled along side. He pointed to the sign on the side of my truck, then to his radio. He picked it up and said, "What have you got goin' on, Little Red?"

I told him the story, and he really got a kick out of the fact that I was going all the way to Washington. He started spreading the word, and from that time on the big trucks took care of me. It didn't matter where I was on the road—if I had a question, they had me covered.

"This is Little Red callin' the big black rig that just passed me," I'd say. "I know there's a truck stop nearby. Can you tell me how far down the road it is?" Another rig would interrupt and say something like, "I passed Little Red about ten miles back, Joe. I'm gonna be stoppin' there, so I can take it from here. Hey, Little Red?"

"This is Little Red."

"At mile post twenty-six you'll see a truck stop on your right. It's got a good restaurant, and we're all parked around to the side. You're only twenty miles away." Sure enough, there would be the truck stop and I'd park Little Red smack dab in the middle of all those big rigs and take a picture. It was great.

My windshield was so old I'd get a blinding glare from oncoming headlights, so driving at night wasn't a good idea. Besides, by the time daylight was petering out, I was ready to look for a gas station and a motel. People at the stations always noticed the sign on the truck, and I got into conversations everywhere. People got a kick out of my story, especially when they saw me writing down the mileage and I'd tell them my gas gauge didn't work.

I'll never forget crossing the Mississippi and taking a picture of Little Red in front of the Arch in St. Louis. Across the state, I walked up the stairs to a Kansas City newspaper office while singing the old Roger Miller song, "Kansas City Star." A writer and photographer there teamed up for a piece on me that was a lot of fun. I pushed on across Kansas, and by the time I reached Hays, the temperature had dropped to freezing. The heater wasn't exactly Little Red's best feature, and there was a lot of cold air rolling onto the floor. My feet were turning to ice, and I knew it was time for some warmer clothes.

I stopped and inspected the bottoms of the doors, which I had never done before. They had rusted, and the rubber gaskets weren't keeping out the air. I drove to a Wal-Mart and bought a pair of overalls, a blanket, and a couple of dish towels, which I laid at the base of the doors. With the overalls on, the blanket on my lap, and the heater wide open, all was well again and I was off down the road looking for a motel.

★★★★

The heater wasn't exactly Little Red's best feature. My feet were turning to ice, and I knew it was time for some warmer clothes.

I was sending the best interviews back to Nashville to be put up on the web site, and I'll never forget the lad I talked to at the gas station in Hays. I noticed him while I was gassing up. He was wearing a motorcycle helmet and riding a three-wheeled bicycle. He got off, walked over to a Dumpster and, with a sharp hook on a long stick, reached in and picked out pop cans he put into a container on his bike. I didn't think much about him until he started asking questions about my truck, talking a mile a minute, like he was auctioning tobacco. I told him a little about the trip, and he said, "This is my third bike. I wore the first one out, and the mailman ran over my second one."

"He ran over it?" I said.

"Yep, and I was on it!"

"The mailman ran over you and the bike?"

"Yep, sure did, and you know the first thing he said when I came to?"

"What did he say?"

"I was lying on the ground and he was looking down at me and he said, 'Thank God you're alive!!'"

We visited some more, and he told me he had seizures and needed the helmet and three wheels under him because sometimes he would have a seizure and fall off his bike while he was riding down the road. He felt a lot safer with a three-wheeler.

He had been collecting cans for years, and he said he also collected model tractors; it sounded like he had hundreds. His wife drove him around the country to shows where he'd enter the tractors and sometimes bring home a ribbon or trophy.

When I finally went into the station to pay for my gas, I learned he used to be a very good accountant for a couple of nearby newspaper offices, but had to quit because of his seizures. He became a real inspiration to me, and I've never forgotten him; to this day I can still see him standing there in that helmet.

After an interview at a nearby newspaper office, I stopped at my friend Bill Duncan's ranch in Sedalia, Colorado, then went on to John and Donna Nelson's place in Colorado Springs, where I did a show for Donna's grade school class. We all had a blast, and afterward we took pictures of the kids and me standing around Little Red.

The next morning, I was off to Cheyenne, Wyoming, where I picked up I-80, a long, straight, cold road with nothing much to see other than deer and antelope. I have to admit I sure didn't want to break down out there. Late in the day I decided it was time to find some gas and ask about a motel. I pulled into a station in a small town holding its annual coyote hunt. A couple of cowboys taking part were filling their truck at a pump next to mine, and when they saw my sign, they asked what I was up to. We talked and laughed for the longest while, and eventually they walked me around to the back of their horse trailer to show me their four-wheelers, telling me all about the hunt. They pointed to a building across the street and said that's where the dinner would be held that night. They asked if I'd like to come along, promising me a lot of laughs. I thought seriously about it, but I knew if I didn't keep moving, I'd never get home. Reluctantly, I passed.

As we said good-bye, I took a picture of them in front of their truck, then asked them to give me their names and addresses so I could send them a copy. One guy's name was Tibbs, and I smiled and said, "Any relation to Casey?" He said, "Yes, he's my uncle." That, of course, led into another conversation about Casey, the world champion cowboy I'd spent a week with on the Rancheros Vistadores ride.

It was clear the three of us could have a ball, and it was also clear that if I stuck around, it could be a couple of days before I hit the road again. So far, the weather had been on my side; getting stuck in a bad Wyoming snowstorm was not something I wanted to risk, and one was headed our way. I thanked them again for the invite, and we shook hands and parted ways. Every now and then I still wonder about the good time I could have had if I'd have stayed, but it's just as well because the snowstorm hit just after I left.

The next stop came in Idaho after I noticed an old airport sitting amid gorgeous green fields, like something out of a picture show from the '30s. I knew I had to get it on film, but finding a road there became a real problem. It seemed like I drove for an hour until I found my way to that little airport.

It turned out to be a crop-dusting service. An old house trailer, which sat near the entrance of a big metal hangar and leaned to one side because of a couple of flat tires, served as an office. The hangar doors were wide open, and the windsock hanging above should have been replaced years earlier. Nearby was the start of a gravel runway with weeds sprouting up through it.

The place looked deserted, but I knocked just to be sure. Nothing. I grabbed my camera and started taking pictures. I walked to the hangar doors and saw a couple of biplanes parked inside. The day was sunny and beautiful, but the hangar took on an eerie darkness once I walked in. I snapped a few photos and noticed how very, very quiet it was. My mind started entertaining the thought that there might be guard dogs, say a Doberman and a Rottweiler, sleeping nearby, and that the slightest noise might wake them and send them, foaming at the mouth, in my direction. The thought became more convincing the longer I stood there. I knew I wasn't going to be able to outrun them from there to my truck without losing some part of my anatomy.

Very carefully, I began backing out of the hangar, wishing I had eyes in the back of my head. Once I got outside, I hustled my fanny to the truck, jumped in, and closed the door—real or imaginary, those dogs had my heart thumping and I was glad to be back in the truck. I was disappointed I hadn't found anyone to talk to and very happy I hadn't encountered any man-eating dogs. I hit the road again with some more shots I knew I'd treasure.

The day after I finally made it to Uncle Bud's house in Thorp, Washington, he and I jumped into Little Red and drove the canyon road to Yakima, where I met up with Jeremy Meyer of the *Herald-Republic*. He wrote a story on my Internet marketing called "Cowboy Poet Lassos Readers with 'Net," which appeared on Monday, November 18, 1996, roughly 3,185 miles into my journey. I had 185 miles to go.

After a relaxing family visit, Little Red and I headed for Snoqualmie Pass and onto the west side of the Cascades. It took about four hours to drive the last leg, and when I drove over Deception Pass Bridge onto Whidbey Island and made the turn onto Cornet Bay Road, that last mile to the house was heaven. What a beautiful sight! I was home.

The trip might have been over, but there was still excitement. Several more write-ups followed in area newspapers. The *Skagit Valley Herald* had a spread titled "Internet Cowboy," and our hometown paper, the *Whidbey News-Times*, ran one called "The Cowboy Poet of Whidbey Island."

I knew that making it back home without any serious trouble was a blessing, and I thank God to this day for helping me beat the Wyoming snowstorm. Spending those thirty days driving that '54 Chevy pickup more than three thousand miles across the country convinced me that if I ever take Little Red on another trip of this kind, I'll have to add another month—and the more I think about it, the more it seems like that still wouldn't be enough time. There are a lot of wonderful people out there and a lot of great things to photograph and write about. I was very glad for the chance to meet, photograph, and write about a few of them.

Just before we left Nashville for good, about a year after that promotional trip, Tom Long and his wife, Belinda, decided we needed a going-away present, and the one they came up with was better than anything we could have asked for. They organized a party that surrounded us with friends who could say, "So long for now," and send us back to Whidbey Island in style. To say they did it up right would be to understate it by a country mile. They held it at Douglas Corner, a nightspot popular with the Music Row crowd that was often used for industry showcases that introduced singers, bands, and songwriters to label and publishing executives. Many of country's finest had graced its stage— Keith Whitley filmed his "I'm No Stranger to the Rain" video there. The place was packed with neighbors, friends in the food business, people from the Opry and the rest of the music world, and folks from our church, including the preacher who married us. It was a night where the love and affection we experienced overwhelmed our hearts, and it's one we'll never forget.

Tom kicked the evening off by asking "our surprise guest—someone Arnie very much admires"—to be escorted to the stage. The place fell apart when two guys walked to the stage on either side of a full-size cardboard cutout of John Wayne and propped him up behind the microphone on center stage. Tom knew I was a huge John Wayne fan, and that night the Duke was part of every act that performed. There were plenty of them, too, as singers and songwriters came up one after the other to perform and tell stories.

The feeling was indescribable. I had come to Tennessee in January 1987, not really knowing anyone. Ten years later, I was part of the music business with a world of show business friends, I had made a promising start in the food business, and I had a wonderful new family to share the rest of my life with. Let me tell you, powerful emotions were welling up inside me.

A few days later, on Easter morning 1997, Joanne, Karen, and I, along with our schnauzer, Munch, pulled out of the driveway of our condo on Boxwood Drive in Franklin and headed toward Whidbey Island. I was driving the biggest diesel truck we could rent, which was packed tight to the roof with our belongings. We were towing Karen's 1976 Chevy Malibu Classic, with two-thirds of a continent to cross. I could write a book about that trip, but nothing can match the feeling as we pulled out of the driveway, basking in the love of all those people who had come to bid us adieu. I felt like Nashville had adopted us and would remain a precious part of our life's journey from then on.

When we got home, we unloaded the truck and turned it in to the rental agency. Joanne took me to the Seattle/Tacoma Airport, where I jumped on a plane and headed back to Nashville. I had one more truck and trailer to drive home. We had packed them to the seams and left them at Buddy Hayes's house. He was waiting for me outside the airport baggage claim when I got back to Nashville, and he slid over as I jumped behind the wheel. He had never been out West, and he was ready for the adventure of accompanying me to Washington to meet the people and see the places he'd heard so much about. After one more continental crossing with its own wealth of stories, I was home for good, moving into the house my parents built for themselves just 150 feet from the house I grew up in.

By the way, that cutout of John Wayne still sits behind the seat of my '94 Chevy truck, where it rode home from Tennessee. It reminds me every time I think about it how lucky I am, how good life is, and how wonderful God is.

[With daughter Laurie (Sis), sharing a hug]

★ ★ ★ ★

Chapter Forty-eight

◆◆◆◆◆◆◆◆◆◆◆◆◆◆◆◆◆◆◆◆◆◆

MAKING IT

◆◆◆◆◆◆◆◆◆◆◆◆◆◆◆◆◆◆◆◆◆◆

I know from experience how important the help, support, and friendship of good people are to achieving goals, but I also know that everything starts with a dream. I had mine long before I got to Nashville, and I know that few people feel theirs as strongly as I felt mine.

I was in a six-month band gig at the American Legion on South Whidbey Island a few months before my move. My son Scott was in that group with me, and we were rehearsing after one of the shows. We went into another room in the Legion, and the manager said, "What do you guys really want to do?"

The other band members kind of hemmed and hawed, and said things that didn't really kick up a lot of excitement.

"Arnie, what do you want to do?" he said finally.

"I want to go to Nashville, Tennessee, and sing on the Grand Ole Opry," I told him. Less than a year later, that's where I was and what I was doing.

Now, maybe I sang to 4,500 empty chairs, but I sang at the Opry. I sang on the stage of the Ryman, too. It was empty, but I've been there. You talk about a dream—this thing has just evolved. People sometimes ask, "Arnie, did you make it in the music business?" Well, it depends on how you look at it. I went down to Tennessee to make it, and twenty-three years later I've got more experience and stories than Carter's got pills. Country superstars helped me realize the dream inside me and helped guide me toward the food business and a line of Cornet Bay products that are in some of the largest grocery chains in the country.

A friend of mine gave me quite a compliment. He said he knows a lot of folks who left home to pursue their dreams and got stuck—so stuck they didn't know which way to turn, so they just went home. He said, "You saw that you needed to make a turn in the road and you did it. Your music helped you along and it's still part of what you do." It's that type of friend who can help you keep the juices flowing.

So how do you look at making it? Have I got a hit where I've got so much money I don't know what to do with it? No, but that's not what I'm after. But have I made it? I don't think you ever make it because if you have the ingredients and you're like me, you're making it happen every day. I could live four hundred years and never achieve everything I want to do, but I wouldn't trade an ounce of anything that has happened since I first went to Nashville. I was going to say I wouldn't trade it for love or money, but I did find love after coming to Nashville. I went home with a gorgeous, wonderful lady who accepted me for what I was and what I had. And that, my friends, is the pearl of great value.

[Son Scott Deckwa on his Harley]

★ ★ ★ ★

Chapter Forty-nine

PRICELESS MEMORIES
FROM A LITTLE YELLOW HOUSE

The little yellow house I grew up in is still standing on this dead-end road named Cornet Bay. The music business and the food business may have taken me a lot of places, including homes big enough that families actually get lost in them, but I've come to realize that the experiences and lessons I carried away from that tiny house are priceless. I wouldn't trade a thing.

We've made changes to the place through the years. In 1995, I came home to be with my mother and my sister, both of whom were hospitalized with serious illnesses, while Joanne stayed in Nashville. Realizing the stay could be a long one, I took a good, hard look at the house, which was then being used only for storage. There was ivy growing inside, and the concrete floor was cracked from one corner to the other. I decided it was time to remodel. I needed something to do between hospital and convalescent home visits, and something in my heart wanted to see the house restored to the wonderful way it had been. So, with the help of some friends and my son Shawn, I went to work. I had always wanted a door on the bedroom my sister and I slept in, so I put one in. I redid some of the interior layout so now you can enter the bathroom from the living room and now there are eight-foot ceilings. The exterior walls are the same as they always were, and so is the size—494 square feet.

Remodeling was a tremendous undertaking, but it was the best medicine I could have taken because I lost both my mom and my sister that year. After the construction was complete, it became our little yellow house by the sea. Joanne and I furnished it with my parents' furniture and rented it out as a retreat. Folks from all over the country came and took in the scenery of Cornet Bay and Ben Ure Island, saw the boats tied to the county dock and marina, walked to the end of Cornet Bay Road and back, and listened to stories about the little house and the generations of life and love it held. One woman liked it so much she stayed several years. After she left, Joanne and I decided to turn it into our office, and I've been writing these stories from my old bedroom.

Before we finish up, I need to update you a little about our five kids, as Joanne and I have always considered all of us to be one family. Scott, of course, was very involved with music from the time he was a teenager and for a while he played bass in my band "The Sunshine Express." During summers while he was still in school, he fished with his grandfather and with other gillnet boat owners in the waters off nearby Neah Bay. Later, he did commercial beach seining for salmon on the shores of Clam Gulch in Alaska.

After he graduated from Langley High School, he got involved in the world of thoroughbred racing as an assistant horse trainer. He worked on many thoroughbred tracks and drove for companies who hauled race horses from Maine to Winnipeg. He later owned his own heavy construction business, installing and fixing city water mains and digging foundations and installing water lines and septic systems for housing developments. Recently, I'm happy to say, he has joined Joanne and me in the Cornet Bay Company. Scott's priority is his children. Courtnie, who is 19, has worked hard in the motel business and child care and is now helping us in the Cornet Bay Company. Ty, who is 14, is a great baseball and basketball player. Scott stayed busy for years coaching his son's teams, and although he has turned that responsibility over to other folks, he still takes him to baseball camps and travels to games where he's seen Ty pitch no-hitters and belt home runs.

Laurie graduated from Oak Harbor High School and worked locally until, while still in her teens, she decided to head for Alaska to work in the fish canneries on the Kenai Peninsula. It didn't take long until she was cleaning fish on a 350-foot processing boat in the Bering Sea. She moved next into the galley as a cook and soon became chief steward, running an operation that fed 80 to 160 people. For 24 exciting years, she often worked two months on and two months off aboard ship in the rough, cold waters off the Alaskan shore. She has enough stories for a book of her own.

On her own time she traveled the world, meeting people and pursuing her passion for music by traveling to concerts all over the country. Recently, back injuries and the demands of that shipboard work have convinced her to change careers, and she will also be helping out our Cornet Bay Company.

As a boy, Shawn loved to spend his summers on his wakeboards, catching as much air as he could. In the winter, there weren't too many Northwest slopes that he and his snowboard didn't come down. I've got a picture of him at 12, coming off a jump, upside down, legs and board up, arms stretched out on each side. Before he gave it to me, he wrote across the bottom, "I made this one, Pops."

After graduating from Oak Harbor High, he put his time in on the water as well, commercial longlining in Hawaii, working the deck of a 350-foot processor on the Bering Sea, fishing salmon on a purse seine boat out of Kodiak, working the rail while fishing for cod in the winter, and sewing commercial nets in Homer, Alaska. During the off-seasons Shawn worked construction and he now works for a company that builds everything from docks to bridges, from commercial buildings to airport hangars. He can build a house from the ground up and run heavy equipment, and he is happily moving up the ladder in the company.

Joanne's son Alan Sullivan was 15 when we married, and he jumped in to help me remodel our first food manufacturing plant in the early days of the company. He loved to learn and was an avid reader who could read and retain six books at a time. He loved role playing and was a master in Dungeons & Dragons. He loved animals and the arts and was a fearless swimmer. It was nothing for him to jump off a 30-foot cliff into a deep pool of river water. He got his first job in the Brentwood Kroger store, and after graduating from Franklin High School and attending college, he went back to work.

Several months after Joanne and Karen and I moved home to Whidbey Island, Alan packed his belongings into his car and drove across country to join us. He delivered pizza, then worked in a management position at PETCO and Best Buy and later became employed at Home Depot. With their cooperation, Alan was able to juggle his responsibilities with schooling at Seattle Central Community College, where he majored in film. As he was earning his degree, we talked and laughed a great deal about our early days together, about the wood-working hobby that had begun to interest him, and mostly about his dream of working in film in California or Texas.

Then, in 2005, tragedy struck. He called my cell phone as I was checking accounts in Seattle and said he'd been sick. He asked if he could come home with us for a while. I picked him up and this kid, who had always been tall, husky and full of fun, slid the seat back and stretched out on our way to Whidbey. I said, "You know, it doesn't matter how old or big our kids get, when they get to feelin' punky, they just want to come home and eat Mom's cookin'." We laughed and headed home, where he stayed a few days, resting and eating some good meals before Joanne took him back to his apartment.

On February 4, I received a call from Alan's dad, Richard, who said Alan had passed away. We were devastated. We lost him to a very rare disease called *Streptococcus milleri*, which has symptoms like a cold or flu but can be fatal in a matter of hours. It has been five years since our loss and we deal with it every day. You never know what's around the corner. It's been one more lesson as to the importance of appreciating every day, of staying close to our Savior, family and good friends, those who help us get through the down times.

Karen was ten when we first met. She was a hoot then and she still is. She was a go-getter who wanted to be involved in everything. She was the one who'd jump from the side of the condo swimming pool and land right on me, laughing all the way. I told you how she helped organized Arnie's Smokin' Salmons and how they danced inside and outside so many Kroger stores. Karen was one of her school's wrestling cheerleaders, and after graduating from Franklin High School she spent a year at the University of Tennessee. After we moved to Whidbey, she worked at an employment agency, then came to work with us at the Cornet Bay Company. Later, she followed a dream and earned a degree in fashion at Seattle Central Community College.

On August 11, 2001, Karen married Craig Griffith. They followed a job opportunity for Craig to Visalia, California, where Karen became manager of a printing company. On February 9, 2009, she gave birth to our grandson, Carter Douglas, and in July of '09 the three of them moved to North Carolina to take on yet another vocational opportunity. She's excited to be back in the

South, where she is back in touch with friends she grew up with. She calls us every day, sometimes twice, and we're very happy for her continued closeness with us. Obviously, we're very proud of all our children. With two of them working with us and two in close touch, we feel like the circle is completing itself. This little yellow house I grew up in rings with the voices of new generations, and I never get tired of walking through the front door and feeling the nostalgia the walls themselves give off. After all these years, it's still great medicine.

[Son, Alan Sullivan, during film school]

[Grandchildren, Courtnie and Ty]

★ ★ ★ ★

Chapter Fifty

THE CORNET BAY COMPANY

Now and then people ask me about my business plan. I just look at them and say, "I got an idea and went to work on it one day over twenty years ago. Then I showed up the next day and the day after that and just kept going. I got more ideas along the way, and when one didn't work, I thought up another and another until I found one that did. And I just kept showing up."

It was a learning process in the old days, and it still is. Do I have a college degree? No. Do I have a high school diploma? Well, I have a GED and a lot of credits in police science. I do have degrees in desire, persistence, and the will to keep this business moving in a direction that feels good and shows a profit.

I'm very passionate about our Cornet Bay Company, and I'm also very lucky to have a wonderful, beautiful, and intelligent wife who works by my side. Joanne has developed seasonings and many of our seafood dips, and she keeps this cowboy from having to handle the detail work; without her expertise and eye for the fine points, this company wouldn't be moving forward. Beyond the things that go with the territory—profit and loss statements, three-year pro formas, full- and part-time help when we need it, and infusions of capital now and then—the most important element is still that passion. In a company like ours, it makes all the difference. You've got to care that the product is as good as you can make it. It's like writing a song—good isn't good enough. You have to work until it's great to have a chance at the big-time. A food product has to have a pleasing look, it has to have an inviting smell when you lift that lid, and then it has to taste great. When you've got all that handled, it has to go into a container with a label that will jump out at a customer walking by in a store. Then you need to find a manufacturing facility that can consistently make your product to your liking—same look, same taste, same shelf life, week in and week out. Since 1995, we have been very fortunate to have that expertise in the making of all of our Cornet Bay and Kroger-labeled seafood dips and spreads thanks to the House of Thaller in Knoxville, Tennessee.

I learned early on that even with all those things lined up, you can't just put the product on the shelves and relax. In fact, that's when the real work starts. When our smoked salmon dips went into Kroger's Nashville Division, I practically lived in the stores. I wanted to show the product to every person who walked by the seafood department, and I wanted to know each and every head seafood clerk who was handling it. "How's it selling?" I'd ask every time I walked in. If it was slow, I'd ask them what they wanted me to do, and it was always a demo—they wanted me in front of those customers demonstrating the product and its uses. Having a product in a store is a wonderful opportunity, and I very much appreciate it. I figure I don't have to build the store, I don't have to pay the rent for the land it sits on, and I don't have to pay the folks who are working to sell my products. All I have to do is help them move those products out the door. I feel pretty darn lucky, and I owe that store all the attention I can give to the task of keeping my product moving.

Of course, some products do better than others, and a store has only so much shelf space, so you've always got to be coming up with something new. If you've only got three products and one is discontinued, that leaves two, and if one more is discontinued—well, you do the math; I had to learn this the hard way. After we'd been in the food business for a few years, I got a phone call from Kroger headquarters in Cincinnati saying they wanted to bring our Smoked Salmon dips into the main warehouse and distribute them to all their stores, and they wanted to put the Kroger name on them! Joanne and I were very excited and flattered. To walk into a Kroger seafood shop and see the Kroger name on our Smoked Salmon Dip, Cajun Style Smoked Salmon Dip, and Southern Style Crab Dip was an incredible thrill. But that was when we began learning what sells and what doesn't, and the importance of having a product to replace one that's not selling for one reason or another. Gradually, we introduced more seafood dips, and Kroger added them to their dip line, including Artichoke Shrimp Dip, Sun-dried Tomato Crab Dip, Smoked Salmon Cheese Ball Spread, and our Chipotle Smoked Salmon Dip, giving us a total of seven dips and spreads. Each new product gave us another thrill.

Once the products were established and selling well, we were able to get them introduced in the Northwest to a Kroger-owned chain named QFC, based in Bellevue, Washington, just across Lake Washington from Seattle. We brought five of the Kroger-named seafood dips into QFC's seafood departments: Smoked Salmon Dip, Cajun Style Smoked Salmon Dip, Artichoke Shrimp Dip, Southern Style Crab Dip, and our Smoked Salmon Cheese Ball Spread. All the dips were well received and the Artichoke Shrimp Dip was a tremendous hit, but we had some lessons to learn. We were shipping a thousand pounds or so at a time from our Knoxville, Tennessee, plant to save shipping costs, and travel time was five days, which cut into the two-month shelf life. There were other shipping problems at times—Hurricane Katrina deserves its own chapter—and selling half a ton of seafood dip in a relatively small number of stores before the expiration date is quite a challenge.

We learned the lessons we had to learn, though. Cornet Bay does a lot of business in QFC's eighty or so stores today, and we love having a big presence throughout the region.

Experience told us the key to our success would be continued growth. We needed to add more products to the Cornet Bay product line. As I often do when there's something big to contemplate, I had a talk with the Man Upstairs, and it didn't take long before things began to happen. We decided to develop some nonperishable items, and we were soon in contact with Colin Postance, owner of barbecuewood.com, of Yakima, Washington, a manufacturer of wooden cooking planks and wraps. I remember eating salmon cooked on a cedar plank wedged into the sand in front of a beachfront bonfire when I was a teenager—it was always wonderful! Cooking on wood adds a flavor to steaks, chicken, and seafood which has made it a very popular cooking technique, both in more and more kitchens and in outlets like the Food Network and gourmet magazines.

We needed a thin piece of wood that could be used for cooking in the oven or on the grill so people could cook on wood year-round. Colin came out with seven different wooden cooking wraps, or grilling papers, and Cornet Bay is offering all of them, giving people a great-tasting way to cook their favorite foods indoors and out, and the Kroger-owned Dillon's chain in Kansas has them in their stores wearing the Kroger label. We've also branded the Kroger label on the six-by-twelve-inch wooden cooking planks and have them in stores throughout the Louisville and Cincinnati Kroger Divisions. We've got them branded with the King Soopers and City Market logos in the Kroger-owned King Soopers chain in Colorado and with the QFC logo for that Kroger-owned chain here in Seattle and Portland.

Joanne and I met a kindred spirit in Ron Elmer, owner of Jamen Foods in Walla Walla, Washington. He approached us about helping him get a number of nonperishable products he markets under the Winsom's of Walla Walla label into store chains around the country. He sent us a bunch of products, and we shared them with friends and relatives until we locked onto the ones we felt would do well in the marketplace. The QFC grocery buyer was as impressed as we were, and we now have twenty-three Winsom's of Walla Walla products, including salad dressings, relishes, mustards, hot sauces, steak sauces, a peach salsa, and a personal favorite named Hot Jalapeno Jelly on grocery shelves in around sixty-five QFC stores. They're fantastic products, and because Ron and I stayed closely involved in the lift-off of the program, doing demos and visiting food shows, the products are selling wonderfully. It's more proof that when a good product comes along and it's marketed properly, it moves off the shelves. I really have to hand it to Ron and his family because they're constantly working their products.

Then there's our friends Randie and Sherri Davis, who, after living for years on the isle of Crete, returned home to Cornet Bay and the house where Randie was raised with some of the finest olive oil I had ever tasted. The Kolymbari Extra Virgin Olive Oil is made from Koroneiki olive trees that are in some cases more than 1,500 years old! The grove is owned by the Ioni (John) Mihelakis family, which goes back several hundred years. Greek legend has it, by the way, that Athena, the goddess of wisdom, placed her magical spear into the ground and the first olive tree appeared, more than 60,000 years ago.

The Koroneiki olive, which originated on Crete about 3,000 years ago, is responsible for the intense, robust flavor in this oil. The olives start with a fruity aroma and end with a peppery taste. Because of the uniqueness of this olive, Kolymbari olive oil needs no blending and is made fresh when ordered. Several months of comparisons with other oils on the market made it clear that there is no other olive oil in the United States that compares with the wonderful taste of this oil.

Our Cornet Bay Company feels very privileged to be working with Randie and Sherri's Cornet Bay Import business and their oil, along with their Balsam Cretan Nectar Dressing and Cretan EMP Natural Honey, which are being distributed throughout QFC and many other fine grocery chains in the Northwest.

All the while, Joanne and I have been developing several new Cornet Bay items and I've been writing this book, so you can bet the midnight oil has been burning. We recently installed sixteen new Cornet Bay items in the QFC grocery division, giving us seventy total items out in the stores, and we have a few more waiting in the wings. There's always excitement in the air here, and when you love food and people as much as I do, it makes for a life I wouldn't trade for anything.

★ ★ ★ ★

Chapter Fifty-one

◆◆◆◆◆◆◆◆◆◆◆◆◆◆◆◆◆◆◆◆◆◆◆◆◆

RUNNING THE BUSINESS HANDS ON

◆◆◆◆◆◆◆◆◆◆◆◆◆◆◆◆◆◆◆◆◆◆◆◆◆

The Cornet Bay Company has always been a hands-on, one-on-one kind of company, whether we're talking supermarket executives or taste-conscious shoppers. That approach led us to revamp our approach to travel a few years back. After years of commercial flights and rental cars, motels and restaurants, it became clear we needed a motor home. That would also let us keep samples on hand and keep my fly rod case from warping in the hot sun under the back window of the car!

So I bought a gasoline-powered 34-foot Newmar with a side slide-out. It had 17,000 miles on it, but it's more than done the job, passing every test we put it through.

I told the salesmen that we were planning a trip to Indianapolis for a Kroger food show and he asked me if I had a place to practice driving it before we left. Now, I don't know who was more surprised after he heard my answer.

SAUCES & MARINADES

★ ★ ★ ★ ★ ★

A **Cornet Bay Sweet Bourbon Glaze**
12 Fl. Oz. – *Tangy sweet and full bodied, our sweet bourbon glaze is the perfect marinade and finishing sauce for beef, pork, poultry and seafood. It makes a uniquely delicious dipping sauce.*

B **Cornet Bay Organic Sesame Ginger Marinade**
12 Fl. Oz. – *The lively ginger and nutty sesame flavors in our organic sesame ginger marinade are the perfect match for beef, pork, poultry and seafood. It makes an excellent dipping sauce. This sauce also makes a great saute for vegetables.*

C **Cornet Bay Zesty Raspberry Chipotle Sauce**
12 Fl. Oz. – *The rich flavor of raspberries is combined with the smoky heat of chipotle peppers to create this unique sauce. Use as a grilling or finishing sauce for beef, poultry, seafood or pork. It makes an excellent dipping sauce and is also delicious over cream cheese.*

D **Cornet Bay Tangy Cherry Balsamic Grilling Sauce**
12 Fl. Oz.– *Our cherry balsamic grilling sauce combines the sweet taste of cherries with the wonderfully tart flavor of balsamic vinegar. This sauce can be used as a marinade as well as a finishing sauce for beef, pork, poultry and seafood. It is also delicious as a dipping sauce.*

E **Cornet Bay Sweet Honey Dijon Marinade**
12 Fl. Oz. – *The sweetness of honey combined with Dijon mustard, sugar and spices makes an excellent marinade and finishing sauce for beef, pork, poultry and seafood. It is also delicious as a dipping sauce.*

F **Cornet Bay Tangy Seafood Cocktail Sauce**
8.5 Fl. Oz. — *Cornet Bay's Tangy Seafood Cocktail Sauce is an amazing blend of tomato, horseradish and worcestershire. It is the perfect complement to your favorite shrimp, crab, oyster, scallop and seafood creations.*

www.cornetbay.com

MUSTARDS

A **Cornet Bay Sassy Vidalia Mustard**
8 Fl. Oz. — *Sweet Vidalia onions have been blended with Dijon mustard to make this product a tremendous addition to any sandwich, grilled chicken or potato salad.*

B **Cornet Bay Sassy Horseradish Mustard**
8 Fl. Oz. — *Just the right "bite" of fresh horseradish has been added to the creamy mustard to enhance the flavor on your sandwich, as well as on roast beef, pork, steak, salmon and crab cakes..*

C **Cornet Bay Sassy Jalapeno Mustard**
8 Fl. Oz. — *The bits of jalapeno peppers blended with mustard give an extra burst of flavor to any sandwich, hot dog or potato salad.*

D **Cornet Bay Gourmet Stout N' Sassy Mustard**
14 Oz.— *This spicy mustard combines the heat of jalapenos with the sweet of brown sugar and molasses to add a bold flavor to any sandwich, roast beef, pork, steak, salmon and crab cakes. Makes a great marinade.*

E **Cornet Bay Gourmet Sweet N' Sassy Mustard**
15 Oz. — *We call this mustard "Sassy" because it combines the sweet heat of red and chipotle peppers with honey to add just a little zip to your everyday dishes. Try it on any sandwich, beef, pork, poultry or seafood. Makes a great marinade.*

www.cornetbay.com

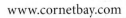

★ ★ ★ ★ ★ ★ ★

A Cornet Bay Louisiana Gourmet Pepper Sauce
5 Fl. Oz. — *For the taste of Louisiana, use our thick and spicy, but not "too hot" gourmet pepper sauce. It's wonderful on beef, pork, poultry and seafood. Also try on eggs and hashbrowns.*

B Cornet Bay Louisiana Steak Sauce
10 Fl. Oz. — *For the taste of Louisiana, use our unique steak sauce on beef, pork, poultry and seafood. Also a great addition in your soup, chili and stew.*

C Cornet Bay Louisiana Worcestershire Sauce
6 Fl. Oz. — *For the taste of Louisiana, use our unique Worcestershire sauce to "kick up" the flavor on beef, pork, poultry and seafood. Try it in your next Bloody Mary for added heat!*

D Cornet Bay Louisiana All Purpose Marinade
12.5 Fl. Oz. — *For the taste of Louisiana, use as a marinade for beef, pork, poultry and seafood.*

www.cornetbay.com

SEASONINGS

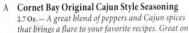

A Cornet Bay Original Cajun Style Seasoning
2.7 Oz. — *A great blend of peppers and Cajun spices that brings a flare to your favorite recipes. Great on beef, pork, poultry and seafood. Try it on the rim of your next Bloody Mary for added heat!*

B Cornet Bay All Around Hot Seasoning
2.9. Oz. — *This seasoning is a blend of spices combined with brown sugar. It adds a flavorful, but not "too hot" touch to beef, pork, poultry, seafood, soups and more. Keep it on your table to perk up any meal!*

C Cornet Bay Joanne's Special Seasoning
2.9. Oz. — *Joanne's Special Seasoning is a combination of spices, including dill and paprika. Try it on beef, pork, poultry, seafood, soups and pasta. Keep it on your table to perk up any meal!*

D Cornet Bay All Around Mild Seasoning
2.5 Oz. — *This is just the right blend of spices combined with brown sugar to give a unique flavor to beef, pork, poultry, seafood, soups, eggs and more. Keep it on your table to perk up any meal!*

E Cornet Bay Garlic Pepper
2.8 Oz. — *Experience the exceptional flavor this seasoning adds to meat, poultry, seafood and vegetables. It's also good on pasta. Keep it on your table to perk up any meal!*

F Cornet Bay Best Steak & Seafood Seasoning
3.1. Oz. — *Our seasoning is a great blend of garlic, salt, pepper and spices. Lightly sprinkle or rub on beef, pork, poultry or seafood. You'll know why we call it "Best Steak & Seafood Seasoning"!*

www.cornetbay.com

A **Kolymbari S.A.**
Extra Virgin Olive Oil-
(Imported from Crete)
This oil is a cold press non-filtered
Extra Virgin Olive Oil with a
fresh, fruity taste. The olive trees
in the Kolymbari Region, Island
of Crete, date back to the Venetian
Occupation about 1500 years
ago. The European Union stamp
Product Designation of Origin
(PDO) is your proof that 100%
of this oil comes only from
the Kolymbari area.

B **ENP Natural Honey-(Imported from Crete)**
ENP Natural Honey is extraordinary natural honey from wild pine flower, thyme and herbs from the
Island of Crete. It is collected by apiarists in the mountainous regions of the Island away from paved roads and
cultivated to keep the natural wild flavor. Crete, with its ideal climate condition and with its rich
flora, constitutes one of the best honey gardens in the world.

WOOD COOKING PRODUCTS
WOOD FLAVORS AVAILABLE FROM CORNET BAY

Alder: *Alder is used to give the delicate smoky and sweet flavor that is*
traditional in the Pacific Northwest. This wood is recommended for fish,
poultry, pork and vegetables.
Cedar: *Cedar planks have become one of the best-known varieties in recent*
years. They give foods a deep yet mild wood flavor. Cedar is recommended
for fish, meats and foods with a bold, spicy flavor.
Cherry: *Provides a slightly sweet and fruity, mellow flavor to your foods.*
Although most often used with poultry, it can be used for cooking all foods.
Hickory: *Hickory is the most commonly used wood for smoking. Your food*
will have a bold and peppery flavor with a hint of sweetness. This wood is
most often used for cooking pork, beef and chicken.
Maple: *Maple is a smoking wood that gives a mild and slightly sweet flavor.*
We recommend using it for fruits and vegetables and all other smoked foods.
Pecan: *Pecan is a favorite flavor of the South and gives a mellow smoke taste*
and can be used with cooking all foods.
Oak: *Cooking with an oak plank gives your food a subtle smoky flavor and*
can be used with cooking all foods.

C **Wood Grilling Papers/Wraps**
These unique grilling papers/wraps give meats, poultry,
seafood, vegetables and fruits a delicious woodsy
smoked flavor while keeping your food moist. You
prepare for cooking by soaking in water, wine, juice or
beer, depending on your desired flavor. Our grilling
papers/wraps can be used in the oven or on your grill
and are also available in a variety of woods.

D **Wood Grilling and Cooking Planks**
Cooking on wood planks helps make your food delicious, tender and juicy with an all-natural smoky flavor. You can
use on your grill or in your oven for cooking meats, poultry, seafood and vegetables. You simply soak, season, grill and
enjoy the results. Our planks are available in a variety of woods and each imparts its own unique flavor.

Salad Dressings

A Winsom's Sweet Onion Poppy Seed Dressing
This dressing is a light, sweet blend of spicy flavors and poppy seeds and Walla Walla Sweet Onions. Our dressing can also be used as a marinade for meat, fish and poultry or served as a dip for fresh vegetables.

B Winsom's Sweet Onion Summer Tomato Dressing
Walla Walla Sweet Onions and juicy, vine-ripened tomatoes are blended with select spices. This dressing is also great as a marinade for meat, fish and poultry. Use it as a sandwich spread or serve as a dip for fresh vegetables.

C Winsom's Sweet Onion Ranch Dressing
Our dressing contains buttermilk, sour cream and Walla Walla Sweet Onions with a hint of garlic, pepper, parsley and selected spices. It is also great as a marinade for meat, fish and poultry. Try it as a sandwich spread or serve as a dip for fresh vegetables.

D Winsom's Garlic Vinaigrette with Olive Oil Dressing
This light vinaigrette contains pieces of sweet garlic and peppers with a touch of olive oil. It is great on your salad greens or served as a dip for fresh vegetables or crusty French bread.

E Sweet Onion Creamy Cucumber Dill Dressing
Walla Walla Sweet Onions and fresh cucumbers are blended to make our deliciously creamy dressing. This dressing can also be served as a dip for fresh vegetables, as a sandwich spread, or as a marinade for fish.

F Winsom's No Fat Creamy Sweet Onion Dressing
A deliciously creamy, lightly seasoned dressing, made with Walla Walla Sweet Onions. Our No Fat – No Cholesterol dressing is great as a marinade for meat, fish and poultry or served as a dip for fresh vegetables.

G Winsom's Sweet Onion Honey Mustard Dressing
Our dressing is a blend of Dijon mustard, pure honey and a hint of Walla Walla Sweet Onions. It is also great as a marinade for meat, fish and poultry. Use as a sandwich spread or serve as a dip for fresh vegetables.

H Winsom's Sweet Onion Bell Pepper Vinaigrette Dressing
Bits of Walla Walla Sweet Onions and sweet red peppers make this golden vinaigrette. It is great on salad greens or served as a dip for fresh vegetables. Use as a marinade for meat, fish and poultry.

I Winsom's Balsamic Herb Vinaigrette Dressing
A wonderful dressing made with balsamic vinegar that is great on salad greens, with crumbled cheese or as a marinade for meat, fish and poultry.

Steak Sauces

A Winsom's Sweet Onion Steak Sauce
This sauce is made with tomatoes, Walla Walla Sweet Onions, mustards and select spices. It makes a great addition to any steak or poultry dish.

B Winsom's Sweet Onion Mesquite Steak Sauce
This combination of Walla Walla Sweet Onions, tomatoes and spices gives a taste of the Southwest to your steak or poultry dish.

C Winsom's Merlot Wine Steak Sauce
The merlot wine flavor added to our steak sauce makes a wonderful finishing sauce or steak sauce for any meat, poultry or ham dish.

D Winsom's Sweet Onion Cajun Steak Sauce
The perfect blend of Walla Walla Sweet Onions and select spices gives a little heat to this sauce for your steak or poultry dish.

Other wonderful products under Winsom's of Walla Walla

include relish, jelly, salsa, mustard, hot sauce and barbeque sauce. Try these great products:
Winsom's Zesty Sweet Onion Relish, Winsom's Green Tomato Relish, Winsom's Sweet Onion Relish, Winsom's Hot Jalapeno Jelly, Winsom's Sweet Onion & Peach Salsa, Winsom's Sweet Onion Mustard, Winsom's Sweet Onion & Orange Hot Sauce, Winsom's Good & Evil Hot Sauce, Winsom's Sweet Onion Barbeque Sauce, Winsom's Sweet Onion & Jalapeno Pepper Hot Sauce Sauce

CANNED SMOKED SALMON

★ ★ ★ ★ ★ ★ ★

A **Cornet Bay Canned Smoked Salmon-Classic**
6. Oz. — *Wild Coho salmon is brined and smoked to our specifications. It is then canned at the peak of perfection and has a "classic" Northwest flavor.*

B **Cornet Bay Canned Smoked Salmon-Red Pepper**
6. Oz. — *Wild Coho salmon is brined and smoked to our specifications. It is then canned at the peak of perfection and sweet red pepper has been added to enhance its Northwest flavor.*

C **Cornet Bay Canned Smoked Salmon-Jalapeno**
6. Oz. — *Wild Coho salmon is brined and smoked to our specifications. It is then canned at the peak of perfection and bits of jalapeno pepper have been added to give a new twist to its Northwest flavor.*

www.cornetbay.com

Kroger Label Seafood Dips

A Kroger Smoked Salmon Dip
This is the seafood dip that started it all! Pacific Smoked Salmon is blended with cream cheese, a secret blend of spices and a hint of dill. It is great as a dip on crackers or as a unique sandwich. Be adventurous and make a special quesadilla (see recipe included in book).

B Kroger Cajun Style Smoked Salmon Dip
Just the right amount of ground red pepper and a special blend of Cajun seasonings have been combined with Pacific Smoked Salmon and cream cheese to make this flavorful dip. You can serve as a dip or add to your fresh lettuce salad for a little punch. This delicious dip will have your family and guests coming back for more.

C Kroger Southern Style Crab Dip
Real crab meat has been blended with Pacific Pollock, mayonnaise, cream cheese and a secret mix of spices to make this special dip. You have the taste of the Northwest with a slightly sweet and peppery Southern twist. This versatile dip is great on crackers and sandwiches, and used for stuffing mushroom caps (see recipe included in book).

To this day, when Joanne and I walk into Kroger stores all across the country and see the Kroger name on our dips, it's a thrill and very flattering. In looking back and realizing it all began in Kroger over 20 years ago, it's still hard to imagine. This has been quite a ride, and it just goes to show that when a product is good, it has staying power.

Now, the next time you are in your Kroger store, be sure and take one of these dips, or all three of them, home with you because you'll love 'em!

Look for our Kroger Smoked Salmon, Cajun Style Smoked Salmon and Southern Style Crab dips in your local Kroger store and our Cornet Bay, Winsom's of Walla Walla and Kolymbari Extra Virgin Olive oil products in the following stores:

QFC Stores	Red Apple	Thriftway
Haggen Food	SAARS	Tacoma Boys
Food Emporium	Snow Goose Market	D&D Meats
Payless-Freeland	Soundview Shopper	Top Foods

"Practice driving?" I said. "I'm taking this RV home, Pal, loadin' it up and we're leaving this week!" He like to have fell over, and after we got underway I began learning the difference between pulling a 30-foot trailer full of horses and driving a motor home.

Joanne and I loaded up our new purchase, including our little schnauzer, Munch, a brand new laptop and a cell phone, and headed for Indianapolis. I was pumped. No more restaurants, since I'm married to the lady who can cook a five-star meal from leftovers in the fridge.

All was going like clockwork until I got into the winds of eastern Washington. I felt like I was about to fly an airplane, especially when passing an eighteen-wheeler, when I had to learn to fight all kinds of wind currents. *This is going to be a long, long trip,* I thought.

We won a blue ribbon for best display at the Indianapolis Kroger Seafood Show (we still have the blue ribbon in the rig), and the folks loved the dips and the chance to meet the people who made them. We loaded up and headed for Nashville, where I had Steer Safe installed. That made a lot of difference in the rig's performance. When we returned home, I had IPD suspension installed and that put it over the top. Katie bar the door! We were on the road and really lovin' it.

We had our Cornet Bay logo painted on both sides of our motor home—it's five feet in diameter, so you can't miss us—and traveled over 50,000 miles, staying in RV parks as we visited the folks who were handling our products in the Kroger and Wal-Mart stores and in Sam's Club.

We had many two- and three-thousand-mile trips and some that were seven- to nine-thousand. We were gone up to seven weeks at a time. More than once we woke up to below-zero weather and snow. Wanting to know the who, what, where, when and why of our products and customers kept us going through all of it.

Many times we left Cornet Bay for California and Arizona to check on our accounts, and from there it was on to Texas, then to Bentonville, Arkansas, where we met with Wal-Mart and the Sam's Club folks. Then it was off to Nashville, visiting one Kroger store after another, and then Louisville and Cincinnati to meet with the Kroger headquarters folks. Then it was on to Michigan, with a few more stops on the way home. One of those was always at a pal's ranch in Colorado, where one morning we woke up to 16 inches of beautiful, freshly fallen snow. We camped in his pasture for three days and nights with the generator running constantly until it became time to leave, snow or no snow. Help on making that decision came from Joanne. One morning I returned to the RV she met me at the door and said, "Take! Me! Home!" That's what seven weeks of hard driving will do, and we went home.

The news got out that our motor home was on the road more than the average RV'er and we were flattered that Sam's Club wanted to do an article on us for their Sam's Club *Shopping Spree* catalog. At that time we had several seafood dips in the Sam's Club seafood department, so they named the article "The Big Dipper." The following year they ran another article, only this time they put it in their Sam's Club *Source Magazine* and titled it "The Wheels Keep A-Turnin'."

Since we were members of the Good Sam Club, word got out that we were being spotted pulling into one of their RV parks in the evening and leaving the next morning. *Highways Magazine* published an article in their *One In a Million* Good Sam Club publication called "The Singing Salmon Man" and shortly thereafter *MotorHome Magazine* published an article titled "Cornet Bay Cowboy."

Our motor home has been resting for a while but as soon as this book comes out we'll be hitting the road again, driving to grocery stores and doing in-store-food-demo/book tours and telling this wonderful, fun story along with showing our products to the stores customers. Great times are ahead.

★ ★ ★ ★

Chapter Fifty-two

LIFE, FOOD, AND PEOPLE

I talked earlier in the book about Cornet Bay itself, and I'd like to do so again as our time together comes to a close. It's where my parents and grandparents lived. It's where I was raised and where Joanne and I now live. It will always be home. I love the fact that our office is in the little house I was raised in. I can walk out on the porch and almost see myself and my friends as youngsters being raised like Tom Sawyer and Huck Finn. I can gaze out at the waters that gave us our livelihood and picture myself as a fourteen-year-old running a commercial fishing boat. I can look back on the love and guidance of my parents, who were my best friends and who supported me as I set out into the world, ready to make a go of it.

As I write this, I'm in the process of putting in this year's garden. I get a lot of thinking done behind a shovel, and as I work the land, every now and then I look down to where our old family garden was. I can still see Grandpa taking a file out of his back pocket and sharpening his garden hoe. I get glimpses of

Grandma coming out to help him or working in her flower garden. Across the field I can see our whole family harvesting raspberries. We were fed from this land, and even though it may be on a smaller scale, we're eating from it again. All of that gives real meaning to my life and to the company, and it keeps my feet on the ground. I always know exactly where I came from. Those are riches money can't buy.

I've told a lot of stories in this book, and there are at least as many I've left out. Otherwise, this book would be four inches thick. As I finish it up, we're already planning the combination book tour and food demos that will take us into many of the stores selling our products. It'll give us the chance to let the public taste many of the delicious foods we sell and to chat about this book and the stories that detail my history and that of the Cornet Bay Company.

Several of the musicians I used to work with have agreed to get back on stage with me when we can work it out at some of our tour stops. We're talking to some of the media outlets that have written about me and Cornet Bay at one time or another, and we're excited about starting another tour scrapbook.

I got started in the food business in Nashville, Tennessee, more than twenty-three years ago with one Smoked Salmon dip I made behind the seafood counter in a grocery store. Since then, we've become a big presence in the Kroger chain and we've been in many others, including Wal-Mart Supercenters and Sam's Clubs.

I'm the kind of guy who's anxious to see what's over the next horizon. I get up every day looking forward to tackling the next challenge, to living the next big adventure. I believe you get out of life what you put into it, and people who know me know I throw myself into it with everything I've got. I love life, I love food, and I love people. I hope that's come across to you as you've read this book.

When this tour takes me to a store in your part of the country, I can't wait to meet up with you. Until then, know that one of these days you'll be hearing the line Charlie Walker first used when I walked into the backstage of the Grand Ole Opry: "Here comes the Singin' Salmon Man."

★ ★ ★ ★

Cornet Bay

RECIPES

Cornet Bay Louisiana Steak Sauce Easy Ideas

- Take 4 cuts of your favorite steak, 1 thickly sliced onion, a container of sliced mushrooms and Cornet Bay Louisiana Steak Sauce. Add to a resealable plastic bag and marinate for at least an hour. Grill the steaks and sauté the onions and mushrooms in a pan. Wonderful and easy! Cornet Bay Louisiana Steak Sauce marinated tri-tip steaks are great sliced on a romaine salad with bleu cheese and sourdough croutons.

- Mix 2 Tablespoons of Cornet Bay Louisiana Steak Sauce into 1 pound of hamburger and sprinkle with Cornet Bay Steak and Seafood Seasoning before cooking for a juicy burger.

- Mix Cornet Bay Louisiana Steak Sauce with ketchup, add to the top of meatloaf before cooking for a tasty glaze.

Other Serving Suggestions for Cornet Bay Raspberry Chipotle Marinade: Use as a barbecue sauce, glaze, or basting sauce for poultry, shrimp, and meats. Pour over a block of cream cheese and serve as a dip with club crackers. Use as a sauce for meatballs or cocktail sausages for a crowd-pleasing appetizer.

Cornet Bay Cajun Chicken Pasta

- 2 chicken breasts, cut into thin strips
- 4 oz of pasta
- 2 tsp Cornet Bay Cajun Style Seasoning
- 2 Tbsp of butter
- 1 sliced green onion
- 1 Cup heavy whipping cream
- 2 Tbsp sun-dried tomatoes, chopped
- 1/4 tsp salt and dried basil, can also use fresh basil
- Large clove of garlic minced
- A pinch of pepper
- 1/4 cup Asiago grated cheese

Cook pasta according to package directions. Place chicken and Cornet Bay Cajun Style Seasoning in a bowl and toss to coat. In a large skillet over medium heat, sauté chicken in butter until chicken is no longer pink, about 5 to 7 minutes. Add green onion, heavy cream, tomatoes, basil, salt, garlic, black pepper. Bring to a light simmer then pour over hot pasta and toss with cheese. Optional: Sprinkle top of dish with more Cornet Bay Cajun Style Seasoning before serving.

Joanne's Special Seasoning Stuffed Jalapenos

- 12 pickled and canned jalapenos
- 1 package of softened cream cheese
- 1 Tbsp Cornet Bay Joanne's Special Seasoning
- 1/2 cup shredded sharp cheddar cheese
- 1/4 cup sliced green onion

Rinse and drain jalapenos. Slit lengthwise on one side. Remove seeds and veins, leaving stem attached. Beat cream cheese and Joanne's Special Seasoning until fluffy. Beat in cheddar cheese and green onion. Stuff each pepper with part of mixture. Arrange on heatproof serving plate or baking sheet. Bake at 350 degrees for 10 minutes, or until cheese melts. Also try wrapping with 1/2 slice of bacon before baking.

Summer Steak Salad with Raspberry Chipotle Vinaigrette

- 1 bag mixed salad greens
- 2 sirloin steaks
- 1 cup cherry tomatoes
- 1/2 medium bell pepper, cut into thin strips
- 1/2 cup red onion, sliced thin
- 1/2 cup sliced carrot
- 1/2 cup sliced cucumber
- black pepper
- Cornet Bay Raspberry Chipotle Marinade
- Olive oil and apple cider vinegar
- Cornet Bay Garlic and Pepper seasoning

To prepare Vinaigrette, add 2 Tbsp of Cornet Bay Raspberry Chipotle Marinade, 1 Tbsp of vinegar and 2 Tbsp of olive oil to a sealable container and shake. Mix salad greens and vegetables in large bowl. Season steaks with Cornet Bay Garlic and Pepper seasoning to taste. Pan fry or grill to your own liking. With one minute left in cooking, brush on some of the Raspberry Chipotle Marinade, let steaks rest for a few minutes then slice. Arrange slices of steak on top of salad. Just before serving, drizzle with Raspberry Chipotle Vinaigrette; toss to coat.

Cornet Bay Honey Dijon Pork Cutlets

- 3 Tbsp Cornet Bay Honey Dijon Marinade
- 3/4 lb lean pork
- 1/2 cup breadcrumbs, fine
- nonstick cooking spray
- 1 medium-sized lemon, cut into wedges (optional)

Slice the pork into 1/4 inch thick slices. Place pork between sheets of waxed paper and pound thin. Spread the Cornet Bay Honey Dijon on both sides of each pork slice, then in the bread crumbs to coat both sides. Lightly coat a heavy 12-inch skillet with the cooking spray and set over moderate heat for 30 seconds. Add the pork and cook about 4 minutes on each side or until crisp and lightly browned. Garnish with the lemon wedges and serve.

Honey Dijon Carrots

- 1 lb baby carrots, steamed until just tender
- 3 Tbsp of Cornet Bay Honey Dijon Marinade
- Cornet Bay seasoning of your choice

Toss carrots with the marinade in a pan and simmer for 2 minutes, sprinkle your favorite Cornet Bay seasoning and serve.

Fast Impress Asparagus

- 1 lb of fresh Washington State grown asparagus
- Cornet Bay Organic Sesame Ginger Marinade

Trim and wash asparagus. Blanch in boiling water for 2 minutes then shock the asparagus in ice water. Return asparagus to a sauté pan and add 3 Tbsp of Cornet Bay Organic Sesame Ginger Marinade and coat well. Sauté for another 2 minutes over med-low heat, then serve and enjoy! This dish is also wonderful served cold. Wrap a piece of ham or turkey around each spear for another way to impress!

Honey Dijon Ham Muffins

- 1-2/3 cups all-purpose flour
- 1/3 cup cornmeal
- 2 Tbsp sugar
- 1 tsp baking powder
- 1 tsp ground mustard
- 1/2 teaspoon salt
- 1/2 teaspoon baking soda
- 2 eggs
- 1 cup buttermilk
- 1/3 cup vegetable oil
- 3 tablespoons Cornet Bay Honey Dijon Marinade
- 1 cup finely chopped fully cooked ham

In a large bowl, combine the first 7 ingredients. Combine the eggs, buttermilk, oil and Cornet Bay Honey Dijon Marinade; stir into dry ingredients just until moistened. Fold in the ham. Fill greased muffin cups three-fourths full. Bake at 375° for 20-25 minutes or until muffins test done. Cool for 5 minutes before removing from pans to wire racks. Great for a brunch! Yield: 14 muffins.

Slow Cooker Raspberry Chipotle Chicken Tacos

- **1 lb frozen boneless, skinless chicken breast**
- **3/4 cup Cornet Bay Raspberry Chipotle Marinade**
- **1 15 oz can black beans (drained)**
- **1 15 oz can no salt added whole kernel golden sweet corn (not drained)**
- **1 can of chopped tomatoes and chilies (not drained)**
- **3 Tbsp chicken stock or water**
- **Flour or corn tortillas**

Mix together the Cornet Bay Raspberry Chipotle Marinade with chicken stock. Place the frozen chicken on the bottom of the slow cooker and cover with mixture. Add the beans, corn and tomato on top. Cook on low for 6-8 hours. Shred up the chicken serve with your choice of tortillas.

Joanne's Special Stuffed Snow Peas

- **1 package cream cheese, softened**
- **36 fresh snow peas (about 1/4 lb)**
- **2 rounded tsp of Cornet Bay Joanne's Special Seasoning**

Blend together the Joanne's Special Seasoning and softened cream cheese, refrigerate overnight.

30 minutes before preparing, let cream cheese mixture sit out. Trim and wash peas, add to plenty of boiling water to blanch for 1-2 minutes. Shock in ice water and pat dry. Gently open pods and pipe the filling in. A quick trick is to use a strong resealable plastic bag to pipe fillings. Simply fill the corner of the bag, twist the top tightly and snip the corner of the bag. Also try Cornet Bay Cajun or Cornet Bay Steak and Seafood Seasoning for more of a kick.

Cornet Bay Salmon Summer Salad

- **4 4oz Wild Salmon fillets**
- **Cornet Bay Organic Sesame Ginger or Raspberry Chipotle Marinade**
- **Panko bread crumb or dehydrated potato flakes**
- **Bag of mixed greens or baby spinach**
- **1 cup sliced cucumber**
- **1/4 cup sliced radish**
- **Olive oil**

Brush the salmon fillets with your choice of Cornet Bay Marinade. Dredge the fillets in your choice of breading (Panko is thicker and crunchy; the flakes make a thinner coating). Heat some oil in a skillet over med-high heat and pan fry salmon 4-5 minutes on each side or until desired doneness. Mix salad and vegetables and place salmon on top. If using Raspberry Chipotle Marinade, dilute with a little olive oil and use as a dressing; no need to dilute the Organic Sesame Ginger Marinade. Optional: Add 2 Tbsp toasted and chopped walnuts to top of salad.

Arnie's Kabobs

- **3 large petite sirloin steaks or boneless pork loin cut in 1 inch pieces**
- **Cornet Bay Organic Sesame Ginger Marinade**
- **Canned pineapple chunks**
- **1 sweet onion cut into chunks**
- **2 green peppers cut into chunks**
- **12 large mushrooms halved**
- **Skewers (soaked in water)**
- **Large resealable plastic bag**

Add all the meat and vegetables to a large resealable bag and add Cornet Bay Organic Sesame Ginger Marinade just to lightly cover. Marinate flat in another container in the refrigerator for 3-6 hours. Prepare the kabobs by alternating the meat and the vegetables on the wet skewers (prevents burning). Grill over med-hot heat for 6-8 minutes or until beef reaches desired doneness. Serve with jasmine rice. Try about 1 lb of large 16-20 count shrimp instead of beef or pork. Your friends and family will think you ordered take-out with these delicious kabobs!

Cornet Bay Sandwich Wraps

SAUCE	MEAT	CHEESE	GARNISHES	CONDIMENTS
Raspberry-Chipotle Honey-Dijon Sesame-Ginger	Turkey Ham Roast Beef Bacon	Provolone Swiss Cheddar Pepper Jack Munster	Lettuce Onion Cucumber Sprouts Tomatoes Cilantro	Mayo Cream Cheese Plain Greek Yogurt

Mix and match any combination for a different sandwich wrap or fun appetizers! Spread whole tortilla with mayo, cream cheese or yogurt, add three slices of meat, and add the cheese. In a bowl, toss lettuce and other vegetables in marinade of choice. Place vegetables on the upper half of the tortilla and roll down towards yourself. Keep the seam down and slice for serving. Insert toothpicks for appetizers.

- **Suggestions: Honey Dijon, Ham, Swiss, Lettuce, Onion, Tomato, Cream Cheese**
- **Raspberry Chipotle, Peppered Turkey, Mixed Greens, Provolone, Cucumber, Yogurt**
- **Sesame Ginger, Roast Beef, Butter Lettuce, Sprouts, Cilantro, Munster, Onion**
- **Honey Dijon or Raspberry Chipotle, Bacon, Cheddar or Pepper Jack, Romaine, Tomato, Mayo**

★ ★ ★ ★

Winsom's of Walla Walla

◆◆◆◆◆◆◆◆◆◆◆◆◆◆◆◆◆◆◆◆◆◆◆◆◆

RECIPES

◆◆◆◆◆◆◆◆◆◆◆◆◆◆◆◆◆◆◆◆◆◆◆◆◆

Winsom's Easy Meatloaf

- 2 lbs ground beef
- 1/3 cup Winsom's Sweet Onion or Cajun Steak Sauce
- 2 Tbsp Worcestershire sauce
- 1 cup Italian bread crumbs
- 1/4 dried parsley
- 1 egg
- 1/2 chopped onion
- 5 or more pieces of bacon

Mix the above, place loaf in pan and squirt ketchup on top. Add cut bacon to the top, and add more ketchup or steak sauce, then dust with cracked black pepper. Bake 350 until done. *Try adding your favorite Winsom's steak sauce to hamburger patties with bread crumbs, make thin patties and add a thick slice of cheese in-between the patties, sealing well.

Winsom's Peach Chicken and Bacon Wraps

- 2 large boneless, skinless chicken breasts cut in 12 cubes
- 12 precooked bacon slices
- 1 jar of Winsom's Sweet Onion and Peach Salsa
- Seasoning salt and toothpicks

Season the cubes, wrap with bacon and secure with picks. Arrange on a greased broiler pan and bake at 450 for 10 minutes. Make a temporary pan with foil, place chicken bites in pan, topping with salsa and finish cooking for a few more minutes, serve warm. *Try using Winsom's Sweet Onion and Orange Hot Sauce, perfect on chicken!

Winsom's Jalapeno Cornbread

- 1/2 cup butter,
- 2 cups buttermilk,
- 2 eggs,
- 2 Tbsp sugar,
- 1 cup flour,
- 2 cups white cornmeal mix,
- 1 can corn well drained,
- 1-1/2 cups Mexican blend cheese and
- 2 Tbsp of Winsom's Sweet Onion and Jalapeno Pepper Hot Sauce

Melt butter in 13x9 pan in 425 oven for 5 minutes. Stir rest of ingredients, tilt pan so butter coats then add butter from pan to the mixture, stir well. Pour back into pan and bake 425 for 30 minutes or until golden brown. Add more hot sauce to top when hot from the oven.

Low Fat Turkey Wrap

- Winsom's Sweet Onion Creamy No Fat Dressing
- Flavored flour tortillas
- Sliced turkey, chopped onion, dried sweetened cranberries and your favorite shredded cheese.
- Shredded lettuce or coleslaw mix

Spread Winsom's dressing on tortilla; add cheese and cranberries, then turkey, making sure to not over lap the edges of the tortilla. Add lettuce, roll and cut into spirals if you wish. If making ahead don't use lettuce; wrap in plastic wrap. Low Carb option: Add all ingredients to a large romaine, leaf or butter lettuce and enjoy like a taco!

Walla Walla Sweet Onion Coleslaw

- 8 cups of shredded mix or 1 med head
- 1 bottle of Winsom's Sweet Onion Poppyseed Dressing
- 2 Tbsp of cider vinegar
- 1 Tbsp of celery seeds
- Salt and pepper to taste

Stir together all ingredients, cover and chill 1 hour.

Serve with Winsom's BBQ Biscuit Cups.

Winsom's BBQ Biscuit Cups

- 1 Bottle Winsom's Sweet Onion BBQ sauce
- 1 large can refrigerated biscuits
- 3/4 lb ground beef (or leftover roast)
- 1 clove garlic minced
- 1/2 Walla Walla Sweet Onion, minced
- Shredded sharp cheddar cheese

Brown beef with onions and garlic, add salt and pepper to season. Drain the fat and add about 3/4 bottle of Winsom's Sweet Onion BBQ Sauce. Press biscuit dough into mini-muffin pans, making a little cup. Add the BBQ beef mixture, then shredded cheese. Bake 10-12 minutes and you have festive finger food!

Winsom's Balsamic Pork Chops

- 5 1/2-inch thick boneless pork loin chops
- 1-1/4 tsp lemon-herb seasoning
- 2-1/2 Tbsp flour
- 1 Tbsp olive oil
- 2/3 c. Winsom's Balsamic Herb Vinagrette
- 1/2 c. chicken broth

Mix the flour with the seasonings. Dredge the pork in the mixture. Pan fry the chops in the olive oil until both sides are lightly brown. Remove and keep warm. Add the Winsom's dressing and broth to skillet, stirring to loosen the bits on the bottom. Cook on med-high heat stirring often for 5 minutes until slightly thickened. Serve over the pork.

Winsom's Greek Salad

- **3 large ripe tomatoes, chopped**
- **1 small red onion, chopped**
- **1 red bell pepper, chopped**
- **1 English cucumber, chopped**
- **3/4 c. Winsom's Sweet Onion Ranch or Garlic Vinaigrette Dressing**
- **1 c. Kalamata olives**
- **3/4 lb feta cheese, about 2-1/4 cups**
- **1-1/2 tsp dried Greek oregano**
- **Salt & Pepper**

Combine all ingredients except the oregano, which is to sprinkle on top before serving.

Try using Winsom's Sweet Onion Poppyseed Dressing

Winsom's of Walla Walla Quick & Easy Ideas

Winsom's BBQ & Merlot Steak Sauce Chicken

In a slow cooker, add bone-in chicken or a whole chicken. Add half a bottle of BBQ & half a bottle of Winsom's Merlot Wine Sauce with 1/4 cup water. Add granulated garlic, salt & pepper to taste. Cook 6-8 hours on low.

Winsom's Peach Salsa Meatballs

Add a bag of frozen meatballs, chopped green bell pepper, chopped onion and one jar of Winsom's Sweet Onion and Peach Salsa to a slow cooker and cook 6 hrs on low or 3 hrs on high.

Try dipping egg rolls in Winsom's Sweet Onion and Orange Hot Sauce.

Winsom's Shrimp Salad Supreme

- 2 c. cooked salad shrimp
- 2 c. sliced mushrooms
- 2 medium ripe tomatoes cut in wedges
- 1 c. sliced celery
- Small can sliced black olives
- 1 c. Winsom's Sweet Onion and Cucumber Dill Dressing
- 3 sliced green onions
- 2 hard boiled eggs cut in wedges
- Crisp lettuce leaves

In a bowl combine the first 6 ingredients. Arrange on the lettuce leaves, then garnish with the green onions and egg wedges.

Winsom's Salad Ideas

Spinach, fresh strawberries, toasted walnuts, thinly sliced onions and blue or feta cheese. Add Winsom's Sweet Onion Poppyseed Dressing or Sweet Onion Creamy No Fat Dressing.

7 Veggie Salad

Cauliflower, chopped cucumber, sliced celery, cherry tomatoes, julienned green pepper, julienned red pepper and sliced green onions. Add Winsom's Sweet Onion Creamy No Fat Dressing.

Winsom's Broccoli Salad

Broccoli, golden raisins, water chestnuts, Walla Walla Sweet Onions, sunflower seeds. Add your favorite Winsom's dressing! Try Winsom's Garlic Vinaigrette with Olive Oil or Sweet Onion Creamy No Fat Dressing..

Tomato Cups Appetizer

Hollow out medium tomatoes and fill with chopped cucumber, fresh mozzarella, and black chopped olives all tossed with Winsom's Balsamic Herb Vinaigrette.

Fish Baked With Winsom's Summer Tomato Dressing

- 4 white fish fillets, about 1/2 lb each
- 1 large tomato, thinly sliced
- 2 c. hot cooked rice
- 2 large Walla Walla Sweet Onions, sliced thick
- 2 garlic cloves, minced
- 1 tsp cumin
- 6 Tbsp olive oil
- 1 c. finely chopped celery
- 3/4 c. Winsom's Sweet Onion Summer Tomato Dressing
- 1 Tbsp tomato paste
- 3/4 c. water
- 1-1/2 tsp salt
- 1/4 tsp ground pepper

In a large skillet sauté onions, garlic & cumin in 4 Tbsp of oil, remove onions with a slotted spoon, set aside. Add celery, sauté a minute, return onions & stir in Winsom's Sweet Onion Summer Tomato Dressing, water, paste, salt & pepper. Simmer until thickened & remove from heat. Brush a shallow pan with 1 Tbsp oil, arrange fish and spread tomato & onion sauce over fish. Top with tomato slices and sprinkle with more oil. Cover with foil & bake for 20 minutes at 350. Remove cover and bake for 10 more minutes. Serve with hot rice.

Basil Ranch Salmon

- 4 fillets of wild salmon
- 1/4 cup Winsom's Sweet Onion Ranch Dressing
- 1 cup salad croutons, crushed
- 1/2 cup grated Parmesan
- 2 tsp dried basil
- 2 Tbsp olive oil
- Black pepper to taste

Place salmon in a greased baking pan. Spoon salad dressing over the fillets and sprinkle with pepper. Combine the croutons, Parmesan and basil. Add the mixture on top the dressing and gently press, drizzle with oil. Bake uncovered at 350 for 15 minutes (for 8 oz fillets).

Winsom's Jalapeno Glazed Pork Medallions

- 2-3/4 lb pork tenderloins
- 1/2 tsp garlic powder
- 1/2 tsp red pepper flakes
- 2 Tbsp oil
- 1/4 cup Winsom's Hot Jalapeno Jelly
- 3 Tb orange juice
- 4-1/2 tsp Worcestershire sauce
- 1-1/2 tsp Dijon mustard
- Salt and pepper

Thinly slice the pork and sprinkle with salt and pepper, garlic powder and pepper flakes. Brown pork on both sides in the oil then remove and keep warm. In the same skillet combine the remaining ingredients, stir and cook over medium heat 3-4 minutes until thickened. Return the pork to the pan and cook another 2-3 minutes.

Winsom's Hot Steak Strips

- 1-1/4 lb boneless rib eye steaks
- 1/4 cup Winsom's Hot Jalapeno Jelly
- 2 Tbsp Cornet Bay Garlic Pepper Seasoning

Add the Cornet Bay Garlic Pepper Seasoning to the steaks. Grill or broil the steaks until desired doneness. For medium rare cook steaks for 10-14 minutes or until meat thermometer reads 145. Medium 15-18 minutes. Whisk the jalapeno jelly and glaze the steaks in the last 5 minutes of cooking. Remove and cover steaks with foil, let meat rest 8 minutes then cut into 1/2" strips.

Fried Ravioli Salad

- **9 oz refrigerated package of cheese ravioli**
- **1 cup Italian bread crumbs**
- **1/4 cup buttermilk**
- **1 egg**
- **2 Tbsp flour**
- **Oil**
- **6 cups mixed greens**
- **1 cup quartered cherry tomatoes**
- **1/4 cup torn fresh basil**
- **1/3 cup Winsom's Balsamic Herb Vinaigrette**
- **Shredded Romano cheese**

Boil ravioli for 5 minutes. Lightly pat completely dry. Dredge the ravioli in the flour. Combine egg and buttermilk, beating well. Add floured ravioli to wet mixture, then lightly toss in bread crumbs. Deep fry in the oil for 2 minutes. Toss the salad greens, tomatoes and basil with the vinaigrette and top with fried ravioli. Sprinkle dish with Romano cheese.

Winsom's Merlot Waikiki Ham

- **3 lb ham or pork roast**
- **1 large can of pineapple slices**
- **1 Tbsp cornstarch**
- **1/3 cup Winsom's Merlot Wine Steak Sauce**
- **1 tsp ground ginger**

Drain pineapple and reserve juice. Combine cornstarch, Winsom's Merlot Wine Steak Sauce and ginger. Blend in pineapple juice and cook over moderate heat until thickened, about 2 minutes. Bake ham or pork at 325 while basting with sauce mixture. After an hour for a precooked ham or hour and a half for a pork roast, place pineapple slices on meat, brush with more sauce and broil about 10 minutes, then brush with remaining sauce.

Tortellini Salad

- 1 package of uncooked refrigerated cheese tortellini
- 1 green pepper, thinly sliced
- 1 large carrots, thinly sliced
- 1 pint of cherry tomatoes, halved
- 1 small can of sliced black olives
- 4 green onions, thinly sliced
- 1/2 cup Winsom's Sweet Onion Bell Pepper Vinaigrette
- 2 Tbsp fresh grated Parmesan cheese

Cook tortellini according to package directions then rinse under cold water. Mix all ingredients together and refrigerate at least 2 hours before serving.

Try adding Winsom's Sweet Onion Creamy No Fat Dressing.

Winsom's Sweet Onion Honey Mustard Crumb Chicken

- 4 Boneless skinless chicken breasts
- 2 eggs
- 2 Tbsp Winsom's Sweet Onion Honey Mustard Dressing
- 1 cup seasoned bread crumbs
- 1/2 cup grated Parmesan cheese
- 1-1/2 tsp onion powder
- 1-1/2 tsp garlic powder
- 3 Tbsp oil

In a shallow bowl, beat eggs and dressing together. In another bowl, combine bread crumbs, cheese, onion and garlic powder. Flatten chicken to 1/4 inch thickness. Dip chicken in dressing and egg mixture, then coat with crumb mixture. In a large skillet, cook the chicken in the oil over medium heat until lightly golden on both sides, about 4 minutes each side. Serve with more Winsom's Sweet Onion Honey Mustard Dressing to dip chicken in.

★ ★ ★ ★

Using Our Dip In

◆◆◆◆◆◆◆◆◆◆◆◆◆◆◆◆◆◆◆◆

RECIPES

◆◆◆◆◆◆◆◆◆◆◆◆◆◆◆◆◆◆◆◆

Smoked Salmon Dip Quesadillas

- **2/3 cup Kroger Smoked Salmon Dip ***
- **2 Tbsp salsa**
- **1 cup shredded Monterey Jack cheese**
- **4 flour tortillas (8 inch)**

Warm smoked salmon dip and salsa over medium low heat and set aside until ready for use. Butter one side of each tortilla. Place tortillas, buttered side down, on a griddle or in a skillet. Sprinkle each with 1/4 cup of cheese. Spread 1/4 of smoked salmon dip mixture over half of each tortilla. Fold over and cook on low for 1-2 minutes on each side. Cut into wedges; serve with guacamole or salsa.

*For a spicier version, use Kroger Cajun Style Smoked Salmon Dip

Smoked Salmon Dip Baked Salmon

- **1-1/2 lb. salmon fillet**
- **2 lemons, thinly sliced**
- **1/3 cup Kroger Smoked Salmon Dip ***
- **Salt & pepper to taste**

Rinse salmon and pat dry. Place a large sheet of foil in a baking dish and arrange a single row of lemon slices down the center of foil. Sprinkle salmon with salt and pepper. Spread smoked salmon dip over top and bottom of fish. Arrange remaining lemon slices in a single row down the center of the fillet. Wrap fillet in foil, sealing edges with a double fold. Bake at 425 degrees for 15-17 minutes per inch of thickness or until flesh turns from translucent to opaque and flakes easily when tested with a fork at the thickest part.

*For a spicier version, use Kroger Cajun Style Smoked Salmon Dip

Mushroom Caps with Crab Dip

- 1/4 cup Kroger Southern Style Crab Dip
- 6 large button mushrooms
- 1 Tbsp breadcrumbs
- Shredded Parmesan cheese

Clean and core mushroom caps. Combine Crab dip and breadcrumbs and stuff mushroom caps. Place in lightly greased glass dish and sprinkle with Parmesan cheese. Cover with aluminum foil and bake at 350 degrees for 6-8 minutes. Remove foil and cook under broiler until slightly brown.

◆◆◆◆◆◆◆◆◆◆◆◆◆◆◆◆◆◆◆◆◆◆◆◆◆◆◆◆◆◆◆◆◆◆◆◆◆◆◆

Recipe Index

[My friend and collaborator Rob Simbeck with Carrie Underwood]

I'd like to introduce you to my buddy Rob Simbeck, the writer who helped me turn a lifetime of adventures into the book you're holding in your hands. We met through our mutual friend Tom Long, and we've been writing off and on together now for twenty years.

Rob's books include *Daughter of the Air, American Music Legends,* and *Tennessee State Symbols.* He's been a ghostwriter or editor on many other books, and his articles have appeared in *The Washington Post, Guideposts, Country Weekly, Field & Stream,* and many others. He's won three national awards for his work in *The Nashville Scene* and two international awards for his writing about the outdoors. He's Nashville Bureau Chief for *Bob Kingsley's Country Top 40,* which counts down the Top 40 on more than 330 stations every week, and he has written press bios for country stars including Tim McGraw, Carrie Underwood, Alan Jackson, Loretta Lynn, Kenny Rogers, Rascal Flatts, Toby Keith, Ralph Stanley, Emmylou Harris, and Hank Williams Jr.

You can learn more about Rob and his work at www.robsimbeck.com.

❖❖❖

Rob, Joanne and I so much appreciate all your hard work, time and patience as you have helped me in the writing of this book. It's been a long couple of years, Pal, but we did it. Thanks, Rob. You're a keeper.

Arnie

As you can tell, I'm very proud of my wife Joanne, and this book wouldn't be complete if I didn't brag on her a little. Joanne has always had a flair for fashion and decorating. The clothes she wore during her years in the corporate world made it clear this lady knows how to put together a perfect wardrobe, as her oufits were all beautiful, and the colors she chooses around the house always match perfectly.

One day, Joanne visited a friend who introduced her to the world of designing and making jewelry. She came home with some books, some borrowed tools and a project she was working on and said, "What do you think?" It wasn't long before she was selling the necklaces and earrings she had made at shows and taking on custom orders. In a short while it became evident she had found a real niche that fits her talents beautifully.

She has attended and put on many jewelry shows in our area and in Tennessee, and she has become part of the Garry Oak Gallery in Oak Harbor, where she displays and sells her creations. Her gifts when it comes to color and design have given her the ability to create one-of-a-kind jewelry time after time.

She loves designing and making jewelry, and it's a blessing to me to see her so proud of what she does. Joanne is in the process of putting together her own website, but for now she can be contacted at

joanne@cornetbay.com
JJD--Joanne's Jewelry Designs
251 Cornet Bay Rd.
Oak Harbor, WA 98277

Joanne J. Deckwa --Designer
Original and Custom Designs
Turquoise ◆ Gemstones ◆ Copper ◆ Sterling ◆ Gold